P9-DFM-190

CARNEGIE LIBRARY
LIVINGSTONE COLLEGE
SALISBURY, NC 28144

MAGNA CARTA

MAGNA CARTA

Katherine Fischer Drew

CARNEGIE LIBRARY
LIVINGSTONE COLLEGE
SALISBURY. NC 28144

Greenwood Guides to Historic Events of the Medieval World
Jane Chance, Series Editor

GREENWOOD PRESS
Westport, Connecticut • London

Library of Congress Cataloging-in-Publication Data

Drew, Katherine Fischer.
  Magna Carta / Katherine Fischer Drew.
     p. cm.—(Greenwood guides to historic events of the medieval world)
  Includes bibliographical references and index.
  ISBN 0–313–32590–1 (alk. paper)
  1. Magna Carta.   2. Constitutional history—England.   3. Law—England—
History.   4. Great Britain—History—13th century.   I. Title.   II. Series.
  KD3946.D74   2004
  342.4202'9—dc22   2004042499

British Library Cataloguing in Publication Data is available.

Copyright © 2004 by Katherine Fischer Drew

All rights reserved. No portion of this book may be
reproduced, by any process or technique, without the
express written consent of the publisher.

Library of Congress Catalog Card Number: 2004042499
ISBN: 0–313–32590–1

First published in 2004

Greenwood Press, 88 Post Road West, Westport, CT 06881
An imprint of Greenwood Publishing Group, Inc.
www.greenwood.com

Printed in the United States of America

The paper used in this book complies with the
Permanent Paper Standard issued by the National
Information Standards Organization (Z39.48–1984).

10 9 8 7 6 5 4 3 2 1

Copyright Acknowledgments

The author and publisher gratefully acknowledge permission for use of the following material:

" 'The Coronation Charter' of Henry I (5 August 1100)," from David C. Douglas and George W. Greenaway, eds., *English Historical Documents 1042–1189*, 2nd ed (London: Eyre Methuen; and New York: Oxford University Press, 1981) © 1981 Eyre Methuen Ltd. Reprinted by permission of the holder of the publishing rights: Routledge, Andover, Hampshire, UK.

"Magna Carta, 1215," "Magna Carta, 1225," "Charter of the Forest, 1225," and "The Additional Articles [Confirmatio Cartarum], 1297," from Harry Rothwell, ed., *English Historical Documents 1189–1327* (New York: Oxford University Press, 1975) © 1975 Eyre & Spottiswoode (Publishers) Ltd. Reprinted by permission of the holder of the publishing rights: Routledge, Andover, Hampshire, UK.

CONTENTS

SERIES FOREWORD

The Middle Ages are no longer considered the "Dark Ages" (as Petrarch termed them), sandwiched between the two enlightened periods of classical antiquity and the Renaissance. Often defined as a historical period lasting, roughly, from 500 to 1500 C.E., the Middle Ages span an enormous amount of time (if we consider the way other time periods have been constructed by historians) as well as an astonishing range of countries and regions very different from one another. That is, we call the "Middle" Ages the period beginning with the fall of the Roman Empire as a result of raids by northern European tribes of "barbarians" in the late antiquity of the fifth and sixth centuries and continuing until the advent of the so-called Italian and English renaissances, or rebirths of classical learning, in the fifteenth and sixteenth centuries. How this age could be termed either "Middle" or "Dark" is a mystery to those who study it. Certainly it is no longer understood as embracing merely the classical inheritance in the west or excluding eastern Europe, the Middle East, Asia, or even, as I would argue, North and Central America.

Whatever the arbitrary, archaic, and hegemonic limitations of these temporal parameters—the old-fashioned approach to them was that they were mainly not classical antiquity, and therefore not important—the Middle Ages represent a time when certain events occurred that have continued to affect modern cultures and that also, inevitably, catalyzed other medieval events. Among other important events, the Middle Ages saw the birth of Muhammad (c. 570–632) and his foundation of Islam in the seventh century as a rejection of Christianity which led to the imperial conflict between East and West in the eleventh and twelfth centuries. In western Europe in the Middle Ages the foundations for modern nationalism and modern law were laid and the concept of romantic love arose in the Middle Ages, this latter event partly one of the indirect consequences of the Crusades. With the shaping of national identity came the need to defend boundaries against invasion; so the castle emerged as a military outpost—whether in northern Africa, during the Crusades, or in Wales, in the eleventh century, to defend William of Normandy's newly acquired provinces—to satisfy that need. From Asia the invasions of Genghis Khan changed the literal and cultural shape of eastern and southern Europe.

In addition to triggering the development of the concept of chivalry and the knight, the Crusades influenced the European concepts of the lyric, music, and musical instruments; introduced to Europe an appetite for spices like cinnamon, coriander, and saffron and for dried fruits like prunes and figs as well as a desire for fabrics such as silk; and brought Aristotle to the European university through Arabic and then Latin translations. As a result of study of the "new" Aristotle, science and philosophy dramatically changed direction—and their emphasis on this material world helped to undermine the power of the Catholic Church as a monolithic institution in the thirteenth century.

By the twelfth century, with the centralization of the one (Catholic) Church, came a new architecture for the cathedral—the Gothic—to replace the older Romanesque architecture and thereby to manifest the Church's role in the community in a material way as well as in spiritual and political ways. Also from the cathedral as an institution and its need to dramatize the symbolic events of the liturgy came medieval drama—the mystery and the morality play, from which modern drama derives in large part. Out of the cathedral and its schools to train new priests (formerly handled by monasteries) emerged the medieval institution of the university. Around the same time, the community known as a town rose up in eastern and western Europe as a consequence of trade and the necessity for a new economic center to accompany the development of a bourgeoisie, or middle class. Because of the town's existence, the need for an itinerant mendicancy that could preach the teachings of the Church and beg for alms in urban centers sprang up.

Elsewhere in the world, in North America the eleventh-century settlement of Chaco Canyon by the Pueblo peoples created a social model like no other, one centered on ritual and ceremony in which the "priests" were key, but one that lasted barely two hundred years before it collapsed and its central structures were abandoned.

In addition to their influence on the development of central features of modern culture, the Middle Ages have long fascinated the modern age because of parallels that exist between the two periods. In both, terrible wars devastated whole nations and peoples; in both, incurable diseases plagued cities and killed large percentages of the world's population. In both periods, dramatic social and cultural changes took place as a result of these events: marginalized and overtaxed groups in societies rebelled against imperious governments; trade and a burgeoning middle class came to the fore; outside the privacy of the family, women began to have a greater role in Western societies and their cultures.

How different cultures of that age grappled with such historical change is the subject of the Greenwood Guides to Historic Events of the Medieval World. This series features individual volumes that illuminate key events in medieval world history. In some cases, an "event" occurred during a relatively limited time period. The troubadour lyric as a phenomenon, for example, flowered and died in the courts of Aquitaine in the twelfth century, as did the courtly romance in northern Europe a few decades later. The Hundred Years War between France and England generally took place during a precise time period, from the fourteenth to mid-fifteenth centuries.

In other cases, the event may have lasted for centuries before it played itself out: the medieval Gothic cathedral, for example, may have been first built in the twelfth century at Saint-Denis in Paris (c. 1140), but cathedrals, often of a slightly different style of Gothic architecture, were still being built in the fifteenth century all over Europe and, again, as the symbolic representation of a bishop's seat, or chair, are still being built today. And the medieval city, whatever its incarnation in the early Middle Ages, basically blossomed between the eleventh and thirteenth centuries as a result of social, economic, and cultural changes. Events—beyond a single dramatic historically limited happening—took longer to affect societies in the Middle Ages because of the lack of political and social centralization, the primarily agricultural and rural nature of most countries, difficulties in communication, and the distances between important cultural centers.

Each volume includes necessary tools for understanding such key events in the Middle Ages. Because of the postmodern critique of authority that modern societies underwent at the end of the twentieth century, students and scholars as well as general readers have come to mistrust the commentary and expertise of any one individual scholar or commentator and to identify the text as an arbiter of "history." For this reason, each book in the series can be described as a "library in a book." The intent of the series is to provide a quick, in-depth examination and current perspectives on the event to stimulate critical thinking as well as ready-reference materials, including primary documents and biographies of key individuals, for additional research.

Specifically, in addition to a narrative historical overview that places the specific event within the larger context of a contemporary perspective, five to seven developmental chapters explore related focused aspects of the event. In addition, each volume begins with a brief chronology and ends with a conclusion that discusses the consequences and impact of the event. There are also brief biographies of twelve to twenty key individuals (or places or buildings, in the book on the cathedral); primary documents from the period (for example, letters, chronicles, memoirs, diaries, and other writings) that illustrate states of mind or the turn of events at the time, whether historical, literary, scientific, or philosophical; illustrations (maps, diagrams, manuscript illuminations, portraits); a glossary of terms; and an annotated bibliography of important books, articles, films, and CD-ROMs available for additional research. An index concludes each volume.

No particular theoretical approach or historical perspective characterizes the series; authors developed their topics as they chose, generally taking into account the latest thinking on any particular event. The editors selected final topics from a list provided by an advisory board of high school teachers and public and school librarians. On the basis of nominations of scholars made by distinguished writers, the series editor also tapped internationally known scholars, both those with lifelong expertise and others with fresh new perspectives on a topic, to author the twelve books in the series. Finally, the series editor selected distinguished medievalists, art historians, and archaeologists to complete an advisory board: Gwinn Vivian, retired professor of archaeology at the University of Arizona Museum; Sharon Kinoshita, associate professor of French literature, world literature, and cultural studies at the University of California–Santa Cruz; Nancy Wu, associate museum educator at the Metropolitan Museum of Art, The Cloisters, New York City; and Christopher A. Snyder, chair of the Department of History and Politics at Marymount University.

In addition to examining the event and its effects on the specific cultures involved through an array of documents and an overview, each volume provides a new approach to understanding these twelve events. Treated in the series are: the Black Death; the Crusades; Eleanor of Aquitaine, courtly love, and the troubadours; Genghis Khan and Mongol rule; Joan of Arc and the Hundred Years War; Magna Carta; the medieval castle, from the eleventh to the sixteenth centuries; the medieval cathedral; the medieval city, especially in the thirteenth century; medieval science and technology; Muhammad and the rise of Islam; and the Puebloan society of Chaco Canyon.

The Black Death, by Joseph Byrne, isolates the event of the epidemic of bubonic plague in 1347–52 as having had a signal impact on medieval Europe. It was, however, only the first of many related such episodes involving variations of pneumonic and septicemic plague that recurred over 350 years. Taking a twofold approach to the Black Death, Byrne investigates both the modern research on bubonic plague, its origins and spread, and also medieval documentation and illustration in diaries, artistic works, and scientific and religious accounts. The demographic, economic, and political effects of the Black Death are traced in one chapter, the social and psychological patterns of life in another, and cultural expressions in art and ritual in a third. Finally, Byrne investigates why bubonic plague disappeared and why we continue to be fascinated by it. Documents included provide a variety of medieval accounts—Byzantine, Arabic, French, German, English, and Italian—several of which are translated for the first time.

The Crusades, by Helen Nicholson, presents a balanced account of various crusades, or military campaigns, invented by Catholic or "Latin" Christians during the Middle Ages against those they perceived as threats to their faith. Such expeditions included the Crusades to the Holy Land between 1095 and 1291, expeditions to the Iberian Peninsula, the "crusade" to northeastern Europe, the Albigensian Crusades and the Hussite crusades—both against the heretics—and the crusades against the Ottoman Turks (in the Balkans). Although Muslim rulers included the concept of jihâd (a conflict fought for God against evil or his enemies) in their wars in the early centuries of Islam, it had become less important in the late tenth century. It was not until the middle decades of the twelfth century that jihâd was revived in the wars with the Latin Christian Crusaders. Most of the Crusades did not result in victory for the Latin Christians, although Nicholson concedes they slowed the advance of Islam. After Jerusalem was destroyed in 1291, Muslim rulers did permit Christian pilgrims to travel to holy sites. In the Iberian Peninsula, Christian rulers replaced Muslim rulers, but Muslims, Jews, and dissident Christians were compelled to convert to Catholicism. In northeastern Europe, the Teutonic Order's campaigns allowed German colonization that later encouraged twentieth-century German claims to land and led to two world wars. The Albigensian Crusade wiped out thirteenth-century aristocratic families in southern France who held to the Cathar heresy, but the Hussite crusades in the 1420s failed to eliminate the Hussite heresy. As a result of the wars, however, many positive changes occurred: Arab learning founded on Greek scholarship entered western Europe through the acquisition of an extensive library in Toledo, Spain, in 1085; works of western European literature were inspired by the holy wars; trade was encouraged and with it the demand for certain products; and a more favorable image of Muslim men and women was fostered by the crusaders' contact with the Middle East. Nicholson also notes that America may have been discovered because Christopher Columbus avoided a route that had been closed by Muslim conquests and that the Reformation may have been advanced because Martin Luther protested against the crusader indulgence in his Ninety-five Theses (1517).

Eleanor of Aquitaine, Courtly Love, and the Troubadours, by ffiona Swabey, singles out the twelfth century as the age of the individual, in which a queen like Eleanor of Aquitaine could influence the development of a new social and artistic culture. The wife of King Louis VII of France and later the wife of his enemy Henry of Anjou, who became king of England, she patronized some of the troubadours, whose vernacular lyrics celebrated the personal expression of emotion and a passionate declaration of service to women. Love, marriage, and the pursuit of women were also the subject of the new romance literature, which flourished in northern Europe and was the inspiration behind concepts of courtly love. However, as Swabey points out, historians in the past have misjudged Eleanor, whose independent spirit fueled their misogynist attitudes. Similarly, Eleanor's divorce and subsequent stormy marriage have colored ideas about medieval "love courts" and courtly love, interpretations of which have now been challenged by scholars. The twelfth century is set in context, with commentaries on feudalism, the tenets of Christianity, and the position of women, as well as summaries of the cultural and philosophical background, the cathedral schools and universities, the influence of Islam, the revival of classical learning, vernacular literature, and Gothic architecture. Swabey provides two biographical chapters on Eleanor and two on the emergence of the troubadours and the origin of courtly love through verse romances. Within this latter subject Swabey also details the story of Abelard and Heloise, the treatise of Andreas Capellanus (André the Chaplain) on courtly love, and Arthurian legend as a subject of courtly love.

Genghis Khan and Mongol Rule, by George Lane, identifies the rise to power of Genghis Khan and his unification of the Mongol tribes in the thirteenth century as a kind of globalization with political, cultural, economic, mercantile, and spiritual effects akin to those of modern globalization. Normally viewed as synonymous with barbarian destruction, the rise to power of Genghis Khan and the Mongol hordes is here understood as a more positive event that initiated two centuries of regeneration and creativity. Lane discusses the nature of the society of the Eurasian steppes in the twelfth and thirteenth centuries into which Genghis Khan was born; his success at reshaping the relationship between the northern pastoral and nomadic society with the southern urban, agriculturalist society; and his unification of all the Turco-Mongol tribes in 1206 before his move to conquer Tanquit Xixia, the Chin of northern China, and the lands of Islam. Conquered thereafter were the Caucasus, the Ukraine, the Crimea, Russia, Siberia, Central Asia, Afghanistan, Pakistan, and Kashmir. After his death his sons and grandsons continued, conquering Korea, Persia, Armenia, Mesopotamia, Azerbaijan, and eastern Europe—chiefly Kiev, Poland, Moravia, Silesia, and Hungary—until 1259, the end of the Mongol Empire as a unified whole. Mongol rule created a golden age in the succeeding split of the Empire into two, the Yuan dynasty of greater China and the Il-Khanate dynasty of greater Iran. Lane adds biographies of important political figures, famous names such as Marco Polo, and artists and scientists. Documents derive from universal histories, chronicles, local histories and travel accounts, official government documents, and poetry, in French, Armenian, Georgian, Chinese, Persian, Arabic, Chaghatai Turkish, Russian, and Latin.

Joan of Arc and the Hundred Years War, by Deborah Fraioli, presents the Hundred Years War between France and England in the fourteenth and fifteenth centuries within contexts whose importance has sometimes been blurred or ignored in past studies. An episode of apparently only moderate significance, a feudal lord's seizure of his vassal's land for harboring his mortal enemy, sparked the Hundred Years War, yet on the face of it the event should not have led inevitably to war. But the lord was the king of France and the vassal the king of England, who resented losing his claim to the French throne to his Valois cousin. The land in dispute, extending roughly from Bordeaux to the Pyrenees mountains, was crucial coastline for the economic interests of both kingdoms. The series of skirmishes, pitched battles, truces, stalemates, and diplomatic wrangling that resulted from the confiscation of English Aquitaine by the French form the narrative of this Anglo-French conflict, which was in fact not given the name Hundred Years War until the nineteenth century.

Fraioli emphasizes how dismissing women's inheritance and succession rights came at the high price of unleashing discontent in their male heirs, including Edward III, Robert of Artois, and Charles of Navarre. Fraioli also demonstrates the centrality of side issues, such as Flemish involvement in the war, the peasants' revolts that resulted from the costs of the war, and Joan of Arc's unusually clear understanding of French "sacred kingship." Among the primary sources provided are letters from key players such as Edward III, Etienne Marcel, and Joan of Arc; a supply list for towns about to be besieged; and a contemporary poem by the celebrated scholar and court poet Christine de Pizan in praise of Joan of Arc.

Magna Carta, by Katherine Drew, is a detailed study of the importance of the Magna Carta in comprehending England's legal and constitutional history. Providing a model for the rights of citizens found in the United States Declaration of Independence and Constitution's first ten amendments, the Magna Carta has had a role in the legal and parliamentary history of all modern states bearing some colonial or government connection with the British Empire. Constructed at a time when modern nations began to appear, in the early thirteenth century, the Magna Carta (signed in 1215) presented a formula for balancing the liberties of the people with the power of modern governmental institutions. This unique English document influenced the growth of a form of law (the English common law) and provided a vehicle for the evolution of representative (parliamentary) government. Drew demonstrates how the Magna Carta came to be—the roles of the Church, the English towns, barons, common law, and the parliament in its making—as well as how myths concerning its provisions were established. Also provided are biographies of Thomas Becket, Charlemagne, Frederick II, Henry II and his sons, Innocent III, and many other key figures, and primary documents—among them, the Magna Cartas of 1215 and 1225, and the Coronation Oath of Henry I.

Medieval Castles, by Marilyn Stokstad, traces the historical, political, and social function of the castle from the late eleventh century to the sixteenth by means of a typology of castles. This typology ranges from the early "motte and bailey"—military fortification, and government and economic center—to the palace as an expression of the castle owners' needs and purposes. An introduction defines the various contexts—military, political, economic, and social—in which the castle appeared in the Middle Ages. A concluding interpretive essay suggests the impact of the castle and its symbolic role as an idealized construct lasting until the modern day.

Medieval Cathedrals, by William Clark, examines one of the chief contributions of the Middle Ages, at least from an elitist perspective—that is, the religious architecture found in the cathedral ("chair" of the bishop) or great church, studied in terms of its architecture, sculpture, and stained glass. Clark begins with a brief contextual history of the concept of the bishop and his role within the church hierarchy, the growth of the church in the early Christian era and its affiliation with the bishop (deriving from that of the bishop of Rome), and the social history of cathedrals. Because of economic and political conflicts among the three authorities who held power in medieval towns—the king, the bishop, and the cathedral clergy—cathedral construction and maintenance always remained a vexed issue, even though the owners—the cathedral clergy—usually held the civic responsibility for the cathedral. In an interpretive essay, Clark then focuses on Reims Cathedral in France, because both it and the bishop's palace survive, as well as on contemporary information about surrounding buildings. Clark also supplies a historical overview on the social, political, and religious history of the cathedral in the Middle Ages: an essay on patrons, builders, and artists; aspects of cathedral construction (which was not always successful); and then a chapter on Romanesque and Gothic cathedrals and a "gazetteer" of twenty-five important examples.

The Medieval City, by Norman J. G. Pounds, documents the origin of the medieval city in the flight from the dangers or difficulties found in the country, whether economic, physically threatening, or cultural. Identifying the attraction of the city in its *urbanitas*, its "urbanity," or the way of living in a city, Pounds discusses first its origins in prehistoric and classical Greek urban revolutions. During the Middle Ages, the city grew primarily between the eleventh and thirteenth centuries, remaining essentially the same until the Industrial Revolution. Pounds provides chapters on the medieval city's planning, in terms of streets and structures; life in the medieval city; the roles of the Church and the city government in its operation; the development of crafts and trade in the city; and the issues of urban health, wealth, and welfare. Concluding with the role of the city in history, Pounds suggests that the value of the city depended upon its balance of social classes, its need for trade and profit to satisfy personal desires through the accumulation of wealth and its consequent economic power, its political power as a representative body within the kingdom, and its social role in the rise of literacy and education and in nationalism. Indeed, the concept of a middle class, a bourgeoisie, derives from the city—from the *bourg*, or "borough." According to Pounds, the rise of modern civilization would not have taken place without the growth of the city in the Middle Ages and its concomitant artistic and cultural contribution.

Medieval Science and Technology, by Elspeth Whitney, examines science and technology from the early Middle Ages to 1500 within the context of the classical learning that so influenced it. She looks at institutional history, both early and late, and what was taught in the medieval schools and, later, the universities (both of which were overseen by the Catholic Church). Her discussion of Aristotelian natural philosophy illustrates its impact on the medieval scientific worldview. She presents chapters on the exact sciences, meaning mathematics, astronomy, cosmology, astrology, statics, kinematics, dynamics, and optics; the biological and earth sciences, meaning chemistry and alchemy, medicine, zoology, botany, geology and meteorology, and geography; and technology. In an interpretive conclusion, Whitney demonstrates the impact of medieval science on the preconditions and structure that permitted the emergence of the modern world. Most especially, technology transformed an agricultural society into a more commercial and engine-driven society: waterpower and inventions like the blast furnace and horizontal loom turned iron working and cloth making into manufacturing operations. The invention of the mechanical clock helped to organize human activities through timetables rather than through experiential perception and thus facilitated the advent of modern life. Also influential in the establishment of a middle class were the inventions of the musket and pistol and the printing press. Technology, according to Whitney, helped advance the habits of mechanization and precise methodology. Her biographies introduce major medieval Latin and Arabic and classical natural philosophers and scientists. Extracts from various kinds of scientific treatises allow a window into the medieval concept of knowledge.

The Puebloan Society of Chaco Canyon, by Paul Reed, is unlike other volumes in this series, whose historic events boast a long-established historical record. Reed's study offers instead an original reconstruction of the Puebloan Indian society of Chaco, in what is now New Mexico, but originally extending into Colorado, Utah, and Arizona. He is primarily interested in its leaders, ritual and craft specialists, and commoners during the time of its chief flourishing, in the eleventh and twelfth centuries, as understood from archaeological data alone. To this new material he adds biographies of key Euro-American archaeologists and other individuals from the nineteenth and twentieth centuries who have made important discoveries about Chaco Canyon. Also provided are documents of archaeological description and narrative from early explorers' journals and archaeological reports, narratives, and monographs. In his overview chapters, Reed discusses the cultural and environmental setting of Chaco Canyon; its history (in terms of exploration and research); the Puebloan society and how it emerged chronologically; the Chaco society and how it appeared in 1100 C.E.; the "Outliers," or outlying communities of Chaco; Chaco as a ritual center of the eleventh-century Pueblo world; and, finally, what is and is not known about Chaco society. Reed concludes that ritual and ceremony played an important role in Chacoan society and that ritual specialists, or priests, conducted ceremonies, maintained ritual artifacts, and charted the ritual calendar. Its social organization matches no known social pattern or type: it was complicated, multiethnic, centered around ritual and ceremony, and without any overtly hierarchical political system. The Chacoans were ancestors to the later Pueblo people, part of a society that rose, fell, and evolved within a very short time period.

The Rise of Islam, by Matthew Gordon, introduces the early history of the Islamic world, beginning in the late sixth century with the career of the Prophet Muhammad (c. 570–c. 632) on the Arabian Peninsula. From Muhammad's birth in an environment of religious plurality—Christianity, Judaism, and Zoroastrianism, along with paganism, were joined by Islam—to the collapse of the Islamic empire in the early tenth century, Gordon traces the history of the Islamic community. The book covers topics that include the life of the Prophet and divine revelation (the Qur'an) to the formation of the Islamic state, urbanization in the Islamic Near East, and the extraordinary culture of Islamic letters and scholarship. In addition to a historical overview, Gordon examines the Caliphate and early Islamic Empire, urban society and economy, and the emergence, under the Abbasid Caliphs, of a "world religious tradition" up to the year 925 C.E.

As editor of this series I am grateful to have had the help of Benjamin Burford, an undergraduate Century Scholar at Rice University assigned to me in 2002–2004 for this project; Gina Weaver, a third-year graduate student in English; and Cynthia Duffy, a second-year graduate student in English, who assisted me in target-reading select chapters from some of these books in an attempt to define an audience. For this purpose I would also like to thank Gale Stokes, former dean of humanities at Rice University, for the 2003 summer research grant and portions of the 2003–2004 annual research grant from Rice University that served that end.

This series, in its mixture of traditional and new approaches to medieval history and cultures, will ensure opportunities for dialogue in the classroom in its offerings of twelve different "libraries in books." It should also propel discussion among graduate students and scholars by means of the gentle insistence throughout on the text as primal. Most especially, it invites response and further study. Given its mixture of East and West, North and South, the series symbolizes the necessity for global understanding, both of the Middle Ages and in the postmodern age.

Jane Chance, Series Editor
Houston, Texas
February 19, 2004

Advisory Board

Sharon Kinoshita
Associate Professor of Literature
(French Literature, World Literature, and Cultural Studies)
University of California–Santa Cruz

Christopher A. Snyder
Chair, History and Politics
Marymount University

Gwinn Vivian
Archaeologist
University of Arizona Museum

Nancy Wu
Associate Museum Educator
Metropolitan Museum of Art, The Cloisters

PREFACE

Magna Carta is an important document in the legal and constitutional history of England. It is also an integral part of the legal and constitutional history of all modern states that have evolved from the former British Empire. On this side of the Atlantic Ocean it is regarded as a central document in establishing the rights later described in the American Declaration of Independence and in the first ten amendments to the American Constitution (the Bill of Rights).

Magna Carta was a product of its time (the early thirteenth century), a time when the outlines of modern European states were beginning to appear, when the people and their rulers were working to overcome the insecurity and devastation of the early Middle Ages, when efforts were being made to work out an equation that would allow modern institutions of government to grow without unduly compromising the liberties of their people.

England was not alone in facing this dilemma. All the states of Western Europe were going through a similar transition and showing tendencies that would end in the creation of nation-states. But the English experience was unique in producing a distinctive form of law (the English common law) and parliamentary (representative) government.

To understand their own institutions, the people of the United States will find the history of Magna Carta to be especially fascinating. It should be borne in mind, however, that in the thirteenth century there was no notion of civil rights or representative government. Rather, the people were concerned with protecting specific "liberties" that their rulers were putting at risk. Furthermore, the concessions obtained from King John in 1215 applied to a minority of the population; the servile villeins (peasants) were only indirectly affected to the extent that they represented property and income for their lords.

Magna Carta should be understood in the context of the social and economic institutions of the time. Although inequality in status was the norm, beginning in the eleventh century the rapidly expanding economy created many opportunities for men of ambition to improve their condition. The baronial rebellion of 1215 that led to the signing of Magna Carta was an aspect of the economic energy that was driving the populace during this period. Yet the issue that prompted their rebellion, the increasing financial demands of the English kings, was also a product of the government's rising costs of providing the many services that were already being taking for granted—namely, peace and security and an impartial judicial system.

It should also be kept in mind that, although Magna Carta marked a first step toward guaranteeing individual rights and limiting the power of the ruler, England was not an isolated country. At that time, England and the western part of France from Normandy in the north to Aquitaine in the south had a common ruler. Thus, the cost of maintaining order in this "empire" and protecting it against absorption into the emerging state of modern France factored into the English baronial rebellion. By the early thirteenth century, the barons not only did not want to serve in an army operating in France, but they also did not want to pay mercenaries hired by the English king to serve in their place.

England was tied in with European developments in more ways than just the French connection and was participating in a growing economy that was stimulated by a vital international trade. It actively participated in the revival of intellectual interests that resulted in the appearance of universities, and its warriors fought in the religious-inspired Crusades that took them far away from home and introduced them to many different ways of thinking and living. Many Englishmen had been abroad as merchants, warriors, students, clerics, or diplomats and brought new ideas and customs home with them. Among the new ideas was an interest in architecture. Churches in the new style—built of brick and stone—followed the new European styles known as Romanesque and Gothic, although they were given a distinctive English flair.

The background for the main drama of this book—the events and developments directly related to Magna Carta—is covered in the first part of this volume, and biographies are provided in the second part. Appendix A provides an overview of the crusading movement. (For an extensive treatment of the Crusades, see the companion volume in the Guides to the History of the Medieval World, Helen Nicholson's *The Crusades*.) Appendix B attempts to explain the medieval trial by ordeal, which was still the accepted mode of proof in criminal cases at the time of Magna Carta.

Magna Carta and its accompanying Charter of the Forest, printed at the beginning of the collected Statutes of the Realm (of England), are legal documents. As such, they contain many specialized legal words that are not part of most individual's working vocabularies. A Glossary is provided to explain these words and to amplify the terms in the text that refer to the customs regarding the holding of property in medieval England. Magna Carta defined these customs not only for the baronial classes—the greater barons and the lesser barons, who came to be known as knights—but for all free men.

KINGS OF ENGLAND AND FRANCE DURING THE MAKING OF MAGNA CARTA

ENGLAND

Alfred	871–899
Athelstan	925–939
Edmund	939–946
Ethelred	978–1016
Cnut	1016–35
Harold Harefoot	1035–40
Harthacnut	1040–42
Edward the Confessor	1042–66
Harold	1066
William I the Conqueror	1066–87
William II	1087–1100
Henry I	1100–35
Stephen	1135–54
Henry II	1154–89
Richard I the Lionheart	1189–99
John	1199–1216
Henry III	1216–72
Edward I	1272–1307

FRANCE

Hugh Capet	987–986
Robert II the Pious	996–1031
Henry I	1031–60
Philip I	1060–1108
Louis VI	1108–37
Louis VII	1137–80
Philip II Augustus	1180–1223
Louis VIII	1223–26
Louis IX (St. Louis)	1226–70
Philip III	1270–85
Philip IV the Fair	1285–1314

CHRONOLOGY

751–68	Pepin I first Carolingian king of Franks.
754	Donation of Pepin. Pepin defeats the Lombards and gives the territory the Lombards had won from Exarchate of Ravenna to pope. Basis for creation of Papal States.
768–814	Charles the Great (Charlemagne) king of Franks.
774–814	Charlemagne king of Lombards.
793	First Danish attack on monasteries of Northumbria in England.
800–814	Charlemagne Roman Emperor, crowned by Pope Leo III.
871–99	Alfred king of Wessex.
878	Danes defeated by Alfred at battle of Edington followed by Peace of Chippingham.
886	Alfred takes London from Danes.
886	Treaty between Alfred and Danish Guthrum.
978–1016	Ethelred king of England.
1016–35	Cnut king of England (also king of Denmark).
1042–66	Edward the Confessor king of England.
1066	Harold, earl of Wessex, king of England.
Sept. 25, 1066	Harold wins battle of Stamford Bridge in Northumbria against a Norwegian claimant to the English throne.
Oct. 14, 1066	Battle of Hastings—Harold killed.
Dec. 1066	William the Conqueror, duke of Normandy, crowned king of England.
1066–87	Willliam I king of England.
1067–71	Rebellion in northen England subdued by William I.

1073–85	Pope Gregory VII.
1077	The *Dictatus*—Papal bull against lay investiture.
1087–1100	William II, second son of William I, king of England.
1089	Death of Lanfranc, archbishop of Canterbury.
1093	William II names Anselm of Aosta archbishop of Canterbury.
1096–99	First Crusade
1097	William drives Anselm into exile.
1100–35	Henry I, youngest son of William I, king of England.
1106–25	Henry V German Roman Emperor married to Matilda, daughter of Henry I of England.
1107	Henry I invites Anselm back to England as archbishop of Canterbury.
1108–37	Louis VI, son of Philip I, king of France.
Early 1100s	*The Laws of William the Conqueror.*
c. 1118	*The Laws of Henry I.*
1125	Matilda returns to England after death of her husband, the German Roman Emperor Henry V.
1127	Henry I marries Matilda to Geoffrey of Anjou (Anjou, a French county adjacent to Normandy).
1128	Geoffrey of Anjou becomes Count of Anjou when father Fulk V goes to Holy Land.
1135	Henry I dies defending Normandy.
1135–54	Stephen, nephew of Henry I, king of England.
1137	Matilda invades England seeking the crown from Stephen; civil war.
1137–80	Louis VII, son of Louis VI, king of France.

1137–52	Eleanor of Aquitaine, queen of France.
1144	Crusading state of Edessa falls to Turks.
1147–49	Second Crusade.
March 1152	Marriage between Louis VII of France and Eleanor of Aquitaine is dissolved.
May 1152	Henry of Anjou marries Eleanor of Aquitaine.
1152–90	Frederick I Barbarossa, German Roman Emperor.
1153	Henry of Anjou, son of Matilda, recognized as heir to King Stephen.
1154–89	Henry II, son of Matilda and Geoffrey, king of England.
1154–89	Eleanor of Aquitaine, queen of England.
Nov. 1164	Henry II and Thomas Becket quarrel about secular criminal jurisdiction over clerks; Becket goes into exile.
1164–70	Becket in exile in France.
1166–89	William II king of Sicily; his aunt Constance is heir.
1170	Henry II and Becket come to terms; Becket excommunicates those bishops and the archbishop of York who had not obeyed him during his exile.
Dec. 29, 1170	Becket murdered in Canterbury cathedral.
1171	The Turk Saladin abolishes the Fatimite Caliphate of Cairo.
1173–74	Rebellion of sons of Henry II of England.
March 1173	Becket canonized by Pope Alexander III.
1180–1223	Philip II Augustus, son of Louis VII, king of France.
1183	Death of Henry, eldest living son of Henry II and Eleanor.

1186	Death of Geoffrey, third son of Henry II and Eleanor.
1187	Fall of Jerusalem to the Turks.
1188	Glanville, *Treatise on the Laws and Customs of England*.
1189	Death of Henry II, sons Richard and John in rebellion.
1189–99	Richard I, second son of Henry II and Eleanor, king of England; Eleanor of Aquitaine is queen-mother.
1189–92	Richard I out of England on Third Crusade.
1190–97	Henry VI, son of Frederick I Barbarossa, German Roman emperor.
1192–94	Richard I of England a prisoner of Emperor Henry VI.
1194–99	Richard I in France fighting to keep his French land out of the hands of Philip II Augustus of France.
1198–1216	Pope Innocent III.
1198	Death of Constance of Sicily; future Frederick II becomes ward of Papacy (Innocent III).
1199–1216	John, youngest son of Henry II and Eleanor, king of England.
1199–1204	Eleanor of Aquitaine is queen-mother.
1202–04	Fourth Crusade
1204–61	Latin empire of Constantinople.
1205	Death of Hubert Walter, archbishop of Canterbury.
1207–1213	Conflict between King John and Pope Innocent III over Stephen Langton as archbishop of Canterbury.
1208–50	Frederick II king of Sicily; 1215–50 German Roman Emperor.

1213	Baronial plot against life of King John; Philip II of France prepares to invade England; John comes to terms with Innocent III.
1214	King John allies with Emperor Otto IV; Otto defeated in battle of Bouvines by Philip II of France; John returns to England in defeat.
1215	Albigensian Crusade, preached by Innocent III, led by the elder Simon de Montfort.
Spring 1215	Barons of England demand that King John accept Henry I's charter of liberties; John refuses.
March 1215	King John takes the cross; part of the barons revolt; London joins the rebels.
c. June 15, 1215	King John meets with the barons at Runnymede; agrees to a preliminary charter.
c. June 19, 1215	A formal charter (Magna Carta) is signed and copies distributed to the counties.
Later 1215	Innocent III releases King John from his oath to accept Magna Carta.
Later 1215	Barons rebel; invite Prince Louis of France to join them; civil war.
Aug. 1215	Stephen Langton recalled to Rome; suspended from archbishopric of Canterbury.
Nov. 1215	Fourth Lateran Council in Rome.
Oct. 1216	Death of King John.
1216–70	Henry III, son of John, king of England.
Late 1216	Regency for Henry III reissues Magna Carta.
1217	Regency for Henry III reissues Magna Carta accompanied by the Charter of the Forest.
1219	William Marshal dies.
1223–26	Louis VIII, son of Philip II Augustus, king of France.

1225	Reisssue of Magna Carta plus Charter of the Forest in final form.
1226–70	Louis IX, son of Louis VIII, king of France.
1232	Henry III of England dismisses Hubert de Burgh as chief justiciar and assumes direction of government himself.
1244	Jerusalem falls to the Turks.
1248–54	Louis IX's first crusade.
1250	Death of Frederick II.
1254	King Henry III of England agrees to allow second son Edmund to accept throne of Sicily in return for assuming papal debt.
1254	King Henry III requests an aid from his council (barons plus two knights from each county); Council grants a smaller aid and makes protest.
1256	Henry de Bracton, *Concerning the Laws and Customs of England*.
1258	Provisions of Oxford—Henry III subject to a council of twelve barons; Simon de Montfort emerges as leader of the barons.
1264	Battle of Lewes; barons defeat king; Henry III and Prince Edward taken captive.
1265	Simon de Montfort's Parliament (two knights from each shire; two burgesses from each borough).
1266	Battle of Evesham; Simon de Montfort and baronial army defeated; de Montfort killed.
1270	Louis IX's second crusade.
1270–85	Philip III, son of King Louis IX, king of France.
1270–74	Prince Edward out of England.
1272–1307	Edward I, son of King Henry III, king of England.

1285–1314	Philip IV the Fair, son of Philip III, king of France.
1295	King Edward I's Model Parliament.
1297	Confirmation of the Charters.
1307–27	Edward II, son of Edward I, king of England.
1327–77	Edward III, son of Edward II and Isabella of France, king of England.
1328–50	Philip VI of Valois, grandson of Philip III, king of France.
1337–1453	Hundred Years War between England and France.
1453	Constantinople falls to the Ottoman Turks.

INTRODUCTION: THE MYTH OF MAGNA CARTA

Magna Carta is the name given to a document that King John of England agreed to sign under pressure from the barons and other notables of England. The signing of this document took place in the summer of 1215 (traditionally June 15, 1215) at a meadow known as Runnymede on the river Thames between London and Windsor. It was a remarkable document for its time, resulting from the rebellion of a significant number of the landed aristocracy against John whom they regarded as having abused his customary rights as lord of England. But although the rebellion began with the barons and the barons received the benefit of many of the concessions made by John, the barons' success was made possible by the fact that John had alienated other influential segments of the population: the Church (both the Roman church and the English church) as well as the rapidly rising mercantile interests of the country symbolized by the city of London. But remarkable as the original agreement was, it acquired its elevated position in the legal and constitutional history of England as much from what men thought it said as from what its provisions actually contained.

This misunderstanding resulted from the course of events that followed the agreement at Runnymede. It soon became apparent that John had no intention of living up to the agreement, and so the barons rebelled again. An invasion from France at baronial invitation faced England not only with civil war but also with the possibility of a foreign ruler. John's unexpected death in October 1216 reversed the situation. The notables of the realm had little difficulty in agreeing to accept the nine-year-old son of John as King Henry III rather than have a French ruler. The young king's advisers took action to placate the barons by immediately reissuing John's charter in 1216 with significant omissions and some editorial corrections, and again in 1217 with a few further changes and with the added Charter of the Forest containing provisions for regulation of the forest issues omitted in the issue of 1216. Following additional baronial unrest, Magna Carta was reissued in 1225 with accumulated omissions and revisions, again accompanied by the Charter of the Forest. It was the issue of 1225 together with the Charter of the Forest that would be reissued in times of future friction between the king and his people and would be the form issued by Edward I (Henry III's son) in 1297 at a time of widespread protest against the financial demands of the crown. It is this issue of 1297 that was placed at the beginning of the collected Statutes of the Realm. Whatever its other protections, Magna Carta and the Charter of the Forest would remain a symbol of the thirteenth-century demonstration that the king was not above the law.

In all the negotiations between the crown and the people in the thirteenth century and after, there was misunderstanding on both sides as to what was being demanded and what was being conceded. The Great Charter (Magna Carta)—as it was now being referred to—was thought to contain a number of "liberties" that had been dropped in the process of revision in the early years of Henry III. These liberties and those that remained in the Charter were embellished by its proponents over the years and utilized in the seventeenth century during a constitutional crisis. This crisis resulted from the clash of Parliament[1] with the Stuart kings,[2] who succeeded Elizabeth I following her death in 1603. Sir Edward Coke, an English common lawyer arguing the parliamentary cause against James I (1603–25) and Charles I (1625–49), could find in Magna Carta such English rights as trial by jury, habeas corpus, equality before the law, freedom from arbitrary arrest, and parliamentary control of taxation. Following the execution of Charles I in 1645, and the expulsion of James II in 1689 by the actions of Parliament, it would be Coke's interpretation, followed by William Blackstone in the eighteenth century, that would prevail in Great Britain and its colonies until the nineteenth and twentieth centuries.

The following chapters provide a background for the making of Magna Carta itself as well as the making of its myth. The documents that follow include what is thought to be a prototype for Magna Carta: " 'The Coronation Charter' of Henry I," "Magna Carta, 1215," "Magna Carta, 1225" together with the supporting document "Charter of the Forest, 1225," and the "The Confirmation of the Charters, 1297."

NOTES

1. Parliament had begun to evolve during the thirteenth century after the king's financial needs forced him to call on his barons for additional aids (money grants). See Chapter 5.

2. The divine-right Stuart kings were James I (1603–25), Charles I (1625–49), Charles II (1660–85), and James II (1685–88).

CHAPTER 1

MAGNA CARTA AND THE CHURCH

The role of the Church in the making of Magna Carta was important in two ways. First, if we regard Magna Carta as the product primarily of a rebellion of the English barons, we have to recognize that the highest ranked churchmen—archbishops, bishops, and abbots—were also barons of the realm because they were landholders who held part, if not most, of their land directly from the crown, that is, the king. They were part of the English landholding system and were as much concerned as the secular barons in demanding that the king recognize the reciprocal obligations between lord and men. (For details on the English system of landholding, see Chapter 3.) Second, the Church was also a spiritual institution that was national in some respects and international in others. The tension between the national and international interests of the Church—that is, between the king as leader and the pope as ruler—would also play an important role in producing Magna Carta.

England's relationship with the universal Christian church as represented by the papacy had been close in the early Anglo-Saxon period beginning with the arrival of Augustine. Pope Gregory I, called the Great, sent Augustine to the southeastern kingdom of Kent in the late sixth century to convert the Angles and Saxons to Christianity.[1] For several centuries thereafter, the tie remained close, but from the late eighth century on, the relationship became weaker as the continental church suffered from the disintegration of Charlemagne's Carolingian Empire. Now lacking a strong secular protector and weakened by the struggles of the local Roman nobility to control the papal throne itself, the papacy lost its spiritual leadership and came more and more under the control of local rulers, including kings, counts, and dukes. The local rulers not only invested (bestowed upon) their higher clergy with the lands that the Church held from them, but also named the holders of church office and invested them with the spiritual symbols of their office.

In this fragmented condition, dominated by the secular authority, the Church under the leadership of the monastery at Cluny in south-central France began in the tenth century to demand and introduce monastic reform. This impetus for monastic reform spread to the western German lands where it developed into a demand for the general reform of the Church. From Germany the reform movement went to Rome, where the leaders were Pope Leo IX (1049–54), Nicholas II (1059–61), Alexander II (1061–73), and Gregory VII (Hildebrand) (1073–85). The goal of this larger reform movement was to eliminate secular control of the Church and ultimately to assert the superiority of the spiritual power over the secular.

Anglo-Saxon England had experienced some monastic reform, but it was not part of the broader church reform movement under way at the time of the Norman conquest in 1066. William, duke of Normandy, in northern France, exploited this situation to obtain papal authorization for his invasion in 1066. He claimed the crown of England from Harold, who had been elected king on the death of Edward the Confessor in that year, by inheritance since Edward had named William as his heir. But William was obviously going to have to fight for that crown, and here the papal blessing would be invaluable. William therefore proposed to introduce reform into the English church, and he was awarded a papal banner to fly at the head of his invading army.

Was the English church in need of reform? The answer depends on how one interprets reform. As far as the morals and training of the English clergy were concerned, the English were probably no better or no worse than their continental counterparts. And a new vitality in organization and learning had begun to affect England as new monastic movements such as that at Cluny began to spread. The great difference between the English church and the continental church, rather, was a product of historical experience. From the time of the Anglo-Saxon invasions of England in the fourth through sixth centuries, a number of relatively small kingdoms had arisen whose boundaries tended to shift from time to time. Into this scene in the late eighth and ninth centuries came the Northmen (Danes in the south and Norwegians in the north and west) who overcame the northern kingdoms and gained control of the land down to a line that ran from approximately London in the south-east to Chester in the northwest. In the end, only the kingdom of Wessex in the southwest and southern part of England, including a part of the Anglian kingdom of Mercia to the north of Wessex, remained outside the Danish-Norse conquest.

The Wessex that emerged under Alfred (871–899) was destined to rally the cause of the Anglo-Saxons and to lead the English (as the newly united people were coming to be called) to unify the land up to the borders of the Celtic lands in the north (Scotland) and west (Wales). In the course of this unification, England became one of the best organized and centralized states of Europe under the leadership of the house of Wessex (replaced briefly by the Danish Cnut and his sons at the beginning of the eleventh century). This unification was accomplished through cooperation and even some consolidation between church and state. Churchmen were useful to the crown because of their literacy and their administrative ability and experience. At the national level, they were ministers of state and counselors of the king. At the local level, they were also very much involved in local administration. There were no separate church courts in Anglo-Saxon England and no separate church legislation. The courts at all levels—hundred, shire (called county after the Norman conquest), and royal—had jurisdiction over all causes. The local ecclesiastical official sat with the court and thus was present when cases that involved the Church (whether disciplinary, administrative, or theological) came before the court. In effect, the state and Church in England were not in competition for jurisdiction.

William of Normandy, with papal support, did conquer England in 1066. It is not necessary to relate here how factors other than simple military conquest were involved. The Saxon king Harold was killed at the battle of Hastings in 1066, and the English had no good candidate to replace him. Since demoralization was widespread, the Anglo-Saxon witan (a royal advisory council made up of the magnates of the realm) agreed to accept William. He was crowned king in December 1066, although he would later have to repress rebellion, especially in the north, on a number of occasions, notably 1067–71.

As duke of Normandy and king of England, William was selective in the ecclesiastical reforms he supported. At William's request, a papal legate came to England and called a church council that deposed Stigand, the archbishop of Canterbury, and many of the other English bishops. In place of Stigand William named Lanfranc, an Italian educated in Roman law at the school of Pavia, who had become abbot of the monastery of Bec in Normandy. Lanfranc was in contact with the continental reform movement; in England he and William worked closely together to reform the church, but not at the expense of the centralized state. William and Lanfranc supported the movement in England to increase the moral authority of the Church, eliminate such evils as the purchase of church office (simony), improve the education of the clergy, and encourage the demand for celibacy of the clergy (a reform that was long in gaining acceptance). They made no attempt to remove the selection of church officials from secular control, a demand that had become a focal point of the reform movement on the Continent. In 1077 Pope Gregory VII issued his bull *Dictatus* prohibiting what came to be known as lay investiture, that is, the naming and investing of church leaders by the secular ruler. This was justified because the Church held much land in every state, and rulers needed loyal followers on that land. In addition, rulers needed these literate individuals to help in the administration of the state. Therefore, lay rulers not only formally invested churchmen with their lands but also bestowed on them the symbols—the ring and the crosier—of their spiritual office. In effect, secular control of the higher church personnel was complete.

William and Lanfranc ignored the demand for the end of lay investiture after 1077 and concentrated on reform of morals, education, and administration. They also fulfilled one of the specific promises William made in return for receiving the papal banner: the separation of church courts from secular courts. Henceforth there would be separate secular and church courts, two different laws, and two different types of court procedure. The secular courts applied Anglo-Saxon customary law (the laws of Edward the Confessor) as modified by local custom and a few royal directions issued by William I and his Norman successors. In contrast, the church courts applied the canon law of the Church, which was in process of being codified—that is, collected and published—and taught at a number of centers of learning, such as, Bologna in Italy and Chartres in France. The result came to be a kind of competition between the two types of jurisdiction: the church courts gradually expanded their jurisdiction to cover not only heresy (belief in false doctrines) and breaches of the rules of Christian behavior, but all offenses involving clerical personnel, including felonies such as murder, and increasingly cases involving contracts, especially marriage.

The potential for conflict between king and pope erupted into a serious dispute during the reign of William's second son, William II Rufus (1087–1100). William II was a more autocratic ruler than his father, and when Lanfranc died in 1089, William let the archbishopric of Canterbury lie vacant which, according to the emerging feudal custom, allowed him as overlord to collect the revenues of the Church during its vacancy. William II also allowed other church positions to lie vacant and appropriated their revenues. He sold office to the highest bidder and blocked English clerical communication with the papacy. But William II became ill in 1093, and fearing death without spiritual support, he repented and named Anselm of Aosta archbishop of Canterbury. Like Lanfranc, Anselm was educated at Pavia and was now prior of the monastery of Bec in Normandy. Since Lanfranc and Anselm had somewhat similar backgrounds, William probably expected Anselm to be as cooperative as Lanfranc had been. But Anselm was primarily a scholar who was completely in sympathy with the reforming papacy. A conflict between king and archbishop rapidly developed over the issue of lay investiture, a conflict that was to have important repercussions in the Church-state disputes leading up to Magna Carta. William recovered from his illness and was soon embroiled in controversy with the archbishop, leading to Anselm's flight to the Continent in 1097, thus forfeiting Canterbury.

In 1100 William the Conqueror's youngest son Henry succeeded to the kingdom of England. Although as strong a ruler as his father and brother had been, Henry sought reconciliation with the papacy in Rome and entered negotiations with Anselm, which eventually led to compromise over the questions of selection of church officials and lay investiture. Church officials would be elected by their clerics in the presence of the king, the king would then invest such persons with those lands held from the king, and then a churchman would invest with the symbols of spiritual office. In effect, the king held a veto over the election by insisting on his own candidate, or he would not invest the property associated with the office. The one significant change was that the secular ruler no longer invested the candidate with his spiritual office.[2] The crown still controlled the personnel of the higher clergy and controlled communications between the English clergy and the papacy.

The situation changed significantly in the next reign, that of Stephen (1135–54). King Henry I had left only one legitimate child, a daughter Matilda,[3] who had been married to the German Roman emperor Henry V. When Emperor Henry died in 1125, King Henry brought Matilda back to England and had his barons take oath to accept her as his heir. In the meantime Henry married Matilda to Geoffrey, son of Fulk, count of Anjou, in northern France to the southwest of Normandy. Unfortunately, Matilda was not in England when Henry I died in 1135. So it was that Stephen, a grandson of William the Conqueror through William's daughter Adela and a nephew of Henry I of England and who held land in both England and Normandy, secured the crown of England with considerable support from the English church and most of the baronage. To get ecclesiastical support, Stephen promised that the English church should be "free." But in practice Stephen tended to treat the Church just as arbitrarily as his Norman predecessors had until an ongoing civil war was initiated by Matilda's invasion of England in 1137 to claim the throne. To retain church support, Stephen made more and more concessions to the Church until, on his death in 1154, the English church was the freest in its history: many higher clergy were elected by their subordinate clergy and confirmed by the pope, papal legates (representatives) passed freely back and forth to England, English clergy traveled to the Continent, and cases from the English church courts were routinely appealed to the papal court in Rome.

The civil war continued intermittently until shortly before Stephen's death. In the war's later phases, Matilda's eldest son Henry pursued Matilda's claims, and in 1153 Henry was recognized as Stephen's heir. Henry II became king of England in 1154; he was already duke of Normandy, count of Maine and Anjou, and duke of Aquitaine, in right of his wife, Eleanor of Aquitaine.

Henry II (1154–89) was determined to restore the powers of the crown as they had been under his grandfather, Henry I, and that included control of the English church. He largely succeeded except in one very significant area, and that was the exclusive jurisdiction of church courts over the personnel of the clergy, even when a cleric was involved in serious secular crimes (i.e., felonies). Henry's defeat in this very important attempt to bring criminous clerks under state control was the outcome of a conflict between Henry and his own choice for archbishop of Canterbury, Thomas Becket. Becket had served as Henry's chancellor from

1155 to 1163 and the two men had worked well together. When Archbishop of Canterbury Theobald died in 1162, Henry pondered a long while before concluding that Becket should fill that office. Accordingly, in 1163 Henry proposed Becket for the office and Becket was duly elected. Henry had expected that Becket would cooperate with him in his attempts to bring the Church under as much control as that exercised by his grandfather, Henry I. But when Henry presented a proposal designed to bring clerks (clergy) accused of felonies (serious crimes against the king's peace) before the royal courts (the Constitutions of Clarendon), the response of Becket and the other clerical members of the king's court was to accept the Constitutions but subject to the limitations of their clerical status (that is, so far as the canon law allowed). This was unacceptable to Henry, who brought charges against Becket that he had misused funds as chancellor and, fearing that he would have to face trial in the king's court, Becket fled into exile in November 1165. Thereafter until final reconciliation in 1170, Becket was supported by Louis VII, king of France, an enemy of Henry's.

During Becket's exile, there were many embassies between the two antagonists, but, both arrogant and egoistic men, neither would compromise his position. Finally in fall 1170, terms were finally agreed upon and Becket returned to his position as Archbishop of Canterbury. He immediately excommunicated those bishops and the archbishop of York whom he regarded as disobeying him and those men immediately appealed to Henry II, still in Normandy. In final frustration, Henry made the unfortunate remark asking why no one would rid him of this problem. Some of his followers took him at his word and proceeded to Canterbury where Becket was murdered before his altar in 1170. Henry did public penance for this act, Becket was canonized several years later, and Becket's shrine at Canterbury became a favorite pilgrimage site in England. Thereafter the English clergy remained free of the criminal jurisdiction of the common law courts until the law reforms of the nineteenth century.

Henry II's defeat regarding exemption for clergy from the criminal jurisdiction of the common law courts was a serious blow to royal control of the Church. This defeat was made more serious because it coincided with increasing tensions between the king and his sons who began to agitate for an increased role in the government of the Angevin Empire. This tension between father and sons was fueled to a degree by the young men's mother, Eleanor of Aquitaine, but increasingly by the young and able new king of France, Philip II Augustus (1180–1223). In the event, Henry II had little time or inclination to seek other ways of bringing the Church under the same degree of control as that exercised by his grandfather, Henry I. Nonetheless, some developments during the later years of his reign would influence future Church-state relations. As part of his penance for the death of Becket, Henry promised to go on a crusade, although he never found time or opportunity to do so before 1187 when the fall of Jerusalem to the Turks increased papal pressure for the crusade. In order to secure financial means to undertake such a military campaign, Henry and his council in 1188 assessed a tax of one-tenth against personal or movable property as opposed to other feudal assessments that directly or indirectly were related to the holding of land—an assessment to be called the Saladin (the name of the Turkish leader) tithe. This would provide an important precedent for later taxes on movable property. All in all, Henry's relations with the Church were fairly amicable during his last years.

While Archbishop Becket was in exile in France, the quarrel between king and archbishop was aggravated by Henry's decision to have his eldest son, Henry, crowned king in his own lifetime, thereby securing the succession. Normally, the archbishop of Canterbury performed the coronation, but since Becket was in exile, the archbishop of York officiated instead, thus adding to the issues dividing Henry and Becket. The young Henry and his father never agreed on a division of authority (the father Henry did not delegate), and so both father and son were still estranged when the young king died unexpectedly in 1183.

When Henry II died in 1189, defeated by the rebellion of his two surviving sons, Richard and John, he was succeeded by his second son, Richard, who had spent his late teens and adult years in Aquitaine. There Richard had represented both his father and his mother against the rebellious nobles of that southwestern part of France. Richard had developed an enviable military record, and his military exploits would determine the relative success of his relations with the Church. In particular, he would soon become the leader in the West's militant crusade to reclaim Jerusalem from Turkish rule.

The city of Jerusalem had fallen to the Turks under Saladin in 1187 (see Appendix A), and a renewed wave of crusading fervor now swept Western Europe, claiming Richard among others—so much so that his succession to the English possessions took second place to his preparations to depart for the east. He returned to England only briefly for his coronation as king and to raise money for his eastern campaign. He raised money by removing many of his father's appointees and naming his own men who paid well for their positions. In addition, he used all of his feudal privileges, including aids, scutages, wardships, and marriage contracts, and he assessed a land tax called a carucage. Though Richard's actions aroused objection, there was little outright protest. Richard left in the company of Philip II of France, but when they arrived in the east they quarreled after capturing the port city of Acre. Philip then returned to France; Richard remained but failed to take Jerusalem, though Saladin did grant Christian pilgrims the right to visit the city. Planning to return to England, Richard feared capture by Philip of France if he returned via the French Mediterranean port of Marseilles, so he traveled incognito through the Adriatic Sea and across the German lands. There he was nonetheless recognized and captured by the duke of Austria and sold to the German Roman emperor Henry VI[4] who held him for an enormous ransom. Richard's mother Eleanor and Hubert Walter, archbishop of Canterbury and chief justiciar, raised the ransom money and Richard returned to England in 1194. But he stayed only long enough to exact money and military service for his war against France where Philip Augustus had been harrying Richard's continental possessions. Richard died in 1199, still fighting in France to protect the duchy of Normandy from French occupation.

Although there was much grumbling among both the secular and clerical baronage over Richard's financial exactions, no overt rebellion developed. Rebellion would come under John, the youngest son of Henry II, who succeeded Richard (an older brother Geoffrey had died in 1186). John's succession was not a foregone conclusion since Geoffrey had left a young son, but Eleanor and the English baronage in general favored the adult John over a minor during a time when France was threatening most of the English possessions in France.

Upon John's accession a crisis developed almost immediately. John had assumed leadership of the Norman campaign, but not being the natural warrior that Richard was, despite his collection of more men and money, by 1204 John had lost Normandy to France, followed shortly by the loss of Maine, Anjou, and Touraine. John continued to collect men and money and spent more time and more money in an attempt to build a coalition against Philip II, but he was unable to mount a continental attack until 1214. In the meantime, John became involved in a bitter quarrel with the Church and faced increasing resistance from the members of the English baronage who began to assert that their feudal military service did not obligate them to serve overseas. Moreover, if they did not need to serve overseas, then they should not pay scutage so that the crown could hire mercenary substitutes.

At the same time the quarrel between John and the Church was expanding. Hubert Walter, archbishop of Canterbury (1193–1205), died in 1205 after a long and able career of service. The monks of Christ Church, Canterbury,[5] seeking to forestall the election of the king's candidate, elected their subprior and immediately sent him off to Rome to receive the approval of the pope, Innocent III (1198–1216). Furious, John then demanded the election of his own candidate, John de Gray, bishop of Norwich; the monks elected him, and he too was sent off to Rome for approval. Determined to assert the supremacy of the spiritual over the temporal, Pope Innocent III declared both elections invalid and named his own candidate, Stephen Langton, an Englishman educated at Paris whom Innocent III had named a cardinal priest in Rome. Although Langton was consecrated archbishop by Innocent, John refused him entry into England. Innocent retaliated by placing England under an interdict—a penalty under which most church services could not be conducted in England. John replied by seizing the possessions of the clergy who observed it. Next Innocent excommunicated John, placing him outside the Christian communion. The stalemate continued until 1213. To this point John's quarrel with the Church had not aroused the people inasmuch as John had confiscated so much church property and assessed so many fines against ecclesiastical property that momentarily John's financial exactions from the secular baronage were less exorbitant than previously. By 1213, however, the situation changed, compelling John to seek reconciliation with Innocent III: in 1212 an outbreak of baronial resistance had culminated in a plot against the king's life, and in 1213 it became known that Philip II of France, with the pope's blessing, planned an invasion of England to depose John. To win Innocent III's help in forestalling invasion and in fighting the barons, John agreed to an astonishing list of concessions. He agreed to accept Langton as archbishop of Canterbury, to receive back the exiled bishops, to compensate the Church for its losses, and to submit England and Ireland to the papacy and receive them back as fiefs of the papacy (see Chapter 5).

In the meantime Stephen Langton returned to England as archbishop of Canterbury and became closely involved in the growing baronial resistance to King John. It may have been Langton who advised the barons of the coronation charter of Henry I (see Document 1 of this volume), which would become a kind of blueprint for Magna Carta. It is not surprising that the first chapter of Magna Carta was a concession to the Church:

> In the first place [we] have granted to God, and by this our present charter confirmed for us and our heirs for ever that the English church shall be free, and shall have its rights undiminished and its liberties unimpaired; and it is our will that it be thus observed; which is evident from the fact that, before the quarrel between us and our barons began, we willingly and spontaneously granted and by our charter confirmed the freedom of elections which is reckoned most important and very essential to the English church, and obtained confirmation of it from the lord pope Innocent III; the which we will observe and we wish our heirs to observe it in good faith for ever.   (Magna Carta 1215, Article 1)

Thus, Magna Carta would formally grant the Church the liberties it had been demanding for so many years. It did not end the struggle over spiritual power against temporal power. Indeed, public opinion did not rest entirely with the Church. During John's quarrel with the Church (1205–13), many English people resented Innocent III for his use of the interdict and excommunication to force John to capitulate. For many, these acts represented foreign interference in a national concern. Even more, Innocent's support of John against the barons and his approval of Philip of France's invasion of England encouraged the concept of an English church under English control.

NOTES

1. The most important kingdoms in Anglo-Saxon Britain were the Jutish kingdom of Kent in the southeast; the Saxon kingdoms of Sussex, Wessex, and Essex, in the south; the Anglian kingdoms of East Anglia and Mercia in the central area; and Northumbria in the north.

2. This English compromise set a precedent for ending the long-lasting quarrel over lay investiture between the German Roman emperor and the papacy.

The Concordat of Worms (1122) concluded between Emperor Henry V and Pope Calixtus II provided that in the German part of the empire, the emperor would have the same veto as in England, but in the Italian part of the empire, the emperor had virtually no control over selection of the higher clergy.

3. Henry's only legitimate son, William, died in a shipwreck in 1120 during his wedding celebration.

4. The medieval Roman Empire was not called the Holy Roman Empire until 1254.

5. The organization of the Church at Canterbury encouraged disputes over election. Canterbury, like a number of other English cathedrals, served not only as a secular cathedral but also as the church of a monastery. Canon law supported not only the claims of the monks of the cathedral to elect the archbishop of Canterbury, but also the claims of the bishops of the province of Canterbury to elect the archbishop. In the case of Henry II and Becket, Henry sought the approval of both monks and bishops. Eventually, the monks won the right, with the result that the archbishop of Canterbury was usually a monk, and monks usually did not have a lot of administrative experience. Because church government had become so bureaucratized by the late twelfth century, there was a movement to establish chapters of secular canons (men who were celibate and lived a common life but worked in the world) at the cathedrals. This was a cause of extreme tension at Canterbury for a number of years.

CHAPTER 2

MAGNA CARTA AND THE TOWNS

Although the merchants of England's towns, especially those of London, played a critical role in the events leading up to Magna Carta, they had already learned to negotiate with the king and other lords in their battle for independence in the conduct of their affairs. Magna Carta specifically acknowledged freedoms and privileges to London and extended them to those towns that had not yet negotiated such rights. In effect, the success of the towns in negotiating with the crown provided an example of what a moneyed class could achieve in dealing with an impoverished monarchy.

This chapter outlines the conditions that allowed the emergence of towns and their acquisition of a wealth and privilege which in turn gave them an influence with the crown that rivaled that of the baronage.

Britain had been a province of the Roman Empire from the middle of the first century to the early fifth century. Roman political organization centered on the *civitas*—a town and its surrounding territory. To create such entities in Britain, the Romans established a number of towns for purposes of defense against the conquered tribes within or enemies from without. Some of these places coincided with the old tribal capitals; others were located in places such as London where some trade had already been established between Britain and the continent; and still others were new foundations. Garrisons were located in certain strategically located towns, and others were administrative centers, but all had to be supplied and otherwise serviced so that a civilian population grew in the towns in addition to the military and administrative personnel. English towns began to develop during early Roman rule, when Roman soldiers, coming to the end of their tour of duty, were given land and began to settle near where they had been stationed.

Roman towns in Britain probably reached the peak of their growth and prosperity in the second and very early third centuries, after which they began to decline. Roman Britain was at the end of a long Roman frontier that had to be defended against constant pressure from without. The Roman economy, already inadequate to support the military forces necessary for such defense, was further burdened by the long dispute over the imperial succession (from 235 to 285). During these years, Roman armies abandoned their frontier posts and marched toward Rome to put their commanders on the imperial throne. The Roman legions in Britain participated in these civil wars, leaving the island with little, if any, protection.

Roman towns in Britain never recovered from these third-century problems. They shrank in size, and town walls were erected around the most important of them for protection. But even inside the walls, the population continued to shrink, and much area lay vacant. The late Roman taxation system placed responsibility for collection of taxes on the local *curiales*, men who had been accustomed to holding local political office; what tax they were unable to collect had to be made up from their own property. This system ruined the *curiales*, the only town class with money. By the end of the fourth century and the beginning of the fifth, when the Roman legions were withdrawn from Britain for the final time, the vitality of town life was gone. Most of the sites were abandoned by the time of the Anglo-Saxon invasions between the mid-fifth and mid-sixth centuries.

The decline of town life affected not just Britain, but all parts of the Western Roman Empire, with the possible exception of Italy; with the shrinking of urban demand, long-distance trade declined. However, the decline in Britain occurred earlier and was more complete than that in other parts of the western empire where town life never completely disappeared but continued on a reduced level. The towns there continued to be occupied by Roman political personnel or by diocesan officers (bishops) of the Church. Therefore, continental towns located on coastal or river trade routes already had a nucleus to attract the settlement of merchants when trade revived in the tenth and eleventh centuries. This revival followed the end of the Northmen, Hungarian, and Muslim invasions and the emergence of more stable political units, which were frequently smaller than the empires or kingdoms of an earlier period.

Nonetheless, Anglo-Saxon towns were not far behind their continental rivals. The revival of trade and the related growth of towns did not, however, depend so much on the favorable location of church administration as on the needs of an emerging nation fighting to survive attacks of Northmen (Norwegians in the north and Danes in the south) from the late eighth to the middle of the tenth century. All the Anglo-Saxon kingdoms fell except the Saxon kingdom of Wessex in the southwestern and southern part of the island and the western part of the Anglian kingdom of Mercia just to the north. The eventual merger of the two kingdoms into an expanded Wessex provided the base for the gradual extension of English rule to the borders of Scotland in the north and to Wales in the west. To control and protect this territory, the English kings, beginning with Alfred in the late ninth century, erected burgs, or fortified enclosures, to provide a place for defense and administrative personnel. As the organization and centralization of Wessex, increasingly referred to as England, grew and internal peace was assured, conditions favorable to the revival of trade developed. Those burgs located on or near where trade routes crossed (on the coast or on rivers or on the old Roman roads that had continued in use) attracted first itinerant merchants and gradually settled merchants. These new "towns" joined a number of older towns: London, which had continued on a small scale to be a trading town throughout the Anglo-Saxon period, and York, which had developed into a town under Norse rule and participated in an active North Sea and Scandinavian trade. In addition, a number of small ports along the English Channel did some trade with the northern part of Francia—essentially modern France—and the Frisian coast on the North Sea to the east of Francia.

By the end of the tenth century and the beginning of the eleventh, a number of mercantile towns were recognized for the personal freedom their inhabitants enjoyed, including the right to move around freely: London, York, Lincoln, Rochester, Canterbury, Bristol, Norwich, Northampton, and Winchester and the southern ports of Dover, Sandwich, Romney, and Hythe. All of these towns were under royal or seigneurial (another lord's) control, their lord being represented by a port reeve (an official named by the lord of the town) who increasingly consulted with the most influential merchants in the community. These men were beginning to be organized into a guild merchant that was influential enough to negotiate for legal and economic rights: personal freedom, mobility, and burgage tenure (the right to hold property for an annual fee and to mortgage or sell that property). The economy was expanding rapidly to include trade with northern and western Gaul, northern Spain, Ireland, and the entire northern world (England was part of a Danish empire under Cnut and his sons in the early eleventh century). As a result, goods from all parts of Europe, northern Africa, and the Middle East found their way to England. In return, England supplied grain, wool, cattle, hides, tin, and hunting dogs, with the demand for wool increasing rapidly.

It is difficult to separate the influence of internal and external trade. With the exception of those coastal ports located favorably for trade with the neighboring continent and the North Sea areas, most inland towns began as royal burgs or other foundations such as monasteries that had a specialized population needing food and services. For many years, the typical medieval urban holding included a building with a shop in front, living quarters above and behind, and a large open area behind it devoted to agrarian purposes. However, as the population was increasing rapidly and the agrarian area was shrinking, eventually the town population failed to produce enough to feed itself. The enterprising landlord would therefore establish a weekly market to which peasants from the surrounding countryside could bring their surplus produce. As population increased in the tenth and eleventh centuries, these market towns proved to be magnets for the surplus country population since servant positions or craft apprenticeships offered more opportunity than the farms. With the revival of long-distance trade, the thriving market towns demanded better goods than was produced locally.

In response to this demand, English traders brought specialized products from other parts of the country. Soon they were delivering goods that had originated overseas, and eventually foreign merchants themselves arrived. The foreign merchants gradually found their way to all the prosperous inland towns, but they were especially attracted to those places where, with the king's license, an annual fair was established for the express purpose of trade. The abbots of Ramsay in Huntingdonshire established such a fair at St. Ives in 1110, attracting merchants from East Anglia as well as merchants from abroad. Other fairs were St. Giles, established by the bishops of Winchester, St. Botolph at Boston-on-the Wash, and St. Bartholomew at Smithfield outside London. Such fairs offered special facilities for the traders to display their merchandise. Special protection was provided for the merchants traveling to and from the fair on roads protected by the king's peace, and special courts—called piepowder courts from the French *pied poudre,* "dusty foot"—were set up where the merchants could get speedy justice according to what was becoming an international law for merchants. The town's landlord profited from all these activities, and in the expansive period between 1100 and 1300, some 140 new towns were established, though not all flourished. Considering all the towns, a variety of landlords were involved, but the crown held the largest number, followed by the monasteries and bishoprics. A few secular lords held the others.

According to Domesday Book (a survey of the kingdom commissioned by William the Conqueror in 1086–87), at the time of the Norman conquest there were a number of old established towns: namely, London, Leicester, York, and the Cinque Ports along the Channel coast. Newer towns, responding to the growing maritime trade, were Newcastle on the northeastern coast and Boston and King's Lynn, on the central eastern coast. By the early twelfth century, the more influential merchants began to band together to negotiate for more privileges from their lords, privileges leading toward self-government. Such groups of merchants formed an exclusive organization that gradually became the spokesman for the town. These merchant associations were called merchant guilds (not to be confused with the later craft guilds) or the guild merchant. It was they who negotiated for increasing independence. By the early twelfth century, a guild merchant had been established in such towns as Oxford, Beverley, York, Leicester, Winchester, and Lincoln. There must also have been one in London, for in 1130 London received its first charter from Henry I allowing the city to "farm"—that is, assess and collect—its own taxes for the town of London and the county of Middlesex in which London was located. As the century progressed, a few other towns received this same privilege either from the king or from another landlord. Invariably, the gift of the privilege was accompanied by a monetary return gift from the town.

The towns gained political influence as the spread of a money economy was felt at all levels of society, including the peasant class. But wealth and power in early medieval society had depended on landholding, a situation that had created a social and political structure reflecting the amount of land controlled by an individual or institution. In England, the result was a pyramid structure with the king at the top, his tenants-in-chief, both lay and ecclesiastical, forming the next tier (eventually called the barons or greater barons), and the subtenants down to the smallest freeholders as well as the landless warriors making up the lowest section (usually known as the lesser barons or knights). Peasants were not part of the power structure.

As the system solidified in England following the Norman conquest, the king, as the largest landholder, was expected to live on the income provided by his feudal dues (for further detail, see Chapter 3). Throughout the rule of the Norman kings (William I, William II, Henry I, and Stephen—1066–1154), this income generally sufficed. As a money economy came to dominate over feudal dues and services during the twelfth century, however, the English kings had to find a way to increase their monetary income. Raising feudal dues and services culminated in protests from the baronage, leading to rebellion in 1212–15; as a result, from the 1190s on, the kings or their representatives increasingly turned to the towns as a source of revenue. The merchants in the towns found that by banding together and for a monetary consideration they could negotiate for ever increasing privileges leading to greater self-government. Prior to 1215, the kings found it easier to negotiate for revenue with the organized towns rather than with the barons who had individual grievances rather than communal interests for which to seek remedies. As can be seen from the events leading up to Magna Carta, it was the example of the towns that led the barons to seek to work out a common set of demands from King John.

In 1130 Henry I gave London its first charter allowing it to collect its own taxes. Later, Henry II deprived London of that right in retaliation for London's having sided with Stephen during the civil war that broke out when Henry's mother Matilda attempted to claim the English throne. In general, Henry II recognized the advantages of founding new towns, but he did not favor the communal movement that had developed in the more organized towns. Even Henry II, however, was increasingly hard pressed to raise the funds needed to rule and protect his widely spaced lands in the British Isles and France, which was often referred to as the Angevin Empire. Continuing the reforms of Henry II, Henry's sons

Richard and John found themselves with increasingly well-organized and efficient town governments, but they also faced new circumstances that made the need for money more critical. For example, Richard I was king for only a few months before joining the Third Crusade to the Holy Land, and on his return he was captured in Germany and held for ransom. It was left to Richard's representatives in England to raise the enormous ransom sum demanded.

London had already profited from the rivalry between Richard's chief justiciar (an official who stood in for the king in the king's absence) and Richard's younger brother John to secure concessions from each. As a result of these unique circumstances, by 1193, London had a charter and the right to elect its own mayor and council of aldermen, in addition to the right to collect its own taxes and deliver them to the exchequer (the treasury). When Richard returned to England in 1194, he needed funds to raise an army and return to France where, during Richard's absence, Philip II Augustus of France had occupied a number of Angevin territories. To obtain these sums, Richard approached the merchants of London and in return for a very large sum of money confirmed their charter and reduced their taxes. In 1200 John, now king, granted the same rights of self-government to the towns of Northhampton and Ipswich in return for significant sums. By 1215, to keep the Londoners' support, John granted them the right to elect their mayor annually (earlier the election had been for life). It should be noted that election did not mean that the towns were moving toward democratic or representative governments. Only members of the merchant guild were eligible for office and could vote.

John's grant to London in 1215 was not enough to retain the support of the Londoners and their own army. It was London joining the baronial rebels that was decisive in forcing John to negotiate with the barons. Article 13 of the charter provided the following: "And the city of London shall have all its ancient liberties and free customs as well by land as by water. Furthermore, we will and grant that all other cities, boroughs, towns, and ports shall have all their liberties and free customs" (see Document 2, Article 13).

Other provisions favored the towns and trade. Article 33 provided that all fish-weirs (fish traps) should be removed from the rivers, allowing merchant boats and barges to move freely; Article 35 provided for uniform weights and measures throughout the kingdom; and Articles 41 and 42 granted merchants the freedom to enter and leave the kingdom and gave them qualified protection during a time of war.

Thus, Magna Carta confirmed and extended those rights and privileges that the towns of England beginning with London had already found they were able to purchase from the king. These purchases were possible because their demands were suitable to all clusters of population that had developed trading needs beyond that provided by a local market. In 1215, with the tutelage of Stephen Langton and William Marshal, the barons were able to translate their individual demands for redress from the king into a single document. This document, which would become known as Magna Carta, detailed those feudal rights and privileges that John had failed to observe. But as will be seen in the following chapters, it was much more than a document detailing baronial rights.

CHAPTER 3

MAGNA CARTA AND THE BARONS

Those who had the most pressing interest in Magna Carta and who received the bulk of King John's concessions were the barons—especially those who were tenants-in-chief of the crown. To understand their complaints and John's concessions, the reader needs to understand English feudalism. Providing a cohesive explanation of feudalism is not easily done, however. Modern historians view the term *"feudal"* as a late Renaissance concept based on a misunderstanding of the varying terminology used in widely scattered geographical areas to describe landholding relations among members of the landed aristocracy. In other words, there is no single "feudal system" but, rather, different regional customs regulating the terms on which a faithful follower (*fidelis*) held land from a superior lord. Speaking of Europe and the Crusading States of the East (see Appendix A) in general, this is true. But special circumstances resulting from the Norman conquest of England in 1066 and the policies of the Norman and Angevin kings before 1215 had encouraged the development of a uniform system of relations between landlord and tenant (both members of what might be described as a landed aristocracy) that could be called an English feudal system. Magna Carta was the document that codified the laws of this "system."

The emergence of the lord–man relationship based on the land grant can be traced back to the late Roman period, but its distinctive medieval characteristics can be more easily seen in the breakup of the Carolingian Empire in the late ninth century. The Carolingian Empire had been created by the Frankish king Charles the Great (Charlemagne) when he had expanded his kingdom (essentially France) to include northern Spain, the Low countries, much of Germany, and Italy into an empire recognized as a renewed Roman Empire by Papal Coronation in 800. This empire was threatened by a new series of barbarian invasions—Northmen from the north, Hungarians from the east, and Saracens (Muslims) from North Africa in the south. Especially when faced with danger from three different directions at the same time, the late Carolingian rulers had inadequate support to provide military defense for the entire area. To provide local defense, local leaders were necessary, and these tended to be the counts who had been named by the king to represent him and oversee the royal lands in his county or other unit of local administration. In some regions, a higher ranking individual who held the title of duke or marquis held a larger area usually close to a frontier known as a duchy or march. In each case, the local individual began as a faithful royal appointee, but as the royal power declined, the position of the local official tended to become hereditary (not necessarily by primogeniture, that is, succession by the eldest son) and the lands he administered for the crown were divided between land supporting himself and his dependents (domain or demesne) and land he bestowed on his own faithful followers to bind them to him and to provide the services that made his position possible. These services were advisory, judicial, financial, and, increasingly important in a time of developing cavalry warfare, military. In such a "system" the king might have had less actual power than some of his "vassals."

These arrangements were in place in northern France in the early tenth century when the Carolingian king of France, Charles the Simple, in order to end the raids of the Northmen, primarily Danes, ravishing France as far south as the River Loire and as far east as the area of Burgundy, bestowed land along the northern coast of France on the Danish leader Rollo. Rollo was to hold this territory that came to be known as the duchy of Normandy as a faithful follower of the king of France. Rollo and his followers accepted Christianity, and in a short time they also accepted the French language and other aspects of the French culture of the region. Rollo and his successors as dukes of Normandy used part of the land they received to reward their followers in the same way as the other French counts and dukes—in return for services they made grants of land to men who were sworn *fideles* of the duke. It was this "system" that the Normans took with them to England.

England was not "feudalized" before the arrival of the Normans—at least not in the French or continental sense. The lord–man relationship did exist, but it had not led to a weakening of the central government. The English kingship was strong, and central institutions such as a treasury and chancery (writing office) were beginning to appear. A professional warrior class (the thegns) increasingly formed the backbone of the army, although all freemen (and many of the peasants were free) were liable for military service (the fyrd). But personal loyalties and protection depended on family ties, and a strong family was still as important or more important than a powerful lord. Justice was administered in public courts, not in private or ecclesiastical courts.

The army that Duke William commanded during his invasion of England was not a feudal army; that is, the men participated not to render military service to their lord but to acquire the spoils of war. Thus, in addition to Normans, the army included Frenchmen from other parts of France, mostly from the northeast and Brittany, and Flemings, Lorrainers, and other adventurers. Serving as the backbone of this army were the mounted knights, although archers and other foot soldiers were also present.

The invasion nearly did not take place because of climatic conditions. William had gathered his army and ships for a summer invasion, but the winds remained contrary for weeks on end. In anticipation, Harold, who had become king of England in January 1066 following the death of Edward the Confessor, had his troops (both thegns and fyrd) lined up along the southern coast. Since the invasion did not occur and the fall harvest was at hand, Harold sent the fyrd home. At this point he learned that a more immediate threat faced him in the north in the form of an invasion by a Norse claimant to the throne, backed by Harold's brother Tostig, who had been exiled a short time before. Therefore Harold and his thegns hurried north. The thegns had horses and rode north, but they fought on foot, marking a major military difference between the Norman and English forces. On September 25 Harold and his army defeated the enemy at Stamford Bridge in Northumbria in northeast England. In early October the winds changed, and William finally landed on the southeastern coast of England. Harold and his thegns hurried south, and the battle between the English and Norman armies took place at Hastings in Kent on October 14. The battle was evenly divided until late in the day when a Norman feint was interpreted as a retreat by some members of the fyrd who had rejoined Harold's army. When they broke ranks to pursue the retreating Normans, the Normans rallied and attacked the disorganized Saxon line. During this attack, an arrow struck Harold in the eye and killed him. Harold's army was demoralized and faded away, while William's army regrouped and slowly made its way to London.

The English, now without leadership, could not mount an adequate defense against the Norman army surrounding London. In the absence of a Saxon candidate with a strong following available to be backed as king, the English capitulated. The English witan thereupon acknowledged William as king. He was crowned king of England by the archbishop of York in December 1066.

William had claimed that the throne of England should be his at the death of Edward the Confessor in January 1066 on the grounds that he was related to Edward, that Edward had nominated him to be his successor, and that Harold had sworn to support his claim.

The English had faced succession crises before: once in 1042 and twice in 1066. In 1042, the second of the sons of the Dane Cnut died without heirs. The Anglo-Saxon witan favored Edward, son of the Wessex king Ethelred II (978–1016) and his Norman queen Emma. Edward had been raised and educated in a monastery in Normandy and accepted the English throne as his responsibility. He was married to Edith, daughter of the powerful Earl Godwin of Wessex, but they had no offspring. Edward brought with him from Normandy a number of his followers—sometimes referred to as the first Norman invasion. Among these followers was Robert of Jumièges, who was appointed archbishop of Canterbury in 1051 during a period when the powerful Earl Godwin and his family were in exile. Jumièges was forced out when Godwin returned a few years later and the Anglo-Dane Stigand was appointed instead—Stigand was never recognized either by Normandy or by the papacy. Norman ecclesiastical architecture was also introduced, the greatest example being Westminster Abbey, completed shortly before Edward's death in January 1066.

Succession presented a problem early in the reign when it seemed unlikely that Edward and Edith would produce an heir. Godwin preferred the succession for one of his sons but was opposed by the other earls as well as by many of the thegns. William of Normandy was a second cousin through Edward's mother Emma, daughter of Duke Richard I of Normandy (942–996). William claimed that Edward had nominated him as successor and that Edward sent Harold (son of Earl Godwin and an influential servant of the crown) to Normandy to take an oath to support William's claim to the throne. The Norman chroniclers backed this version, but the Anglo-Saxon chroniclers tended to ignore it. When Edward died in January 1066, a meeting of the most important advisers of the crown, the witan, had little difficulty in recognizing Harold of Wessex, the most powerful man in the kingdom, as king. Harold would face challenges from Norway as well as from William of Normandy. The battle of Hastings was by no means a foregone Norman victory. Harold and his thegns had stood firm on foot behind their shield wall throughout the day and had repulsed a number of cavalry charges. The death of Harold was the decisive event.

William's most effective claim to the throne was that England was his by the right of conquest. At any rate, William took the bulk of the land for himself and began to divide the rest among his troops as the spoils of war. Not only would he distribute the lands of those English who had fallen at Stamford Bridge and at Hastings, but he would also confiscate the lands of those involved in the various rebellions between 1067 and 1071. Since the rebellions occurred primarily in the northern part of the kingdom and William devastated this area thoroughly in putting them down, almost all the northern territory was the king's to be granted.

At the time of the Norman conquest, the landholding system in Normandy was evolving in the direction of what would later be called feudalism. The system was based on landholding patterns that were in place at the time the duchy was granted to the Dane Rollo, whereby the future duke of Normandy held of (that is, received possession of the duchy from) the king of France in return for loyalty, and the duke's men held of him in return for loyalty. But prior to the eleventh century the precise meaning of loyalty was not well established, and many of the larger landholders behaved as independent rulers. William the Conqueror's predecessors had made some progress in asserting their authority and in requiring some service in addition to loyalty, but much of this progress had been undone during the minority of William when he and his advisers were not strong enough to assert control. By 1066, however, William had his duchy well in hand, and the outlines of a system of landholding had begun to emerge; it was this system that the Normans introduced into England. In England, the king granted land in return for loyalty and certain services and certain payments. The services were already pretty well defined: military service (called knight service in England) and service at court (ceremonial, advisory, and judicial). The payments, to be known as feudal aids, were made on three occasions: on the knighting of the lord's eldest son, on the marriage of his eldest daughter, and as a contribution to ransom if the lord were captured in battle. The irregular payments that were just beginning to be accepted as part of the landholding system were known as feudal incidents, the most important of which were relief, wardship, and marriage, which were covered in detail in Magna Carta.

Although the Normans introduced the landholding customs they knew in Normandy, the resulting relationships had a very different focus. In France, the duke held the duchy as a sworn follower (vassal) of the king of France. In England, the king of England held of no one—in effect, he was an independent ruler.[1] In bestowing land on his followers, William insisted that all swear loyalty (fealty)—that is, do homage—to him in addition to rendering specified service. In an unusual move, however, he required that the subtenants of his tenants-in-chief take an oath of first loyalty to the king himself. Even those relatively few surviving native English tenants continued to hold their land only by becoming sworn followers of the king. The higher English clergy were over time replaced by Normans or their allies so that by 1087 all were Norman. The entire landed aristocracy was Norman by the time Domesday Book[2] was compiled in 1087.

The king bestowed land directly on his tenants-in-chief, the tenants-in-chief bestowed on their tenants, and the tenants in turn on their subtenants. The practice was driven by the amount of knight service demanded by the king. In the case of a very large grant, the tenant-in-chief might owe the service of many knights. When called to arms, the tenant could serve as one knight, but he would have to get the rest from his household knights and his subtenants. In theory, a clerical tenant would have to obtain all of his service from his household knights or his subtenants, although occasionally a cleric served in person. The subtenants would have to fill out their quotas from their own followers, and so on down until the holdings might be so small as to owe the service of only one knight or a fraction of a knight. This process would later become known as subinfeudation.

The most common incident was relief, which was a payment a tenant's heir had to make to the lord in order to receive (inherit) the grant of land from his father; or, if there were no male heir, some other heir would have to make the payment. If there were no heir, the fief escheated (went back) to the lord. The size of the relief was not fixed, but at the subtenant level the extension of the royal common law to cover all disputes over land tended to protect the subvassals from arbitrary assessment by their lords.[3] The tenants-in-chief had to answer to the king's court rather than to the common law courts, and thus they were not protected by the common law from arbitrary demands by the king.

Other incidents were wardship and marriage. In the case of a minor heir (an heir under age), the lord exercised wardship over the heir until he came of age. During this time, the lord was responsible not only for the ward but also for his property, and in return he enjoyed the income from that property. Magna Carta would detail the lord's privileges and responsibilities during a minority. The incident known as marriage referred to the marriage of women. Since women could not perform all of the feudal services, especially military, their marriage was important to their lords since their husbands would perform the service. Therefore, the marriage of a female heiress was in her lord's control, and the remarriage of the widow of one of the lord's men was also in the lord's control. Magna Carta would place severe limitations on the lord's power to marry such a widow to just anyone whom the lord might choose.

At the time of the Norman conquest in 1066, the nature of military service was beginning to change. The feudal host (army), made up of trained knights serving for a limited period of time, was not well suited for long campaigns, whereas hired mercenaries might be kept in the field as long as they were paid. In addition, not all aristocratic landholders were eager to fight in person with the frequency that medieval warfare necessitated. So almost from the beginning of Norman rule arrangements were made whereby military service could be avoided by payment of a monetary sum called scutage. During the twelfth century, with the growth of a monetary economy the payment of scutage became customary. The major items in dispute involved when it was owed and how much it should be—should it be only for the number of knights owed by the tenants-in-chief, or should it be at a rate that included all of the service owed by the subtenants? Should it cover only campaigns in England, or should it cover wherever the king deemed it necessary?

These were some of the issues treated in Magna Carta, but they were raised as the result of rebellion in 1215. On the surface, it would appear that the rebellion was a direct result of King John's policies which required him to increase his monetary exactions from England. From his brother Richard he inherited a war with France over Normandy, which he intended to pursue. When he failed at that and lost Normandy to France and Philip II in 1204, followed shortly by the loss of Anjou and Maine, John was determined to resume the war in the future and to reestablish the Angevin Empire as it had been built by his father, Henry II. Both policies demanded money and allies, and John, heir to the administration built up by Henry II and Hubert Walter, Richard's justiciar and John's chancellor, used all the means under the crown's control to increase his revenues. These means affected all aspects of the social and economic life of the country, but the group of actions raising the most vocal protest affected those men who held their land directly from the crown (the tenants-in-chief). It seemed to these men that although their own men were protected in their landholdings from arbitrary demands from their lord in the common law courts, the tenants-in-chief had to answer to their own lord (the king) in the king's court where John himself was likely to be present.

John was the first English king since the conquest to spend most of his time in England, rather than in some part of France under English control, and John knew the English system intimately. Although not a great military leader, he was an effective administrator, and accordingly the government's policies were attributed directly to the king. John was not a likable person. He had the formidable Angevin temper, he played favorites, and he could be exceedingly cruel. It would be easy to ascribe the rebellion to John's actions and his unsavory character, but the rebellion had much deeper roots.

During the reign of the second Norman king, William II (1087–1100), protests began to be heard from the landholders of England against the arbitrary policies followed by the king. These protests seem to have begun with the clerical tenants who had become accustomed to the rather benevolent treatment pursued by William I and his archbishop of Canterbury Lanfranc. Although canonical election of church officers was not allowed, at least they named able men to these offices and during a vacancy preserved the income from the land for the new holder. After Lanfranc's death early in the reign, William II allowed the archbishopric of Canterbury to lie vacant and treated its properties as he would a minority in a lay (secular) fief. He took over the land as guardian and enjoyed the revenues. As other church positions fell vacant, William treated them similarly, thus significantly increasing the royal revenue. William

II also continued his father's policy of increasing the royal forest and im-
posing exceedingly harsh penalties for violations of the forest law. All
landholders affected, lay and clerical, aristocratic and peasant, found
themselves unfairly impoverished by the royal forest policy.

So vociferous were the protests against William II that immediately
following his unexpected death in 1100 (a result of a hunting accident
in one of the royal forests), his successor, Henry I, the youngest son of
William I (1100–35), not only took the traditional English coronation
oath promising peace, justice, and equity but at the same time issued what
is referred to as a charter of liberties. "The Church is made free from all
the unjust exactions; and the kingdom from the evil customs; to the English people are restored the laws of King Edward with the Conqueror's
amendments; the feudal innovations, inordinate and arbitrary reliefs and
amercements (fines), the abuse of the rights of wardship and marriage,
the despotic interference with testamentary disposition, all of which had
been common in the last reign, are renounced."[4] Henry I certainly recognized what the complaints against William II were. As far as the ecclesiastical complaints were concerned, he worked out a compromise
with Archbishop of Canterbury Anselm regarding election to ecclesiastical office which allowed the crown to continue to control appointments, but spiritual investment was now to be performed by an
ecclesiastic. Henry disregarded the other promises made in his charter
when it pleased him, and he, too, was able to increase his revenue beyond what the original enfeoffments (grants) would provide.

The reign of Stephen (1135–54), a grandson of William the Conqueror and a nephew of Henry I, set the stage for the reign of Henry II
(1154–89), grandson of Henry I and the first of the Angevin (Plantagenet) kings of England. Stephen had not been Henry I's choice as his
successor. Henry I had had only two legitimate children; the son had died
in 1120, and the daughter had been married at an early age to the German Roman emperor Henry V. This daughter, Matilda, was still in her
twenties when the emperor died. Her father brought her back to England
and presented her to the barons as his successor. She was then married
to the younger Geoffrey of the French county of Anjou, who would succeed his father Count Fulk V when Fulk went off to the Holy Land in
1128 to marry the heiress of the kingdom of Jerusalem and to found a
dynasty there. Meanwhile, Henry I became involved in a war defending

the duchy of Normandy; he was injured and died as the result of his wounds (1135). The nephew Stephen who, though French, had received extensive English properties from Henry I, was close at hand, and upon learning of Henry's death, immediately made his way to England where it was apparent that most of the English baronage had little desire to support Matilda. After some negotiation, Stephen was accepted and crowned king. He took the usual short English coronation oath, and then, as the barons sought concessions in return for their support, he promised to observe many of the liberties, especially those involving the Church, outlined in Henry I's charter of liberties.

Stephen proved a weak king. To keep support, he made further concessions whereby the barons, both lay and ecclesiastic, were allowed to build fortifications and to organize what were essentially private armies. These men tended to follow their own interests whether to support Stephen or Matilda or to become practically independent rulers. To gain support to face Matilda and his own rebellious followers, Stephen used the royal lands to make lavish gifts to his own followers, many of whom were regarded as foreigners in England. A virtual state of anarchy followed as Stephen alienated the most important members of Henry I's administration. In spite of Stephen's weakness and mistakes, Matilda was never able to capitalize on her victories or to keep the support she had. Later when the leadership of her cause had passed to her eldest son Henry, a compromise was arranged whereby Stephen remained king but recognized Henry as his successor. When Henry II succeeded in 1154, he faced a baronage out of control, a judicial system that was in shambles, a church that had become virtually independent, and royal revenues that were sharply reduced.

It was in trying to restore conditions to what they were in the reign of his grandfather Henry I that Henry II undertook those measures that would reform almost all aspects of the English government: the legal system, the judicial system, and the military and financial institutions of the state. In doing so, Henry offered good government and firm control but at the same time he had to withdraw many of the concessions that Stephen had agreed to make. Many of the protests against John originated in the "reforms" of Henry II. (Henry's relations with the Church and with the towns have been covered in previous chapters; his relations with the law and the judicial system will be covered in the next chapter.)

Henry II's successor, Richard I (1189–99), was essentially an absentee king. As already noted, at the beginning of his reign he visited England only long enough to be crowned and to raise money to participate in what is known as the Third Crusade. This involved collecting all the royal revenues, selling offices, and granting privileges in return for money. On his return from the crusade Richard was captured and held for ransom. The queen mother Eleanor and Richard's justiciar Hubert Walter (one of Henry II's well-trained administrators) used every device possible to raise the ransom money. When Richard returned from captivity in Germany, he remained in England only long enough to raise more money to return to France to recover those lands that had been lost to France or were being challenged by that country. But despite the king's absence and the heavy exactions in money and military services, and although there were complaints, there was no rebellion under Richard. The government reorganized by Henry II managed very well without the presence of the king.

When John became king in 1199, he inherited a war in Normandy against the aggression of King Philip II of France, during the course of which Richard had been wounded and killed. To John's lack of effective military leadership were added difficulties over his matrimonial adventures. In 1200 he had received an annulment from his childless marriage to Isabel of Gloucester, and perhaps on his way to Portugal to seek a Portuguese princess as his bride, he visited one of his vassals in France, the count of Angouleme. With the count's consent, John married the count's daughter Isabelle. But Isabelle was already betrothed to another of John's vassals, and this vassal demanded the compensation customary for such breach of promise from John, who was his own overlord. When John failed to provide such compensation, Hugh de Lusignan, the offended suitor, appealed to John's overlord, the king of France. In 1202 Philip II cited John to appear before the king's feudal court in Paris. After a number of summonses that John ignored, Philip's court declared John contumacious (a rebel against his lord) and thereby forfeited all of his French fiefs. John's response was inadequate, and by 1204 Phillip II occupied Normandy, Maine, Anjou, and Touraine. Although he levied a number of scutages to pay for a war of reconquest, John lacked any sustained drive. In the circumstances, those members of the baronage who had fiefs in both England and Normandy found it necessary to choose between England and France. Although a few families continued to have a French branch and an English branch, those with holdings in England increasingly regarded themselves as English and resisted rendering military service abroad or paying scutage so that the king could hire mercenaries.

In 1205 Hubert Walter, archbishop of Canterbury, died, and a controversy arose between the monks of Christ Church Canterbury[5] and the king over the right to name the successor. This conflict played into the hands of Pope Innocent III, who declared both elections invalid and named his own candidate, the Englishman Stephen Langton, whom John refused to accept. The conflict that followed between king and pope lasted from 1207 to 1213, during which time England lay under an interdict and John was excommunicated. John responded by outlawing—placing outside the protection of the law—those clergy who observed the interdict, and so they were forced into exile. In the case of those bishops who went into exile, John treated their lands as vacant and collected their revenues for himself. With these revenues and heavy fines against those clergy who remained in England, John somewhat relaxed his relentless financial pressure on the secular tenants-in-chief of the crown.

During this time, John remained in England, continuing to lay plans for resuming the war against France, hopefully in conjunction with the German Roman emperor Otto IV (a cousin—Otto's mother was John's sister). But in 1212 a baronial uprising took place against John that threatened assassination of the king, followed in 1213 by Philip II of France's announced invasion of England to depose John with the backing of Innocent III. Faced by internal and external dangers, John came to terms with Innocent III. This action transformed Innocent III from an implacable foe into a staunch supporter, who would retract his support of Philip II's invasion of England and back John against the barons of England.

In the meantime John continued his plans for war against France. He planned to lead an English invasion from the remaining English possessions in the southwest of France; John's ally Otto IV of the German Roman Empire would lead an invasion from the east. In the west John enjoyed some success in the county of Poitou, but encountering an army under Prince Louis, son and heir of the French king Philip II Augustus, and fearing the disloyalty of his own men, many of whom were there because John had threatened to seize their property or families, John retreated. In the east Otto IV did invade and encountered the main French army under the king. The defeat of the emperor Otto IV at the battle of

Bouvines (1214) in eastern France spelled the end of John's hope to recover his lost French territory. It also spelled the loss of much baronial support in England

Baronial resistance had been moving toward confrontation with John since the second half of 1213. The rebellious barons had met a number of times that fall, and on one of these occasions someone (possibly Stephen Langton, archbishop of Canterbury, who met with the barons) produced a copy of the Coronation Charter of Henry I, Henry's charter of liberties (see Document 1). Henry I had issued this charter in an effort to reconcile baronial discontent with the arbitrary policies of the previous king, Henry's brother William II. Many of the "liberties" promised by Henry sounded much like the corrections in John's policies desired by the rebels; Henry's charter became a kind of blueprint for what would later become Magna Carta.

When John returned from France in late 1214 in utter defeat, the rebellion, which had been centered in the north and East Anglia (northeast of London), spread when a number of barons who had been with John in France and were disgusted with him joined the revolt. By early spring 1215, the rebels were presenting their demand that John agree to accept the Charter of Henry I. John refused, and the rebel barons began to arm, preparing to resist John. In March 1215 John took the cross (he promised to go on a crusade to rescue Jerusalem, captured by the Turks in 1187), bringing Innocent III even more thoroughly on John's side. When John refused to make concessions to the barons, the barons denounced their allegiance to John and began war. John still refused to meet with the barons until the town of London joined forces with the rebels. This was a major blow to the crown, and after a number of postponed meetings, John eventually agreed to meet with the barons.

While these actions were taking place, a number of the king's faithful counselors, including Stephen Langton and John Marshal, shaped the disorganized individual demands of the rebels into a coherent list of demands that began with the "liberties" of Henry I and incorporated additional items from a long list of rectifications specific to the injuries suffered by an individual or family. This document is usually known as the Articles of the Barons. A meeting with the king was set for June 15, 1215, at the meadow known as Runnymede on the Thames River between London and Windsor. Here John agreed to this "rough draft," and between June 15 and June 19 (the exact dates are not known) the draft was turned over to the royal chancery to be converted into the form of a formal charter that has come to be known as Magna Carta. It was this version that was given the royal seal, and copies were sent out to be read in all the county courts.

The barons still mistrusted John, and John himself appealed to Innocent III to release him from his promise to observe the charter on the basis of canon law, according to which oaths given under duress (force) are not binding. Innocent granted John's appeal, thereby releasing him from his oath and instructing Stephan Langton to excommunicate those barons who had again taken up arms. In turn, the barons then offered the crown of England to Louis, son and heir of Philip II of France, if he would join them in overthrowing John. But now John, who had been listless since his return from defeat in France, threw off his lethargy and led a series of vigorous campaigns in the central part of the country. Under this extreme pressure John became seriously ill with dysentery. This condition seems to have been aggravated by the news that his baggage train containing some of the royal treasure had been lost in quicksand while trying to skirt the Wash, a bay that penetrates deep into the eastern English coastline between Lincolnshire and Norfolk. He could no longer walk or ride and died on October 18, 1216, after naming protectors for his nine-year-old son Henry.

The civil war continued. The advisers of the young Henry III immediately (late 1216) issued a significantly revised charter of liberties under the seal of the long-time royal servant, William Marshal, and Gualo, papal legate in England. A more carefully revised version was issued in 1217. Gradually, the civil war was put down, and the rebels accepted peace with little loss of status or property. As a further reassurance to the baronage, the charter that was coming to be referred to as the Great Charter (Magna Carta) was reissued in 1225 with still further revisions. This revision of 1225 was the form in which Magna Carta was reissued numerous times in the thirteenth century and by Edward I in 1297; this was also the form recorded at the beginning of the collected Statutes of the Realm.

The barons received a number of articles in Magna Carta that dealt with matters involving only themselves. In addition, they enjoyed a number of benefits that were extended to all freemen. The "liberties" that adhered to the barons alone are articles 2, 3, 4, 5, 6, 7, 8, 9, 10, and 21 (from Magna Carta 1215). These articles regulate the so-called feudal incidents: How much could a lord charge for relief (inheritance) of a fief? When could a lord claim guardianship over a ward? How much could he take from his ward's land for his own revenue? In what order must the lord turn over the land when the heir comes of age? The articles also covered how widows should have their marriage portions and dowers and be free to remarry so long as they did not marry an enemy of the king. A lord might not seize a vassal's land as long as his chattels were sufficient to satisfy the debt. Earls and barons must be judged by their peers.

A number of articles dealing with royal forests, forest law, and the administration of the forest law (articles 44, 45, 46, 47, 48, and 53 from Magna Carta 1215) were omitted in the reissue of 1216 but were included in a Charter of the Forest that accompanied the reissues of 1217 and 1225. The two charters were always issued together in the thirteenth and later centuries (see Documents 2, 3, and 4).

In addition to the articles noted above that applied primarily to the landholding baronial aristocracy, many articles in Magna Carta applied to free landholders of nonbaronial status and others included persons of even humbler status. These sections will be considered in the next chapter.

NOTES

1. Note that the pope had argued that William held England as a fief of the papacy. William successfully denied this claim.

2. See Chapter 4 for a description of the inquest procedure followed in compiling the Domesday Book.

3. Also see Chapter 4 for the extension of the king's justice (i.e., the common law) over all land disputes, eventually even covering peasant tenures.

4. William Stubbs, *The Constitutional History of England in Its Origin and Development*, Vol. I, 5th ed. (Oxford: Clarendon, 1906), pp. 330–331.

5. See Chapter 2 for the relationship between the monks of Corpus Christi, Canterbury, and election of the archbishop of Canterbury.

CHAPTER 4

MAGNA CARTA AND THE COMMON LAW

Magna Carta is not directly related to the growth of the English common law. However, a number of provisions in the document refer favorably to developments in the common law and its court system or regulate certain common law procedures. What was this English common law and why was it strong enough by the time of Magna Carta to resist the powerful growth on the Continent of a common law (*ius commune*) based on the revival of Roman law in the late eleventh, twelfth, and thirteenth centuries?

The revival of Roman law began in Italy in the schools of Pavia and Bologna, and then spread to southern France and northern Spain, and thence to the rest of France, insofar as it supported royal absolutism, and to the German areas in central Europe and into some parts of eastern Europe. England had felt some of this influence inasmuch as William I's archbishop of Canterbury Lanfranc and William II's and Henry I's archbishop Anselm had been trained in Roman law at Pavia. Lanfranc had been especially influential since he was a close adviser to the king in establishing separate church courts in England. He took advantage of his familiarity with written documents to regain a number of properties that had been lost to Canterbury during the uncertainties that had accompanied the removal of the Saxon Stigand from the archbishopric of Canterbury and the appointment of the Norman Lanfranc in his place.

During the reign of Stephen, the then archbishop of Canterbury Theobald (1138–61) had brought an Italian by the name of Vacarius to England to advise him in his disputes with King Stephen and his brother Henry, bishop of Winchester, who had obtained appointment as papal legate in England. Vacarius was trained in Roman law and taught Roman law for a time at Oxford at a very early stage in Oxford's development as a university; he also wrote an early textbook of Roman law in England. Undoubtedly, these contacts with Roman law had some influence in England (certainly in the case of canon law and the inquisitorial procedure of the church courts[1]), but the native English tradition of law was strong. By the end of the Anglo-Saxon period, a series of well-organized public courts had developed, and a number of the English kings, most recently Ethelred (978–1016) and Cnut (1016–35), had issued extensive codes of law for their emerging unified kingdom. The English tradition of law and public courts was taken over by the strong Norman kings and developed into a system of royal courts administering a royal justice common to the entire realm.

At the time of the Norman conquest of England in 1066, the English had a well-developed written law, whereas Norman law was as yet unwritten. One of William the Conqueror's first acts was to reassure the English people that they would continue to enjoy the laws of King Edward the Confessor (1042–66). The Normans, however, would continue to use the unwritten law of Normandy. This was essentially a resort to personality of law (a man is judged by the law of his homeland, not by the territory in which he resides), a legal concept that was strong during the period of the early Germanic kingdoms (fifth through ninth centuries). This dual legal system foundered in Norman England, however. Although the higher aristocracy became mostly Norman, the two peoples, Norman and Saxon, came into close contact and began to merge almost immediately. Many a Norman lord married a Saxon woman; Henry I (1100–35) married Matilda, a descendant of the house of Wessex. The way was set for a merging of the two laws.

Anglo-Saxon law was written and was applied in public courts, which were organized by territorial units. The lowest territorial unit was the hundred (called wapentake in the Danelaw[2]) court, which was presided over by a hundredman and the parish priest. (There were no separate church courts in Anglo-Saxon England.) The hundred court was attended by the men of the hundred who "spoke" the customary law of the community. The next larger unit was the shire court, which would be called county court after the Norman conquest. (The complete division of the country into shires had been accomplished in the ninth and tenth centuries.) The shire court was presided over by the sheriff, a royal appointee, and the diocesan bishop, and it was attended by the influential men of the shire who spoke the customary law of the shire. Above all was the king's court presided over by the king and attended by his witan—the king's ministers and other influential men of the kingdom. Of particular value to the king were a number of churchmen versed in Old English and Latin.

Although Anglo-Saxon law was written, Anglo-Saxon England was for the most part an illiterate society. Its court procedure was essentially north Germanic. The hundredman who presided over the hundred court, the sheriff who presided over the shire court, and even to some extent the king who presided over the royal court, were not trained in the law and were not expected to declare the law. That function was carried out by the men of the community (usually the oldest and/or the most influential) who attended the court and who spoke the law—that is, the customary law of the community. Basic English legal principles remained the same throughout the land, but local customs varied widely in such matters as marriage, the composition of the family and inheritance, the holding and transfer of property, and the making of gifts and endowments.

The early Germanic peoples did not distinguish between civil and criminal law. All cases were handled as essentially civil suits with the injured party or his family bringing suit (making an appeal) against a defendant before a court. The members of the court decided the kind of proof that would be required to establish guilt or innocence. The Anglo-Saxons used two forms of proof. If the accused was of good reputation, he would be allowed to present proof by compurgation—he would give his own oath and, in addition, present the number of oathhelpers prescribed by the court. If the accused was of poor reputation, he would be required to undergo the proof by ordeal. The ordeals used were hot water, cold water, or hot iron. (For a description of these ordeals, see Appendix B.) The person proved guilty had to pay composition (compensation) to the injured party—the amount of the composition was set by law—in addition to a fine paid to the court. The whole system relied on a close association of community and church. A churchman provided the sacred objects on which the oath was taken. In cases of proof by ordeal, a churchman observed the preparation and result. In each case the proof was an appeal for divine intervention.

The Normans' settling in England introduced some changes to this system. Separate church courts were established, eliminating the clerical element from the hundred and shire (now county) courts. The clerical element, however, did not disappear from the king's court. The archbishops, bishops, and abbots all held most of their land from the king and were summoned to meetings of the king's court. By the late twelfth century and more especially in the thirteenth, the higher clergy (archbishops and bishops primarily) were university-trained men who had studied civil (Roman) and canon (church) law. They were also men who served the crown as well as the Church. They thus served as royal justiciars and in that capacity presided over the common law courts, but they also served as judges or judges delegate (delegated by the pope) presiding over the canon law courts. It was through these men in the thirteenth century that the influence of Roman law entered the common law. The extent of this influence has never been determined.

The Normans introduced their own custom regulating the holding of property by feudal tenure, including proprietary (private) courts. Each lord held a court attended by his followers (vassals) that could hear cases between the lord's vassals or between the lord and his vassals. The king's court was now a feudal court attended by all his tenants-in-chief and the language spoken in court was now French and Latin. But in addition to this large feudal king's court (sometimes called the great council), there was another smaller king's court (*curia regis*). This smaller court was made up of the men who served the king directly and were in almost constant attendance on him. In addition to its administrative duties, this smaller court could act as a court of justice when actions involved breach of the king's peace. The king's responsibility to assure the peace of the land had been inherited from the Anglo-Saxons, but now the tendency was to extend the number of offenses that constituted a breach of the king's peace. With this expansion of the king's peace, the small king's court became a very busy judicial court following the king, and a way needed to be found to take the royal justice to other more accessible courts. The way found was to use the county courts by sending a royal justice or justices to preside over the county court—it then became a royal court.

Under the Normans when an entire hundred was held by a single lord, the lord's private (proprietary) court tended to absorb the hundred court, so that the hundred courts tended to decline. The county courts continued as in the past under the shire reeve—the sheriff, an appointee of the king, usually a Norman from the lesser baronage. The law applied was either English or Norman, depending on the parties to the suit, but in addition to proof by compurgation or the ordeal of water, the usual ordeal in the twelfth and early thirteenth centuries, the Normans added the ordeal of trial by battle in the case of disputes over land.

The Norman kings issued little formal legislation, but several unofficial collections have survived from the early twelfth century. In the first of these collections, known as *The Laws of William the Conqueror*, William promised peace and security to both Englishmen and Normans. Every freeman was to be under oath to be faithful to the king; the laws of King Edward should be observed as modified by William. The death penalty was to be replaced by blinding and castration (however, the death penalty continued to be used). No one should sell a man outside his native land. Somewhat longer and more diverse in content was the series of laws written as *The Laws of Henry I* in about 1118.[3] This was an extensive collection of Anglo-Saxon laws as modified by Norman custom.

The substance of the law in Norman England thus came to be a merging of the Old English law with the Norman law. But the key to the development of a law common to all of England is in the extension of the range of pleas (cases) that should come before a royal court. In the process, there gradually developed a distinction between civil and criminal jurisdiction. The expansion of the criminal jurisdiction of the king's royal courts was accomplished by extending the concept of the king's peace to include an ever larger number of offenses that were called felonies. The Norman treatment of the land facilitated the expanding civil jurisdiction of the king's court. William and his successors regarded the land of England as theirs by the right of conquest and divided it among their followers who came to be known as the king's tenants-in-chief. These tenants-in-chief bestowed some of that land upon their own followers, and they on their subtenants, and so on further down the line (in a process known as subinfeudation). In continental feudalism the tie was between a lord and his man and would not extend to the subtenants. In contrast, in England all tenants owed their first loyalty to the king; hence the king had an interest in all land transactions. In other words, all land was held directly or indirectly from the king.

Royal justice expanded rapidly under the Norman kings, and the king's court came to have a number of very experienced justices whose expertise was increasingly sought out. But the king's court was constantly moving from one part of the country to another, and when the king went abroad, sometimes for years, as to Normandy, he took his court with him. To make the royal justice more available, the king began to send out one or more of his experienced justices to preside over the county courts. When a king's justice presided, the county court became a royal court. This practice becomes identifiable during the reign of Henry I (1100–35), although regularization of these visits by itinerant (traveling) justices would not come until the reign of Henry II (1154–89). The royal justice was very popular because it was administered by men who had become experts in this field, and they could call upon a law that was uniform throughout the country, a law that later would be called the English common law.

At this point, it is important to note why Roman law did not become more influential even though the teaching of Roman law had been available in England from the time of Vacarius in the middle of the twelfth century. Roman law was a university subject in the twelfth century, and only those destined for the higher clergy took instruction in civil (Roman) and canon (ecclesiastical) law. Knowledge of Roman law was therefore available in England and was largely responsible for the development of procedure in the church courts of England. However, during the twelfth century when the universities were getting their start, the English kings chose their advisers and civil servants from the lesser baronage (or even from the burgesses as in the case of Thomas Becket). These men were not university trained but learned the law by experience, much like an apprentice system. The law they learned was that applied in the public and royal courts, which was the modified English-Norman law discussed above. In the thirteenth century, more of the justices were university men and some Roman law came in then, but there remains great controversy about how much.

The next important developments in the growth of the common law came during the reign of Henry II. Henry identified useful procedures, as in the case of the itinerant justices, and regularized them. Henry II is also responsible for utilizing irregularly used procedures and thus creating that distinctly English institution, the jury system. At the time of Magna Carta there were two different juries: the presentment jury in criminal procedure and the recognition jury in civil procedure. Neither of these was new, but their use was regularized and extended during the second half of the twelfth century.

The presentment jury was based on the inquest. Anglo-Saxon England may have known the inquest, but it was more likely brought to England by the Normans. Roman in origin as an information-gathering procedure, the Franks adopted it at the time of Charlemagne (768–814) as a means of checking on local conditions of government in the far-flung empire created during that reign. William I used the inquest to learn about property holdings in England, information that would be compiled in Domesday Book. The information was obtained by sending royal representatives into all the boroughs and counties of England. The good men of the community were called before the king's men and placed on oath and then asked questions about all property holdings in their community. The questions included information not only about landholders, but also about the terms on which the land was held, how many servile tenants were on the land and how much they owed for it, even how many animals they had. On numerous occasions, William I's Norman successors had used similar inquests to learn about local conditions. Henry II adapted the inquest for use in the criminal jurisdiction of the king's courts.

Use of the presentment jury allowed a community to take action against criminals, whereas in earlier times the injured party or his family had to bring an appeal (accusation) against the one who had injured him. This made it very difficult for a poor or weak man to bring a successful suit against one who was richer or more powerful than he. By using the inquest procedure, a royal justice could be sent to a special session of the county court. A number of good men of the community would be summoned to the court and placed on oath and asked to identify individuals suspected of certain crimes since the last session of the court. If there appeared to be some consensus that some individual was responsible for a certain crime, the jury would present him—that is, it would indict him. He would be arrested by the sheriff and held for the next regular session of the court where the trial would be accomplished by the ordeal. Trial by jury in criminal suits was not yet contemplated, and serious steps toward working out the functions of a trial jury would not be developed until after the clergy was prohibited from participating in the ordeal by a decree of the Fourth Lateran Council in 1215.[4] If the clergy did not participate in the ordeal, then the fiction that the ordeal put the decision of guilt or innocence in the hand of God could no longer be maintained.

The recognition jury had occasionally been used before, but it now became the normal means of resolving a dispute over property or property rights. Again, the community would be involved in an action of a royal court. An individual could bring a civil action against another person or corporation by purchasing a writ from the royal chancery—a division of the king's court that handled written communications under the direction of an individual called the chancellor. The writ was an Anglo-Saxon device for sending out brief written instructions from the king's court, which now were in Latin instead of Old English. At first during Henry II's reign, there were four possessory (i.e., concerning the possession of property) writs or assizes, although in the thirteenth century after Magna Carta the number of writs increased to cover many other civil complaints. (This is where the influence of Roman law may have come in.) The possessory writs were utrum, novel disseisin, mort d'ancestor, and darrein presentment. The writ *utrum* was utilized in disputes over whether a property was held by the tenure of free alms, that is, held for the service of prayer only, in which case it came under the jurisdiction of a church court, or held by lay (secular) fee, in which case the king's court claimed jurisdiction. The writ *novel disseisin* was purchased to claim recent dispossession (that is, novel disseisin) of property. The writ *mort d'ancestor* (death of ancestor) was purchased to claim a heritable tenement if one was the heir to a man who possessed the property at the time of his death. The writ *darrein presentment* (last presentment) was purchased to settle a dispute over advowson, that is, who had the right to name a priest or other churchman to a vacancy. Many churches were founded by endowment from individuals or families and were regarded as "belonging" to that individual or family and their heirs: they are thus known as proprietary churches. Therefore, when the position of priest became vacant, it was the individual's or family's right to name the successor. The same was true of monastic foundations. The church reforms of the eleventh and twelfth centuries aimed at removing secular control of church appointments did not extend to these usually small private foundations.

All of the possessory writs entitled the purchaser to have his case settled in a royal court before a recognition jury. At a meeting of a county court presided over by a royal justice, the sheriff was instructed to impanel a jury, usually twelve respected men of the community, who were placed on oath and asked what the community believed about the justice of the writ that had been purchased. The use of the recognition jury in civil suits was very popular. It was a much more rational way to settle property disputes than by compurgation or the ordeal (including battle). Moreover, since it could be used only in a royal court, the royal courts absorbed most of the land disputes from the county and private baronial courts, just as use of the presentment jury had taken over most of the serious criminal jurisdiction of the hundred and county courts. The recognition jury was not an impartial jury. It did not hear evidence, but since it was made up of members of the community, the members were expected to know what was going on in their community; if not, they should find out.

The use of juries so expanded the work of the royal courts that Henry II regularized the circuits of the itinerant justices. Even more importantly, a number of specialized royal courts gradually appeared, and instead of following the king's court as it traveled around, they were settled permanently in London or its suburb Westminster where petitioners could always find them. These courts were the court of the Exchequer (treasury), which handled all disputes over money due to the crown; the court of Common Pleas, which handled cases not involving the crown; and the court of King's Bench, which handled cases involving the royal interest.

These procedures so strengthened the system of common law that was growing in England that it could hold out against the revival of Roman law that was developing on the Continent. The common law system inspired a book of law written by one of the justices who had served the king for many years and knew the law at first hand: the *Treatise on the Laws and Customs of England* (1189). (Although it is not known who actually wrote this treatise, it was early ascribed to Ranulf Glanville, chief justiciar of Henry II, and it still goes by his name.) A subsequent treatise that included developments of the first half of the thirteenth century was written by Henry de Bracton in about 1256 and is called *Concerning the Laws and Customs of England.*[5]

Magna Carta contained a number of provisions regarding these legal developments (the article numbers that follow refer to the 1215 version of Magna Carta). Article 17 provided that the court of Common Pleas should be held in a fixed place. Article 18 provided that suits deriving from the writs of novel disseisin, mort d'ancestor, and darrein presentment should be held in the county courts in which the property involved was located; the king or his justiciar would send two royal justices through each county four times a year (later reduced to once a year) to preside over these courts. Article 19 provided that a sufficient number of recognitors (potential members of recognition juries) should be summoned so that if all the cases scheduled could not be heard in one day, they could be heard on subsequent days. Article 24 provided that no sheriff, coroner, or other local officer could hold royal pleas (i.e., preside over a royal court). Article 39 provided that "No free man shall be arrested or imprisoned or disseised [dispossessed] or outlawed or exiled or in any way victimized, neither will we attack him or send anyone to attack him, except by the lawful judgment of his peers [equals] or by the law of the land." Article 40 stated: "To no one will we sell, to no one will we refuse or delay right or justice."

Clearly, as the provisions about law or legal process show, Magna Carta in the form that John was "forced" to sign had been modified from the narrow baronial interests of the rebel barons into a document that covered all free men in the land, some of whom were of very modest status. In addition, the common law was already stretching its jurisdiction toward the servile villeins. We have already noted articles 39 and 40 where the protection of the law (that is, the law applied in the royal courts, the common law) was not limited to the landholding classes but was extended to all free men. In fact, the last sentence of Article 1 (the bulk of which guarantees the liberty of the Church) closed with the statement that the king has "granted to all free men of our kingdom . . . all the liberties written below." Article 20 regarding limiting amercements (fines) to reflect the seriousness of the offense but protecting the culprit's livelihood applied to all free men, merchants, and villeins. Villeins were servile dependents who would ordinarily not be subject to the royal or public courts but to their lord's manorial (agrarian) court. Articles 23, 28, 30, and 31 had to do with protections of such a humble sort that they cannot be regarded as causes of baronial rebellion: freedom from making bridges and limitations on royal officials demanding food, horses, carts, or timber without paying for them. Article 37 listed the free tenures that were held without owing knight service (i.e., the nonfeudal tenures): fee-farm, socage, burgage (all held for rents), or petty serjeanty (held for a negligible rent, an annual arrow, knife, or some such petty rent). Article 45 recognized the importance of law in the promise to appoint as justices, constables, sheriffs, or bailiffs men who "know the law and mean to serve it well." Article 35 of Magna Carta 1225 (expanding Article 18 of 1215), provided that the sheriff on one of his two visits (tourns) a year to the hundred courts should hold a view of frankpledge to determine that all men without a lord be in a tithing group. A tithing group was an association of ten men (or more) who were mutually responsible for the behavior of everyone in the group, a device inherited from the Anglo-Saxons to help to keep the peace. If a man had a lord, the lord was held accountable for his actions.

The Charter of the Forest was first issued in 1217 to replace those articles in the 1215 version of Magna Carta dealing with forest issues (articles 44, 47, and 48). From that time on, Magna Carta and the Charter of the Forest were always issued together as if they formed two parts of one document.

The Charter of the Forest is even clearer than Magna Carta about the rights of persons of humble status. Article 4 expressly included freeholders along with persons of the baronial classes who had woods inside the royal forest. Article 7 forbade the king's foresters from demanding ale, wheat, oats, lambs, or piglets from dwellers in the forest. Article 13 stated that any free man shall have the raptors (hunting birds) and honey from his own woods. Article 14 protected men who purchased forest products in the king's forest from arbitrary road taxes when they took their purchases out by horse or cart; if they carried them out on their back, they paid nothing.

The barons and other free men of the kingdom approved of the royal courts and the emerging common law, but they were concerned that the king not abuse the courts or law in the royal interest as all of the Angevin kings had done. King John, however, did it more frequently and more consistently than his predecessors.

As the result of the activities of the common law courts, members of the baronage as well as members of the knightly class had much experience with local government and with the juridical members of the king's court. This experience would give them the knowledge and expertise to enter into negotiations with the crown's representatives that led to the formulation of Magna Carta. It would also provide the political experience that encouraged subsequent parliaments to increase their power at the expense of the king.

The legal provisions of Magna Carta and the Charter of the Forest provide proof that the "liberties" involved were not limited to the baronial order but rather extended to all free men. For the time being, that excluded in most cases the servile villeins, who constituted the bulk of the population. But already the towns offered freedom to those who made their way there. The interest of the common law in land would reach out and gradually absorb even disputes over servile tenures. The common lawyers and parliamentarians of the seventeenth century could well argue that Magna Carta protected the liberties they were asserting against royalist claims.

NOTES

1. The procedure of the canon law courts depended heavily on taking written depositions in response to questioning by a magistrate of the court.

2. The Danelaw was the area of England north and east of a line running approximately from London in the southeast to Chester (on the border of Wales) in the northwest. This was the area most heavily settled by Danes and Norse in the ninth and tenth centuries.

3. For the laws of William I, see Carl Stephenson and Frederick George Marcham, *Sources of English Constitutional History* (New York and London: Harper, 1937). See also A. J. Robertson, ed. and trans., *The Laws of the Kings of England from Edmund to Henry I* (Cambridge: University of Cambridge Press, 1925). For Henry I, see L. J. Downer, ed. and trans., *Leges Henrici Primi* (Oxford: Clarendon Press, 1972).

4. The pope called Lateran councils at irregular intervals to discuss church problems and issue decrees for the regulation of the Church. These councils did not necessarily meet in Rome, but the term *Lateran* comes from the pope's diocesan church, St. John Lateran, in Rome.

5. See M. T. Clanchy, *The Treatise on the Laws and Customs of the Realm of England Commonly Called Glanvill* (Oxford and New York: Oxford University Press, 1993). See also Samuel E. Thorne, ed. and trans., *Henry de Bracton's De Legibus et Consuetudinibus Angliae: On the Laws and Customs of England,* 4 vols. (Cambridge, UK: Published in Association with the Seldon Society [by] the Belknap Press of Harvard University Press, 1968–77).

CHAPTER 5

MAGNA CARTA AND PARLIAMENT

The responsibility of Magna Carta for the growth of Parliament is part of the myth surrounding the document since the men responsible for determining the provisions of Magna Carta had no concept of an institution such as the English Parliament would become. In fact, their solution to the problem of forcing the king to live up to his promises and what they regarded as the law of the land was to claim the right of feudal rebellion against an unjust lord. In 1215 the solution had the barons select a group of twenty-five barons (one of whom was the lord mayor of London) who were to monitor the actions of the king and to receive complaints against him if he failed to observe the rights and liberties set out in the charter. If the king or his officers did not remedy the grievance within forty days, "those twenty-five barons together with the community of the whole land shall distrain [seize property] and distress us in every way they can, namely, by seizing castles, lands, possessions, and in such other ways as they can" (Article 61, Magna Carta, 1215). And the barons did rebel against John (with Innocent III releasing John from his oath to observe Magna Carta, annulling Magna Carta, and decreeing the excommunication of the barons). Civil war and a French invasion followed, and only the unexpected death of King John in October 1216 removed the main source of the rebellion. The barons who acted for the new king (the nine-year-old Henry III) immediately reissued Magna Carta minus a number of key provisions. The provisions omitted in the 1216 reissue as well as in all subsequent reissues included the arrangements for calling a meeting of the "common counsel of the kingdom" to approve a levy of additional scutages (a money assessment in place of knight service) and aids (requests for money grants). Also omitted was the barons' right to establish a group of twenty-five barons to oversee the actions of the king.

Baronial attempts in the thirteenth, fourteenth, and early fifteenth centuries to limit the power of the king all relied on replacing royal control with control by a group of barons. None of these attempts at baronial rule was successful for more than a very short time.

In the meantime, without any deliberate planning Parliament was gradually evolving, motivated by the increasing cost of running the increasingly bureaucratized government of England and its military needs. Although the provisions about the king's needing the consent of the "common counsel" in order to assess additional payments to the crown had been omitted from the reissues of Magna Carta, it was a widely accepted feudal principle. From the king's standpoint, the problem in seeking consent to another levy against the greater barons, who would attend such a meeting, was that the greater barons were rich in land but not in the money that the kings increasingly needed. And so Henry II, Richard, and John sold charters granting such rights as freedom of person, the right to come and go, the right to assess and collect their own taxes, and even the right to elect their own mayor and aldermen (council men) to the towns. These kings had found that the towns were where the money was.

But the idea of summoning representatives of these monied groups to give consent for a money aid was to be combined with calling representatives of certain groups to discuss the concerns of that group with a royal policy or with the actions of royal servants at the local level, especially the actions of the sheriff. John had on occasion summoned representatives of certain ports or boroughs and certain counties, but the purpose had been not the raising of money, but the local response to a particular concern or the gathering of information. A number of such summonses occurred during the reign of Henry III before 1254 when Henry was involved in an ultimately unsuccessful campaign in Gascony (part of Aquitaine, the last English holding in southwest France) and was in great need of money. In his name (Henry was abroad in Poitou), the king's great council—the common counsel of the greater barons as described in Magna Carta 1215, articles 12 and 14—was summoned to a meeting at Westminster. In addition, the sheriffs were to have elected two knights (lesser barons) from each county to attend the meeting and be prepared to state "what sort of an aid [money grant] they will give us in so great an emergency."[1]

Henry III got his aid in 1254 but not as much as he had asked and not without protests. By this time there was widespread dissatisfaction with his policies. As long as Henry continued to have the help of those officials who had been trained in his father's and grandfather's bureaucratic Angevin government, things went well enough. But Henry very much wished to run the government himself and so dismissed his last justiciar, Hubert de Burgh, in 1232. (William Marshal had died in 1219.) Henry had been well educated, but his interests lay in culture and the arts, not in the business of good government. He continued to believe that he owed his throne to the intervention of the pope, and he remained subservient to the papacy. He also came under the influence of several groups of foreigners.

Henry married Eleanor of Provence, in the southeastern part of what is now France, and she brought many relatives with her to England. Her uncles particularly took advantage of their relationship to the queen to receive many offices and benefices (endowments providing income), and they were severely resented by the English baronage. Another group of foreigners came in the persons of Henry's half-brothers. His mother Isabelle, after King John's death, returned to France and married the man to whom she had originally been betrothed at the time John married her. This later union gave Henry III four half-brothers, all of whom came to England where they became members of the royal court. The English barons resented the wealth these Frenchmen accumulated and their influence over the king.

Although Henry's foreign favorites contributed to a growing English resentment of foreign interference in England, Henry lost more support through his disastrous military campaigns. Dreaming of restoring the Angevin Empire of his grandfather Henry II, he led a number of unsuccessful campaigns in Brittany and southwestern France. He won nothing back and even lost the rest of Poitou. He would probably have lost more if the French king had not been Louis IX (canonized as St. Louis), who did not take advantage of Henry's military ineptness. Henry lost much respect as a result of his failures in France. He lost even more respect by his failures with Scotland and Wales, both of which refused the homage (the swearing of loyalty) won by Henry II.

Adding to English resentment against foreigners at court and in the government was Henry's support for a number of papal projects. After the death of Innocent III in 1216, the papacy had become increasingly immersed in Italian politics as it attempted to prevent Emperor Frederick II from squeezing the Papal States between his territory in northern Italy (as part of the German Roman Empire) and Frederick's own kingdom of Sicily (that included southern Italy and the island of Sicily).

The Papal States, an area in Italy under the political control of the papacy, were the remnant of the Exarchate of Ravenna, which had been created after the Byzantine conquest of the kingdom of the Germanic Ostrogoths in 552. Byzantine rule was challenged by an invasion of the Germanic Lombards in 568. The Lombards gained control of northern Italy (the Po Valley and Tuscany); they also controlled a central area to the east and north of Rome and a southern area to the south of Rome. This left Rome and its territory extending north and south and a corridor stretching northeastward to a point somewhat north of Ravenna on the Adriatic Sea. This area remained under Byzantine control until the mid-eighth century when the Byzantines had weakened to the point that conquest by the Lombards seemed inevitable. Although the Lombards had become Catholic by this time, the Lombards and the papacy were bitter political enemies. Since the papacy no longer received support from the Byzantine Empire, the popes now turned for support to the Franks who had established a kingdom in what is now France and the German Rhineland. The time was opportune because a dynastic revolution was under way in Francia. The ambitious and able "mayors of the palace" who had been the virtual rulers of the Franks for some time wanted to become kings to replace the much weakened Merovingian dynasty. The pope agreed that he who actually ruled should have the title of king; the alliance was created and a new Carolingian dynasty recognized. When the Lombards threatened Rome in 754, the pope appealed to King Pepin of Francia for aid. The Franks invaded, defeated the Lombards, and by a grant known as the "Donation of Pepin" gave the former Exarchate of Ravenna to the papacy. Thus was created the Papal States that would remain under the temporal control of the papacy down to the time of Italian unification in 1862. Nonetheless, even then the papacy refused to recognize the Italian state until an agreement was finally reached in 1929 restricting papal political control to Vatican City.

Northern Italy was in the process of breaking up into a number of semi-independent city-states and resisted the imperial authority. The papacy backed the city-states in their resistance to Frederick by supplying them with money to hire mercenaries. This war went on intermittently until Frederick's death in 1250, but throughout the struggle the papacy was relying heavily on revenues from England to pay its costs for resistance to Frederick. The English clergy paid heavy papal exactions and protested that the freedom of election of higher church offices guaranteed by Magna Carta was now denied by the popes who increasingly claimed the right to fill church vacancies with their own candidates. The English clergy protested, but King Henry backed the pope. However, Henry's relations with the papacy went too far when he became involved in a papal scheme to take the kingdom of southern Italy and Sicily from the heirs of Frederick II. The throne of Sicily was declared escheated (forfeited) to the papacy on the ground of rebellion (the kingdom had been created as a fief of the papacy in 1130), and a new ruling dynasty was sought. In 1254 Henry III concluded an agreement with the papacy whereby he would allow his second son, Edmund, to accept the Sicilian throne in return for Henry's paying the papal debt, which was enormous and getting larger. By 1257 Henry could not meet his financial commitments to the papacy and the pope threatened excommunication—so far had the church reform movement fallen! And by 1257 the barons were ready to unite to bring the king under control.

In 1258 Henry called an assembly of the greater barons—the "common counsel" of the kingdom. Such occasions were already being called parliaments.[2] In response to Henry's demand for aid, the barons refused and demanded a committee be appointed by the king and barons to draw up a program of reform. The program that was produced—the Provisions of Oxford (the meeting with the barons had been at Oxford)—called for the establishment of a council of twelve barons who effectively controlled the king. This council dominated the government for two years and then began to fall apart because the barons could not agree on just what reforms should be undertaken. The leader of the barons who wanted continued reform was Simon de Montfort, earl of Leicester. The reformers carried the day for the moment and issued the Provisions of Westminster in 1259. These provisions confirmed the baronial decisions taken since the Provisions of Oxford. But the reform party split in 1260: Henry's oldest son Edward was now able to form a royal party that attracted the more moderate barons, and in 1261 the pope released Henry from the oath he had taken to observe the Provisions of Oxford. It seemed that the baronial reform party was doomed when a key baronial leader (not de Montfort) rejoined the reform movement.

To avoid civil war, de Montfort and Henry agreed to submit their quarrel to Louis IX (St. Louis) of France who had a widespread reputation for justice. Louis supported Henry as king. Failing to win by peaceful methods, de Montfort declared war and led the baronial army against the king. This baronial army defeated a royal army led by Henry III and his son Edward at the battle of Lewes in Kent (1264). Both king and his heir were captured, leaving Simon de Montfort the real ruler of England, although he ruled in Henry's name with a council of nine barons.

To broaden the base of his support, de Montfort called for a "parliament" in that same year (1264). In addition to the greater barons who would be invited to a great council, he summoned four knights from each county. Then in the next year (1265), in addition to the greater barons, he summoned two knights from each county and two burgesses from each borough, thus bringing together all the groups that would eventually appear in Parliament. This meeting is usually called Simon de Montfort's Parliament, but it should not be regarded as a precedent for Parliament, for there would be many years of continued experimentation before the makeup of the English Parliament would be set.

De Montfort's baronial government did not last very long. Before the end of the year 1265, the baronial party split in reaction against de Montfort's policies, and the young prince Edward escaped from captivity and reformed a royalist party. Edward, who would prove to be a more than competent military leader, led a royalist army against a baronial army that was no longer wholly supporting de Montfort. The royalists won the issuing battle of Evesham (1266), and de Montfort was executed on the battlefield.

Hereafter, Henry III was recognized as king until his death in 1272, but it was increasingly his son Edward who ruled England. Recognizing that the claims of the barons had to be reconciled, king and council in 1267 formally issued the Statute of Marlborough containing many of the baronial demands of the Provisions of Oxford and Westminster.

Edward was so successful in reestablishing the royal government that he was able to leave England in 1270 and to remain abroad until 1274 even though Henry III had died in 1272. Edward left England to join Louis IX (St. Louis) of France in Louis' second crusade to recover the Holy Land from the Turks. Unfortunately, Louis was following the advice of his younger brother Charles I, the new king of Sicily who in 1266 had become king with papal backing to replace the Hohenstaufen dynasty of Frederick II.

Charles I (1266–85) established the Angevin dynasty as kings of Sicily (1266–82), and thereafter his descendants ruled the kingdom of Naples while an Aragonese dynasty ruled the kingdom of Sicily. (A rebellion in Sicily in 1282, called the Sicilian Vespers, drove out the Angevins and called in the Aragonese.) The two kingdoms were reunited in 1435 when the same person inherited both kingdoms. The "new" state thus created was known as the Kingdom of the Two Sicilies. Charles, hoping to extend the region of his influence along the neighboring coast of north Africa, urged Louis to begin his crusade in Tunisia and work eastward toward Jerusalem. The attack upon the city of Tunis was not successful, and Louis became ill and died in Tunisia, bringing his crusade to an end. Edward, however, continued to travel across north Africa to Egypt and Palestine, returning by way of southern Italy and Sicily. Then instead of returning immediately to England he stopped in Aquitaine where he remained until he had reestablished order in that unruly province.

Back in England in 1274, Edward I proved to be a strong and able king. In addition to his accomplishments in the realm of law and his subjugation of Wales and attempts to subdue Scotland, Edward played an important role in the emergence of Parliament. First as virtual regent in the last years of Henry III and then as king, Edward I continued experimentation in calling representatives of certain groups to meet with the great council to discuss concerns specific to the group or groups summoned or to request approval of an additional aid to enable the crown to pursue its policies. These expanded meetings of the great council were usually referred to as parliaments.

In 1295 Edward summoned one of these parliaments. This meeting is usually referred to as the "Model Parliament" because it contained all the elements that would eventually attend Parliament: (1) the greater barons, both lay and ecclesiastical, who attended in their own right; (2) the representatives of the lesser barons who came to be known as knights of the shire; (3) the representatives of the burgesses from the larger towns of England; and (4) the representatives of the lesser clergy. But this meeting did not immediately lead to a final form of parliament. Edward continued to experiment with parliaments of various composition throughout his reign. It would not be until the middle of the fourteenth century during the reign of Edward III (1327–77) that the composition of the assembly would become recognizable. After years of indecision, the representatives of the lower clergy dropped out and, following continental procedure, made their grants in the two convocations (synods or assemblies) of York and Canterbury (the two archbishoprics or provinces of the Church in England).

Edward had received a grant or aid from the Parliament of 1295 (the Model Parliament), but it was not enough to pay for the high costs of his wars in Wales and Scotland as well as his preparations for a war with France. France was now ruled by the able and aggressive Philip IV (known as Philip the Fair) (1285–1314), who was determined to bring under royal control the two remaining great fiefs of France, the county of Flanders and the duchy of Aquitaine. Unable to obtain further money from his parliaments, Edward assembled a small group of barons and obtained from them a grant to apply not only to themselves but also to all barons and burgesses. He also levied a customs tax on the export of each bale of wool. (Wool had become the chief English export, supplying the weavers of Flanders and northern Italy.) Having done this, Edward sailed to Flanders to negotiate an alliance against France. In his absence, the most influential groups in the realm under the leadership of the barons refused to pay the tax until Edward had agreed to reconfirm Magna Carta and the Charter of the Forest and agreed to certain additions, the most significant of which are as detailed in the Confirmation of the Charters 1297: "and we have likewise granted for us and our heirs to the archbishops, bishops, abbots, priors and other folk of holy church, and to the earls and barons and all the community of the land that for no need will we take such manner of aid, mises [taxes] or prises [assessments] from our realm henceforth except with the common assent of all the realm and for the common profit of the same realm, saving the ancient aids and prises due and accustomed" (Article 6), and "and because by far the greater part of the community of the realm feel themselves greatly burdened by the maltote [bad tax] on wool, . . . we at their request have completely relieved them and have granted that we will not take this or any other in future without their common assent and their goodwill" (Article 7) (see Document 5). This grant provided future parliaments with their claim to control taxation.

At the beginning of the fourteenth century, all the members of a parliament would gather to hear the agenda of the meeting. If knights of the shires and burgesses were present, the agenda always included a request for supply (aid, grant). When it came time to deliberate on the supply, the knights of the shire, who were lesser barons, joined the greater barons for this discussion and the burgesses were sent off by themselves. But as the fourteenth century progressed, parliaments were frequently called because of the financial strain of the Hundred Years' War with France (1337–1453). This war was the one anticipated by Edward I, but it did not begin until 1337 during the reign of Edward III. It was a war begun by England ostensibly because Edward III claimed the French throne through his mother, a daughter of Philip IV, but the French preferred a male candidate whose claim did not come through the female line (Philip VI of Valois). This was not a continuous war. It was a war in which the English won the major battles (Crécy, Poitiers, and Agincourt), but the French won the war.

Because Parliament was frequently asked for supply during this long war, the organization of that assembly changed. The modification was caused primarily by social and economic changes due to the rise of a money economy and the decline of feudal warfare. The change affected the role of the knights of the shire who as lesser barons met with the greater barons to vote supply. By this time, however, the knights were not knights in a military sense but simply well-to-do country gentlemen who no longer held their land by feudal tenure. The growth of the common law had effectively ended subinfeudation, and the courts regarded their land as held by proprietary right (i.e., not held as a vassal of a lord). Therefore, the qualification to be a knight of the shire no longer depended on the status of lesser baron but on annual income. Under the circumstances, the interests of the knights were more similar to those of the burgesses since both were merely the elected representatives of their constituents and did not attend Parliament in their own right, as did the greater barons. So it was natural for knights and burgesses to combine to form the commons. Thus the English Parliament came to have two houses, Lords and Commons, instead of an assembly made up of the three traditional medieval estates (lords spiritual, lords secular, and commons) as found on the Continent.

By the middle of the fourteenth century, Lords and Commons were using the concessions made by Edward I in the Confirmation of the Charters, that "he and his heirs would not assess aids or other taxes without the consent of the greater ecclesiastical and secular barons and the community of the realm," to claim control over taxation. This control, combined with Edward III's unending financial needs, led to Parliament's bargaining with the king—no further money unless the king accepted Parliament's petitions, most of which came from the commons. By this means Parliament gained a role in the making of legislation, so that by the end of the fourteenth century it was accepted that legislation came from "the king in parliament" and that a bill (proposed law) became a statute only with the consent of all three elements—king, lords, and commons.

During the reign of the Lancastrians[3] in the fifteenth century, the weak claims of this dynasty to the throne provided Parliament with the opportunity to increase its powers at the expense of the king. At the same time, the Commons was able to establish that all money bills must originate in the Commons.

Although Parliament did not increase its powers in the sixteenth century under the strong Tudors, it did not lose any, and its organization and efficiency continued to evolve. The Tudor dynasty came to the throne in 1485 following a long struggle for the throne between the Lancastrians and Yorkists known as the Wars of the Roses. The Lancastrians ruled until the defeat and imprisonment of Henry VI in 1461, when Edward IV (1461–83) established the Yorkists. On the death of Edward IV, the throne passed briefly to his minor son Edward V, but the boy was soon pushed aside and presumably murdered by his uncle who took the title Richard III (1483–85). The Lancastrians threw their support to Henry Tudor, son of Margaret Beaufort, descended from John Beaufort, an illegitimate son of John of Gaunt, duke of Lancaster. With strong support, Henry Tudor invaded, and Richard III was defeated and killed. Parliament recognized Henry Tudor as Henry VII (1485–1509). Although Henry had some difficulty getting all of England to recognize the legitimacy of his rule, the dynasty was firmly established by the time his son, Henry VIII (1509–47), became king.

When the new Stuarts came to the throne on the death of Elizabeth I, the last of the Tudors in 1603, Parliament was ready to oppose the absolutist claims of the Stuarts.[4] The Parliamentarians, led by Edward Coke, successfully argued that Magna Carta guaranteed such English rights as trial by jury, habeas corpus, equality before the law, freedom from arbitrary arrest, and parliamentary control of taxation. England was well on the way to becoming a constitutional monarchy.

NOTES

1. Carl Stephenson and Frederick George Marcham, eds. and trans., *Sources of English Constitutional History, A Selection of Documents from A.D. 600 to the Present* (New York and London: Harper, 1937), No. 46J, pp. 139–40.

2. The English word "parliament" comes from the French word *parler* meaning "to talk." The word "parliament" or "colloquium," a coming together to talk, was used to refer to meetings of the council of the greater barons from the early thirteenth century.

3. The Lancastrian dynasty replaced the Angevin or Plantagenet dynasty on the deposition of Richard II (1377–99), grandson of Edward III. The Lancastrian claim came from John of Gaunt, duke of Lancaster, third son of Edward III.

4. James VI of Scotland became James I of England following the death of Elizabeth I in 1603. James was the son of Mary Stuart, Queen of Scots, executed in England in 1581 following a plot against the life of Elizabeth I. Mary Stuart was a great granddaughter of the Tudor king Henry VII. Mary was Catholic but her son was Presbyterian. Scotland had followed the Continent in adopting the absolutist principles of Roman law. The new king, James I, found it difficult to accept the parliamentary claims relating to the essential role that parliament had come to have in the government of the state, especially in the area of finances.

BIOGRAPHIES

Alfred of Wessex

Alfred, known as Alfred the Great since the sixteenth century, was king of the Anglo-Saxon kingdom of Wessex from 871 to 899. He became king just as the attacks of the Danes were shifting from raids for plunder to invasions seeking land for settlement. Wessex, with its long coast along the English Channel, was vulnerable to landings at many places. In addition, it was vulnerable to attacks by Danes who had been transported in their ships up the Thames River, forcing the men of Wessex to face Danes from two directions at the same time.

Alfred's succession to the kingdom was in accordance with his father's will that provided for the succession in turn by his sons. Alfred was preceded in the kingship by his two older brothers. That this did not lead to outright rebellion on the part of Alfred's nephews may well be due to the fact that in 871 the Danes defeated the forces of Wessex in a number of encounters and Alfred had to go into hiding on occasion to avoid capture. But Alfred persisted and gradually was able to bring more men into his army from a number of outlying places. With such an enlarged army, Alfred defeated the Danes decisively in 878 at the battle of Edington followed by the Peace of Chippingham. When Alfred and his forces occupied London in 886 (the Danes had been in possession for some years), the almost continuous conflict came temporarily to an end, and Alfred could turn to reorganizing his kingdom in preparation for possible further invasions.

For coastal defense, Alfred divided his army in two parts and rotated the parts at strategic spots along the coastline. He built a navy of ships designed to offset the fast maneuverable boats of the Vikings. And with unexpected consequences, he built a series of fortified towns (burgs) throughout his kingdom where garrisons were located and where the population of the surrounding countryside could take shelter in case of attack. As Alfred and his helpers and successors continued to press the Danes back, new burgs were built. This policy would provide nuclei for expanding trade in the next century. The Danes did return in 892 with an exceptionally large army, but the measures that had been taken for defense proved adequate for the job and by 896 the immediate Danish threat to Wessex was over.

Alfred's role in political history was thus assured by his resistance to and defeat of the Danes, a defeat that marked the beginning of English expansion at the expense of the Danelaw—an area of Danish-Norse settlement north and east of a line running roughly from London in the southeast to Chester in the northwest. As the area under the control of the kings of Wessex expanded, it was organized as one unified kingdom. This expansion took place under Alfred's successors of the house of Wessex, a remarkably able series of rulers until late in the tenth century, when the Danes would return again.

Alfred's political importance is paralleled by his accomplishments in law and education. He issued a code of laws based on earlier codes issued by kings in Wessex and Kent. And he entered into an agreement known as the Treaty with Guthrum, the Danish leader defeated in 886. This "treaty" is a very interesting and enlightened document. It is actually an outline of legal relations between the English and Danes in those areas where the two populations lived close to one another and where part of the Danish population was still pagan.

Alfred's interest in learning may well have been influenced by at least one and possibly two trips to Rome as a boy. His contribution to education came as the result of the serious decline in monastic learning that had resulted from Danish raids and devastation, which had been especially hard on the monasteries. As a result, by the later ninth century there were very few people who could read and write. Following the example of Charlemagne, Alfred sent abroad for scholars to staff a school where the sons of his followers could be taught. There Alfred instituted a program of translations from Latin into what is now known as Old English; Alfred himself did a number of the translations. As a result, a significant improvement in the level of learning in England took place, and those who served in church and royal courts would be fluent in Old English and Latin.

Thomas Becket (St. Thomas)

Thomas Becket was born in London probably in 1120. His father was a merchant, and both his father and mother were of Norman descent; they were of the middling rank of merchants. The origin of the name "Becket" is unknown. Thomas always referred to himself as "Thomas of London" until such time as he obtained an office that identified him. He received a basic education, learning to read and write Latin and French, in England and with the encouragement of his mother, went briefly to Paris. He was never, however, much of a student, and on his mother's death, when he was twenty-one, he left school. A year later, he took service with a London banker for several years and learned those administrative and financial skills that he would later use to great advantage.

By 1146 Thomas had become a clerk in the household of Archbishop of Canterbury Theobald where he advanced to the rank of archdeacon despite competing against a number of better-educated young men. During this time he may have been allowed to study law at Bologna for a short time, and he was probably involved in the negotiations that brought Henry II to England in 1154 where he was crowned king by Archbishop Theobald. The next year Henry consulted with Theobald to find someone with legal and financial experience for the position of chancellor. On Theobald's recommendation, Henry II offered Thomas the chancellorship; Thomas was both archdeacon of Canterbury (a strong and influential position) and chancellor of England between 1155 and 1162. During this time, Thomas served Henry faithfully and the two became good friends. Thomas was used in a large number of capacities for which he was rewarded generously. He maintained a large retinue, and his household was impressive in dress and manners. The two worked together to strengthen and improve the organization of the king's government in whatever part of Henry's realm they were in at the time. Thomas was often sent on diplomatic missions for the king, missions that he carried out with pomp and circumstance.

When Archbishop Theobald died in 1162, Henry pondered for some time whom he would recommend as a successor. He and Theobald had worked well together. Theobald had not been subservient; he had often counseled patience or moderation to the impatient king. Above all, Theobald had been loyal. Henry believed that Becket, too, had these qualities. The two of them had worked well together for seven years, and if Becket continued as chancellor and became archbishop as well, Henry's plans to restore the powers of the crown as they had been in the time of his grandfather Henry I should go forward easily. Accordingly, in 1163 he recommended Becket to the monks of the cathedral and to the bishops of the province. Perhaps reluctantly, since Becket was not a monk or even a priest, the monks elected Thomas and the bishops approved; Becket was ordained into the priesthood and installed as archbishop of Canterbury.

Becket did not live up to Henry's expectations. From a staunch supporter of the king he became a champion for the liberty of the Church, and Becket unexpectedly, from Henry's standpoint, resigned the chancellorship. Perhaps it was inevitable that two such self-confident and egotistical men should disagree, following which neither man could back down.

The issue that divided them was the matter of criminous clerks—clerks responsible for committing a felonious crime that would ordinarily come before a royal court. However, the church reformers of the late eleventh century (known as the Gregorian reformers) aimed to separate the Church entirely from secular control and, in the advanced form of the reform movement, to assert the superiority of the spiritual over the secular. If this reform were carried to its logical conclusion, no member of the clergy (no clerk) could be subject to a secular court. Under the previous king, Stephen, who had to make concessions in order to obtain and keep the throne, the jurisdiction of the church courts had expanded. When Henry became king, he received complaints about the number of violent crimes the Church had failed to punish other than to deprive the clerk of his office. Henry knew, or at least was advised, that the problem was that nobody knew exactly what the canon law of the Church was. A number of attempts had been made in the late eleventh century to codify the laws of the Church, but the state of records was so incomplete and contradictory that the result of these attempts had been more confusion.

In 1140, however, shortly before Henry became king of England, a successful codification was achieved by a canon lawyer known by the name of Gratian, who worked in the Italian city of Bologna where a famous law school was being developed. Gratian succeeded where others had failed because he applied the dialectic method to the contradictory canons (church laws) and deduced a single rule out of the confusion. Although this collection of canon law, known as the *Decretum,* was never pronounced to be an official collection, it was treated as such and was responsible for a remarkable development of the canon law courts in the second half of the twelfth century. When Henry became king of England, however, these developments had not yet occurred. It seemed to Henry that the only way he could provide peace and security to his people (and this was a main provision of the English coronation oath) was to take action against criminals, whoever they were. Henry presented to his barons assembled in council (and the bishops were there as barons of the realm) a program of reform that demanded support for the "ancient customs of the realm," which meant before the innovations of Stephen. Becket and the bishops would take the oath but added the qualification, "saving their order"—that is, provided the customs were not contrary to canon law. This qualification was not acceptable to Henry II.

Adding to the tensions created by what Henry interpreted as disloyalty was the position of the papacy. There was a split election in the college of cardinals in 1159. One pope, Victor IV, was backed by the German emperor, Frederick I Barbarossa; the other pope, Alexander III, who favored the north Italian towns and Norman Sicily against the emperor, needed some stronger support and looked to France and England for it. France recognized Alexander III first and the pope took up residence in France, usually in Sens a short distance south of Paris in territory under the control of the king of France. Henry held church councils in England and Normandy and on their advice also recognized Alexander III. Alexander was thus very dependent on France and England; in the coming conflict between Henry and Becket, he was frequently forced to take evasive action in order not to give a final answer in favor of one or the other. As it happened, Alexander outlived four anti-popes and Thomas Becket as well and died in 1181. In return for Henry's support, Alexander issued a bull canonizing the Anglo-Saxon king Edward the Confessor (he later canonized Thomas Becket as well).

The quarrel continued, with Henry determined to get what he wanted and Becket determined to resist. Both men were very unreasonable in their statements and were counseled to show patience and to negotiate. The ecclesiastical barons were torn. They would have been happy to have the whole question of the jurisdiction of secular and church courts left undefined, but Henry wanted everything stated in writing in a document known as the Constitutions of Clarendon. Thomas and the bishops said no to approval of the constitutions, but then under pressure, Thomas relented and said yes, and although Thomas later retracted his consent, the bishops were never able to trust him completely, even those who went into exile with him. Brought to trial over monies Becket collected as chancellor, Becket feared what Henry would do and fled the kingdom in November 1164 with a small party of followers. One of his secretaries, John of Salisbury, had gone ahead to seek supporters.

Becket's exile would last until 1170. During this time, he had little independent income and was mostly dependent on Louis VII of France, who regarded it as worth the cost to offer protection to an enemy of his enemy, Henry II of England. During the years of exile, many persons tried to mediate the quarrel, and although there were many embassies between the two, neither was willing to retreat in his demands. This was embarrassing to the English church and to Alexander III, but Louis VII was probably amused. Terms were finally agreed upon in the fall of 1170, while Henry was in France, and Thomas made preparation to return to Canterbury, which had been administered by the king's men during his absence. Among other things, he excommunicated those clergy whom he regarded as having disobeyed him, including the archbishop of York, an action that aroused great resentment. It was obvious that not everyone was glad to have Thomas back, and Thomas replied by taking an extreme stand vis-à-vis his opponents and about the properties that had not been restored to him.

When the excommunicated bishops reported all this to Henry II in Normandy, he exclaimed aloud and wondered why anyone could allow such treatment from a low-born clerk. Four of Henry's knights immediately plotted to remedy this matter, although it seems that they did not know how they were going to do it. The knights made their way to England where they were joined by additional men, and on Tuesday, December 29, 1170, they made their way to Canterbury in the late afternoon when there were services in the cathedral. They found Thomas in a chamber off the great hall of the monastery in conversation with a number of his clerks. When Thomas did not respond to their demands, they armed themselves, and when Thomas made his way into the cathedral the knights followed him. He defied them and was cut down before the altar.

All eyewitness accounts of the murder agreed that Thomas could have saved himself and he was urged to do so by his men, but Thomas remained unmoved. The witnesses said it was as if he wished martyrdom, and indeed he almost immediately became a martyr. He had won against Henry since Henry accepted responsibility for speaking the words that inspired the knights. Henry was assigned physical penance for his part, which he performed publicly. Louis VII condemned the murder and made the most of Henry's discomfiture. Nonetheless, although Henry made no further attempt to impose the Constitutions of Clarendon, his relations with the Church during the rest of his reign were amicable enough.

In Canterbury, miracles almost immediately began to occur beside Becket's tomb, and his canonization took place in March 1173. Canterbury became the site of pilgrimages to St. Thomas' tomb, and a cult of St. Thomas grew up to the great advantage of the monks of Canterbury.

Charlemagne and the Carolingian Empire

Charlemagne (Charles the Great) (768–814) became king of the Franks in 768 on the death of his father, Pepin I. He added the title king of the Lombards in 774 upon his defeat of the Lombards in northern and central Italy. In 800 he was crowned Roman emperor by Pope Leo III, thus establishing an ill-defined link between the empire and the papacy.

The Franks were a Germanic people, some of whom began settling in the northeastern part of Roman Gaul to the west of the Rhine River in the fourth century. For the next century they lived in this area more or less in peace with the Roman authorities. They were allowed to live there on terms that made them federate allies of the empire—that is, they were allowed to settle there in return for guarding the area against further Germanic penetration. The Franks fulfilled their defensive obligations until the late fifth century when the weakness of the Roman frontier defense encouraged more Franks to cross the Rhine. These Franks lived in loosely organized bands under a number of petty kings until one group under the leadership of a family known as Merovingian (from its mythical leader Merovech) defeated rival kings and began to consolidate those Franks living west of the Rhine into a single kingdom. In 481 a man by the name of Clovis (an early form of the name Louis) became king of these Franks on the death of his father. Clovis began to expand his kingdom, first to incorporate those Franks living east of the Rhine, known as Ripuarian Franks, into his kingdom, then to defeat the remnants of Roman authority in northern Gaul centered at Soissons (a short distance south of Paris), then back east to establish some kind of authority over other Germanic peoples living just east of the Rhine, the Alamanni and the Bavarians. By this time Clovis ruled all of northern Gaul down to the Loire River. Some time during this expansion, the Franks were converted to Christianity. Thus, in Clovis' move against the Germanic Visigoths who had established a kingdom in southwestern Gaul in 418 but were still Arian Christians, Clovis had the support of the Gallo-Roman Christian clergy. He defeated the Visigoths at the battle of Vouillé, south of the Loire near Poitiers, and by the time of his death in 511, Frankish control had been extended almost to the Pyrenees Mountains between modern France and Spain. By 534 Clovis' sons had added Burgundy in southeastern Gaul.

Frankish Gaul under the Merovingians therefore covered most of what is modern France as well as a strip of territory in Germany that had never been under Roman control. This was not, however, a consolidated state, for the Franks had no such notion. Rather, the history of Merovingian Gaul is a picture of division first among all the sons of a dead king followed by warfare among them until all but one had been eliminated; and then division once more among all surviving sons. In this way by the end of the seventh century, a number of "natural" divisions had appeared. The main strength of the Frankish kingdom lay in the north where the eastern part with its capital at Aachen was called Austrasia. To the west was the kingdom of Neustria centering on Paris, to which the former kingdom of Burgundy in the southeast was frequently added. That left the southwest, known as Aquitaine, to break free whenever the opportunity presented itself.

The history of Merovingian Gaul displays constantly changing alliances as the royal contestants sought support from the strong aristocratic families. This support was bought with gifts, especially landed gifts at the expense of the royal domain. Gradually, one family—the Arnulfings or Pepinids (ancestors of the Carolingians)—gained more power than the others. The heads of this family dominated the land through their hereditary position as mayor of the palace (chief of the household officials) in Austrasia. This family's attempts to replace the Merovingian dynasty as the royal rulers of the Franks were unsuccessful until the middle of the eighth century when a mayor of the palace by the name of Pepin, known in history as Pepin the Younger or Pepin the Short, took center stage. Pepin utilized the strength of his position among the Franks, as well as the need of the pope for allies against the Lombards, to obtain ecclesiastical sanction for the transfer of the crown from, according to historical sources written by supporters of the new Carolingian dynasty, the weak and incapable hands of the Merovingians to the strong and capable hands of the Carolingians.

Pepin ruled the Frankish kingdom, including Austrasia, Neustria, Burgundy, and Acquitaine, from 751 until his death in 768 when he divided his kingdom between his sons Charles and Caroloman. Caroloman died soon thereafter, and Charles claimed the entire kingdom for himself, overlooking any claims of Caroloman's sons and sending Carloman's family into exile. Charles' answer to the problem of making gifts to keep the important families on his side was to lead the Franks into almost yearly military campaigns of conquest to provide land for these gifts. The Merovingians had eroded the royal domain by their gifts, and the sparseness of their gift giving was partly the reason they were unable to retain the throne. Charles' father and grandfather (Charles Martel) had made extensive use of church property to make what were presumed to be gifts for the lifetime only of the recipient but tended to become hereditary. Charles chose not to use church lands for this purpose, thus retaining the support of the clergy, but he led the Franks on almost yearly military campaigns. The Franks apparently expected constant fighting as the death of each ruler had for centuries been followed by civil war to eliminate rivals. Moreover, Charlemagne had little difficulty in getting the support of his followers on the occasion of the annual meeting of his "men" at the Marchfield or Mayfield. As long as he could lead his men in war and add territory to be distributed, they followed loyally. And so three borders of the Frankish state, which came to be called Francia, were extended southward across the Pyrenees into the northeastern part of Spain (a campaign that can be regarded as the beginning of the Christian reconquest of Spain from the Muslim Moors who had overthrown the now Catholic Visigothic kingdom in 711); into Italy (overthrowing the Lombard kingdom in 774); and deep into Germany by reconfirming rule over the Alamanni and the Bavarians, pushing further eastward by conquering and converting to Christianity the Saxons, Thuringians, and Frisians, and establishing protectorates over some of the Germanic and Slavic peoples living even further to the east.

Meanwhile, Charlemagne undertook a number of reforms to improve the administration of his kingdoms. As part of this movement, he instituted an educational reform by establishing a palace school and inviting a number of scholars from abroad to come to Francia and work there. Among those scholars was the Anglo-Saxon Alcuin, who came from a school at York. The purpose of this educational reform was to provide the Church and the kingdom with literate men. This reform helped to replace the old hardly legible Merovingian script with the elegant Caroline script that is still used today; aided the issuance of new laws and the reissue of old laws; and encouraged participation in the many religious controversies of the day. To such men it was natural to equate Charlemagne's realm with the western Christian Church headed by Rome, over which the Franks had assumed a sort of protectorate (there was no formal break between eastern and western churches at this time). If there was a Roman emperor in the east protecting the Church headed by the patriarch of Constantinople, Charlemagne held such a position in the west. Charlemagne was crowned Roman emperor by the pope in Rome at Christmas 800. (For this coronation and the subsequent history of the imperial title, see the biography of Frederick II.)

In making plans for the future of his kingdoms and empire, Charlemagne intended to divide his realm among his sons. It was only an accident of history that on his death in 814, only one son, known as Louis the Pious, survived. Thus, the territorial empire survived, but things were not the same. While later generations would look back to the rule of Charlemagne as being successful and enlightened, he left serious problems for his successor. Charlemagne retained the support of the aristocratic families by keeping them actively involved in military conquest and allowing them to share in the spoils. By the time of his imperial coronation, he was already too old and ill to lead those constant campaigns, and so powerful aristocratic families reemerged and struggled among themselves for influence. The local officials appointed to administer the royal domain, the counts, increasingly regarded their offices as hereditary and the royal domain as their own. In addition, Danish raids along the northern coast that began in the opening years of the ninth century continued during the reign of Louis the Pious. Since Louis was not a military leader, local officials were left to provide defense, again adding to their independence. Louis himself, trained in the new schooling, may have held an imperial ideal, but his own sons reverted to the Frankish type and insisted on division of the land. Thus, the centralization of power that seemed to have been established under Charlemagne merely masked the reality. Charlemagne's successors in France were therefore essentially at the mercy of their great feudatories until a reversal of fortunes took place in about the year 1200 under Philip II Augustus of France.

Eleanor of Aquitaine

Eleanor (c. 1124–1204) became countess of Poitou and duchess of Aquitaine on the death of her father, Willliam X, in 1137. She became queen of France in 1137 following her recent marriage to Louis VII. She became queen of England in 1154 when her then-husband became King Henry II. Following the death of Henry II in 1189, she became queen-mother during the reigns of her sons, Richard I (1189–99) and John (1199–1216) until her death in 1204.

Such in bare outline is the life of Eleanor of Aquitaine, but beneath these facts lies a very colorful personality who, to a remarkable degree, considering the restraints attending women in her position, controlled her own life and influenced events around her. She was born and raised in Aquitaine, the southwestern part of France, an area notorious for its independence of control by the French crown. She was the descendant of dukes whose quasi-independent position went back to Carolingian times. She was also the granddaughter of William IX of Aquitaine, a romantic poet and crusader, whose fame may have accounted for some of the legends that grew up about Eleanor and the courts of love. In 1137 she was heiress to a territory extending from the Loire River in the north to the Pyrenees in the south, a territory dwarfing in size the land actually under the control of the king of France. When her father William X went on pilgrimage to Santiago de Compostela in Spain (he soon after died there), Eleanor was left to the guardianship of King Louis VI of France. It is not surprising that King Louis, facing imminent death, immediately arranged for his son Louis to marry her. At the time of the marriage Eleanor was about thirteen and Louis was seventeen; they became king and queen of France a short time later.

Eleanor was apparently not a very happy queen of France. The royal palace in Paris was dark and gloomy, and the atmosphere was dull in contrast with bright sunny Aquitaine where life was full and joyful. She was also overshadowed by the queen-mother who was openly contemptuous of her when, after six years of marriage, Eleanor had produced no children; after all, producing a male heir was the primary consideration in royal marriage.

The situation changed in 1144 when she met the famous Cistercian abbot, Bernard of Clairvaux, who told her she would have a child. She did indeed have a child, but unfortunately, it was a girl (named Marie, who would later be the patroness of poets, Marie of Champagne). The year 1144 also saw the fall of the easternmost of the crusading states, Edessa, to the revitalized Turks and the spread of a crusading fervor throughout the Christian west, preached by Bernard of Clairvaux at Vézelay in eastern France in 1146. Louis VII took the cross, and Eleanor prepared to accompany her husband when he left in 1147 on what is known as the Second Crusade.

On the Second Crusade Louis VII led a large French army, and Conrad III of the German Roman Empire led a large German army. Both armies suffered separate defeats by the Turks in western Asia Minor, although the remnants of the two armies made their way to the eastern Mediterranean by sea. The French contingent reached Antioch, and there Louis VII, Eleanor, and their surviving troops remained for some time, entertained by Eleanor's uncle, Raymond of Toulouse, who was prince of Antioch. After the hardships of the land journey to Constantinople and defeat in Asia Minor, Antioch offered palatial luxury and gay entertainment. Louis and Conrad, at the suggestion of the resident defenders of the Christian states, decided to attack Damascus instead of trying to free Edessa. This attack was a complete failure and served to indicate that the interests of those Christians who had lived in the east for some time differed from those of recent arrivals intent on defeating the Turks at all costs. The result would be some decline in the crusading fervor in Europe.

As for Eleanor, relations between her and Louis VII deteriorated during the stay in Antioch. She no doubt enjoyed the sophisticated atmosphere prevailing under Raymond, who was not much older than Eleanor herself, and her conduct and reluctance to leave in order to visit Jerusalem may have led to rumors that the queen was intimately involved with him. At any rate, it was at Antioch that Eleanor raised with Louis the possibility that their failure to produce an heir might be due to the illegal nature of their marriage since they were within the prohibited degrees of relationship for canonical marriage (i.e., marriage approved by the laws of the Church). For the moment, Eleanor submitted to Louis' demand that they go on pilgrimage to Jerusalem. On the way back to France, however, they visited Rome to consult Pope Eugenius III about the illegality of their marriage, but the pope encouraged them to stay together and not to think of dissolution. He blessed the pair and persuaded them to think of having more children. Eleanor did have another child when they returned to France, but unfortunately it was another girl, Alix or Alice. Probably the only reason Louis did not immediately proceed for divorce at this time was the opposition of Suger, abbot of St. Denis just outside Paris, who had served Louis VI and was now the chief adviser of Louis VII. Suger foresaw only political loss to France if it were to break the connection between the crown and Aquitaine. Louis VII was duke of Aquitaine in the right of his wife; even if there were no male heir, his older daughter would inherit Aquitaine and possibly inherit France— there was no firm rule of succession in the twelfth century. Upon Suger's death in 1151, however, Louis was free to consider his own future. He concluded that continued life with Eleanor was impossible, and accordingly he approached the higher clergy of France to hear his case. He was able to demonstrate that he and Eleanor had a common ancestor in Robert II of France (996–1031), Louis in the fourth degree from Robert and Eleanor in the fifth degree. Canon law at this time prohibited marriage within the seventh degree; this would be reduced to the third degree at the Lateran Council of 1215. The marriage was declared dissolved in March 1152, and Eleanor immediately left court for Poitiers in Poitou, the northern part of Aquitaine.

Eleanor married Henry, count of Anjou and duke of Normandy, in May 1152; Henry was nineteen and Eleanor twenty-eight or twenty-nine. This marriage was just as important as the earlier marriage to Louis VII. The duchy of Aquitaine, added to Henry's territories in the north, gave Henry control of almost all the western coast of France, making him a much more powerful person than his overlord, the king of France. Henry of Anjou, as he is known, was the grandson of Henry I of England and Normandy, the son of Matilda, Henry I's only surviving legitimate heir after 1120. Matilda had been married to the Roman emperor Henry V until his death in 1125 when Henry I brought her home to England and had his barons swear to accept her as their ruler on his death. Henry I then married her to Geoffrey of Anjou, the young son of Fulk V of Anjou. Henry of Anjou, the future Henry II of England, was the first of three sons of this marriage. Matilda never became queen of England or duchess of Normandy, for the barons of both of these territories preferred her cousin, Stephen of Blois (1135–54), a grandson of William I of England (William the Conqueror).

Geoffrey of Anjou sought to take Normandy from Stephen in the name of his son Henry, while Matilda sought to take England. Matilda herself did not succeed in overcoming Stephen in England, although she came close. Her son Henry was more successful, and Stephen recognized him as his heir before his death in 1154. Geoffrey was successful in Normandy. By 1150 he had all but the eastern part of Normandy under control, after which he sought the help of his overlord in France, Louis VII, for aid in completing the conquest and recognizing his son as duke of Normandy. It was while these negotiations were taking place in Paris that Henry and his father Geoffrey became acquainted with Eleanor. When news of the impending divorce became known, Henry apparently opened secret negotiations with Eleanor herself. (Count Geoffrey had died in 1151.)

Henry and Eleanor were married in Poitiers where their first son was born in August 1153 (he died in 1156). Henry became duke of Aquitaine in right of his wife. They became king and queen of England following Stephen's death in October 1154. Henry II is generally acknowledged to have been one of the great medieval kings. He traveled incessantly, using the institutions and customs of the various entities which he held and rounding out the boundaries of his "empire." These included England with its centralized institutions and a loose lordship over Wales, Scotland, and Ireland. On the continent his lands included the duchy of Normandy, the counties of Anjou, Maine, and Touraine, and the duchy of Aquitaine, including the counties of Poitou and Gascony. He selected the men to attend his inner court and to carry out the functions of his government from the lesser barons or even the burghers. These were usually not university men but men trained at the court in many different kinds of activities, political, financial, and legal. He selected his men well and, with the major exception of Thomas Becket, they remained loyal to him.

Henry spent much more time in his continental possessions than in England, and his court followed him. Eleanor usually remained in England where she served as regent until 1163, although she was sent to the Continent from time to time on ceremonial occasions. She also had seven more children, four sons and three daughters; the last child, John, was born in 1166. Hers was certainly a busy life, but it was very much one at the command of Henry, who was domineering and subject to fits of rage; he was also not a very faithful husband. At any rate, by the time of John's birth, Eleanor and Henry were not on good terms. Also the period between 1163 and 1170 was one of conflict between Henry and Becket with much accompanying tension at court.

Then in 1168 Eleanor's life changed drastically: she was sent to Aquitaine to try to control the rebellious barons of that duchy. From her court at Poitiers she administered her lands, issuing charters, giving judgments, and discouraging the warfare that every baron thought his right to wage. Eleanor remained in Aquitaine until 1174. It is to this period that romance has assigned her presiding over courts of love and her son Richard's emergence as a troubadour. In 1170 Henry indicated a future disposition of his territories among his sons: Henry, the oldest, would have England, Normandy, and Anjou; Richard would have Acquitaine; Geoffrey would have Brittany (he was betrothed to the heiress of Brittany); and John, the youngest, would have only a number of strong castles (he received Ireland in 1177). None of the sons was satisfied with this arrangement, with each thinking he should have more. When it became obvious that Henry would delegate no real power to any of them in their "own" territories, they rebelled (1173–74) and accepted the backing of Louis VII. When Eleanor sided with her sons, Henry had her captured in 1174 and returned to England where she was allowed no independence of movement as long as Henry lived. The exception was the period 1185–86 when she was sent to Aquitaine to try to bring a rebelling Richard under control.

Eleanor remained a captive until Henry's death in 1189 which occurred during yet another rebellion of his sons. Richard and John were the only ones alive by this time, the young Henry having died in 1183 and Geoffrey in 1186. Eleanor was immediately freed, whereupon she prepared England to receive her son Richard as king, offsetting some of the opposition by freeing those whom Henry II had imprisoned without a regular trial. When Richard finally arrived in England, Eleanor was beside him in his court. (Richard was not married at this time.)

Since Richard was above all interested in embarking on the crusade to which he was already committed, he remained in England only long enough to appoint men to office, for which they paid, and to raise as much money as possible from all the various incomes of the crown: scutages, marriages, wardships, privileges to the towns, monopolies, and so on. He then left for the east, stopping along the way in Sicily where one of his sisters was queen. It was to Sicily that Eleanor brought Berengaria of Navarre, a small kingdom on the southern boundary of English Gascony, across the Pyrenees Mountains, partly in Spain and partly in France. Richard and Berengaria were married in Cyprus on the way to the Holy Land.

In Richard's absence, England was under the control of a chief justiciar who was not very popular and would be replaced by Hubert Walter, bishop of Salisbury. Walter, along with Archbishop of Canterbury Baldwin, had gone on the crusade and arrived in the Holy Land ahead of Richard. Baldwin died in the Holy Land, but Walter was present at the fall of Acre to the Christians and remained there with Richard until Richard left the east in 1192. Walter returned to England as chief justiciar, where he and Eleanor worked together to maintain peace and loyalty in the continued absence of the king. Eleanor's role was especially important after Richard was captured on his way home from the Holy Land. (He never secured Jerusalem, but he did negotiate with Saladin the right of Christian pilgrims to visit there.) Richard had avoided going back through France, which was now under the rule of his fellow-crusader Philip II Augustus, because he rightly thought that Philip might find an excuse to attack him. Instead he went up the Adriatic Sea and landed incognito in the land of the duke of Austria. He was recognized, however, made captive, and then sold to the emperor Henry VI, who held him for an enormous ransom. Richard's brother John, taking advantage of Richard's absence and then captivity to argue that Richard was never coming home, maintained that he, John, should be made king. In this bold move, he had the backing of Philip II of France. Eleanor played an important part with Hubert Walter in deflecting John's claims and raising the money for the ransom. And when Richard finally came home in 1194, she continued to support him as he raised money for an army to fight on the Continent where Philip II had taken advantage of the king's absence to occupy some of Richard's territories. Normandy was especially hard pressed. So it was that Richard was again in England only a few months before he left once more. He would never return to England: he died in 1199, fighting in Poitou. Eleanor was at his side at his death.

Eleanor participated in the deliberations about the succession. Richard had left no heir, although Berengaria was in Normandy. John demanded the throne, but there was another possible heir, the young Arthur, heir to Brittany, son of John's older brother Geoffrey who had died in 1186. The rules of succession were not fixed at this time, and many of the barons of Normandy and Anjou favored Arthur's claims, as did Philip II of France. But Eleanor, Hubert Walter, and William Marshal all favored the adult John over the minor Arthur who would be under French influence. Accordingly, John became king.

Eleanor remained active during John's reign, although she had "retired" to the nunnery of Fontevrault on the south side of the Loire in Anjou but close to Poitou. She was especially important in maintaining English control in the south of France. And in a short period of truce between John and Philip II, it was she who in 1200 traveled to Castile in order to lead one of her granddaughters, Blanche of Castile, to Paris where she was the intended bride of Louis, son of Philip II. Blanche would be the mother of Louis IX, St. Louis, of France.

Eleanor of Aquitaine died in 1204 and was buried at Fontevrault beside Henry II and Richard I. John was buried at Worcester in England.

Frederick II

Frederick II (1195–1250) was king of Sicily (1208–50) and (German) Roman emperor (1215–50). It was Frederick's involvement with the papacy throughout the first half of the thirteenth century that indirectly led to the baronial rebellion of 1258 against Henry III of England. To understand this event, we need to look at a number of continental developments revolving around Italy.

During the ancient Roman Empire, Italy was the capital province of an empire that included Gaul, Spain, and Britain in western Europe. This unified western world was destroyed following the Germanic barbarian invasions in the fifth and sixth centuries, which resulted in the establishment of a number of separate early Germanic kingdoms. The medieval Roman Empire was created in 800 when the Frankish king,

Charles (Charlemagne) (768–814), was crowned emperor by the pope, thus establishing a link, though undefined, between empire and papacy. The basis for this re-creation of the Roman Empire was Charles' territorial campaigns which extended the Frankish boundaries beyond Frankish Gaul south into northern Spain, east into Germany, and southeast into Italy. It was the Frankish expansion into Italy at the expense of the Lombard kingdom that lay behind the coronation. Lombard power had been centered in the Po Valley and Tuscany, although there were two more Lombard duchies, Spoleto to the northeast of Rome and Benevento further to the south just east of Naples. These southern duchies tended to be almost independent of royal Lombard control.

The eighth-century Lombard kings had been encroaching on the territory known as the Byzantine (East Roman) Exarchate of Ravenna, which stretched from Rome in the southwest to Ravenna in the northeast. This strip of territory cut the main Lombard kingdom off from the more southern Lombard duchies, and with the weakening of Byzantine power in the eighth century, the Lombards began moving into this territory, threatening even Rome itself. Unable to get aid from the East Roman Empire with its capital at Constantinople, the popes turned to the Franks. The way for this request was paved in the mid-eighth century when the pope recognized the overthrow of the older Merovingian ruling family of the Franks and its replacement by a new Carolingian dynasty, thus establishing a precedent for Frankish-papal cooperation.

The sources do not reveal where the idea for a revival of the imperial title originated, although Charlemagne's biographer Einhard, writing years later, claimed that the king said he would not have attended Christmas services in Rome in the year 800 if he had known what the pope had in mind. In any event, the coronation was mutually advantageous. To Charles' titles king of the Franks and king of the Lombards was now added the imperial title, a title that in theory made him the equal of the Roman emperor in the east. That the pope could create an emperor marked a tremendous increase in his potential power. From this time on, the secular and spiritual powers were so intertwined that friction was unavoidable.

The connection between Italy and Germany resulted from the breakup of Charlemagne's empire following the death of his son Louis the Pious in 840, when the empire was divided among his three surviving sons. The western part of the empire came to be known as the kingdom of the west

Franks, the eastern part as the kingdom of the east Franks, and between was a long narrow middle kingdom that included Italy. Italy was assigned with the imperial title to the eldest son. The rulers of the west and east Franks combined against the middle, defeated its ruler, and divided the upper part of the middle kingdom between themselves leaving Italy and the imperial title as well as part of Provence (extreme southeastern Francia) to the heirs of the eldest son. The imperial title continued to remain associated with the ruler of Italy but who held Italy was frequently disputed and so Italy was the scene of frequent civil wars for over a century.

The association of Germany and Italy was firmly established in 962 when the German king Otto I (936–973) intervened in Italy, reestablished order, and was crowned emperor in Rome by the pope. The German kings thereafter claimed Italy and the imperial title, but were prevented from exercising very much power there by numerous rebellions at home. The north Italian towns had always been centers of economic activity, and with the revival of trade in the tenth and eleventh centuries, the towns expanded rapidly and their merchants became extremely wealthy. The north Italian towns would become centers of anti-imperial activity in their desire to become self-governing.

In the middle of the peninsula by the late ninth century, the papacy was controlled by several powerful Roman noble families who fought among themselves to fill papal vacancies. Under the circumstances, the popes lost their spiritual leadership. This change, combined with similar conditions in the rest of the Church, inspired a reform movement that began at the monastery of Cluny in south-central France and moved to the Rhineland where it was endorsed by the emperor Henry III (1039–56). When Henry went to Rome in 1046 for his imperial coronation, he found the papacy disputed by three men representing three factions of the Roman aristocracy. All three were summoned before a church council called by Henry; all three were deposed; and Henry named one of the German reformers as pope. Henry's first three reforming popes had very short pontificates; then he named Leo IX (1049–54), and the reform movement became well established in Rome.

The papacy was reformed at the initiative of the emperor, but inasmuch as removing the Church from secular control, as well as ending such abuses as simony (the purchase of church office) or nepotism (the naming of relatives to office), was part of the reform program, a reformed papacy was sure to oppose the common practice of secular rulers naming the higher church officials such as archbishops, bishops, and abbots to office and then bestowing on them the symbols of their landed fiefs (property) as well as the symbols of their spiritual office. An overt quarrel over this issue began during the pontificate of Gregory VII (1073–85) when Gregory, in 1075, issued a papal bull entitled *Dictatus* prohibiting what came to be called "lay investiture." The Church and the states of Europe quarreled over this issue throughout the rest of the eleventh century and well into the twelfth, with various compromises being worked out similar to the one worked out in 1107 by Henry I of England during the controversy with his archbishop of Canterbury, Anselm. In this agreement, the king retained control of naming church officials, but the Church obtained control of investing with the symbols of the spiritual office. Nonetheless, the Church continued to press for freedom in the election of its higher officials. The English Magna Carta would be a step in resolving this controversy.

In Germany, a new ruling family, the Hohenstaufen, became kings of Germany and Roman emperors in the twelfth century. The Hohenstaufen, especially Frederick I Barbarosa (1152–90), showed more interest in Italy than their predecessors. Frederick's attempts to reassert imperial control over the north Italian towns prompted the formation of an alliance of mercantile towns known as the Lombard League. In the League's attempts to forestall the reassertion of imperial authority, it had the support of the papacy. Frederick was finally defeated and came to terms with the north Italian towns whereby the towns were to be largely self-governing in return for their loyalty and for recognizing Frederick as emperor.

Defeated in his designs for the north Italian towns, Frederick I achieved success in the marriage he arranged for his son and heir, the future Henry VI (1190–97). In 1186 Henry was married to Constance, the aunt and heir of the king of Sicily, a kingdom that included southern Italy as well as the island of Sicily. At the time of this marriage, the pope as feudal lord of Sicily raised no great objection since no one expected Constance to inherit from William II (1166–89) of Sicily. But William died in 1189 and Frederick I died in 1190 while on the way to the Holy Land on the Third Crusade. Henry VI had already been crowned king of Germany and Italy; he was now emperor-elect. Constance had already inherited Sicily, which Henry had to fight to secure since the Sicilian aristocracy objected to a German ruler.

Henry VI funded his Sicilian campaign with the ransom money he raised from England in order to release the English king, Richard I, captured on his return from the Holy Land on the Third Crusade. It was during the fight for Sicily that Henry's queen, Constance, gave birth to a son, Frederick, who could expect to inherit both the German-Italian Hohenstaufen lands and the kingdom of Sicily. Henry had partially pacified Sicily when he unexpectedly died in 1197. Constance had no luck in controlling the rebellious Sicilians, and prior to her own death in 1198 she turned over her three-year-old son as ward to the papacy as guardian. Innocent III (1198–1216) was one of the strongest popes of the Middle Ages. Having no desire to see the Papal States (see Chapter 5) squeezed between Hohenstaufen power to the north and Hohenstaufen power to the south, during the minority of the future Frederick II Innocent tried to arrange affairs so that Germany and Sicily would never be united.

In Germany there were two candidates for the German imperial inheritance: Philip of Swabia (brother of Henry VI) who was the Hohenstaufen candidate and Otto of Brunswick (grandson of Henry II of England), who was backed by the papacy. Philip died in 1208, leaving Otto without strong opposition. After requiring a number of strong oaths from Otto promising that he would never seek the Sicilian throne and would guarantee the pope's sovereignty in an enlarged Papal States, Innocent III approved Otto's coronation in 1209. But Otto IV almost immediately forgot his promises and took a German army south in order to capture Sicily from the young Frederick II, who had just begun to rule, and to bring order out of the chaos that had befallen Sicily during his minority.

Meanwhile, many of the southern German princes began to resent the highhandedness of Otto and to object to his use of local property to reward his followers. Dissatisfaction with Otto encouraged them to turn back to the Hohenstaufen, of whom Frederick was now the leading candidate. The southern German princes invited Frederick to come to Germany to seek election as emperor. Frederick's position in Sicily was not so strong that he could afford to leave at once, and his advisers did not want him to try to obtain Germany and the empire. By 1212, however, Frederick was ready to try his hand in Germany. Frederick was in Germany rallying the princes of Germany when Otto IV and King John of England concluded their alliance aimed at defeating Philip II Augustus of France, who was attempting to push the English out of their remaining French territory. It was an unusual alliance, for at the time it was made, both rulers were excommunicate—John for his refusal to recognize the rights of the Church in the matter of accepting Stephen Langton as archbishop of Canterbury and Otto IV for his refusal to abandon an attempt to add Sicily to Germany and the empire and for his refusal to recognize the sovereign rights of the papacy to all of the territory Innocent III wanted as part of the Papal States. At this point the papacy backed Philip II of France and even encouraged the French to invade England to seek to overthrow John.

In 1213 John faced a baronial rebellion and an attempted assassination. To improve his situation he sought an understanding with Innocent III. He agreed to accept Langton as archbishop, to receive back the exiled bishops, and to restore all the church properties that he had seized. Furthermore he agreed to turn England and Ireland over to the pope and to receive them back as fiefs of the papacy. Innocent agreed to these conditions, lifted the excommunication, and raised the interdict; further, he forbade Philip II to invade England.

John, moving to take advantage of his new position, made plans with Otto IV for a joint English-German attack on France in 1214. John would lead an English force northward from English Aquitaine in southwest France, and Otto would invade France from the northeast. John failed in his attempt partly because of the strength of a western French army under the command of Louis, the heir to the French throne and partly because John could not trust the loyalty of his own barons. But the decisive engagement occurred at the battle of Bouvines in the east where Otto led a German army to defeat by an eastern French army under the command of the French king. Otto would lose the remainder of his support for the position of emperor, and John would agree to Magna Carta. Frederick II would be elected king of the Romans (the title of the emperor-elect) in 1215, and he would be crowned Roman emperor in 1220. John would repudiate Magna Carta and be released from his oath to support it by Innocent III. Continued baronial rebellion brought on civil war in England, to be relieved by the unexpected death of John in October 1216; Innocent III had died in July 1216. (For further details, see Chapter 3.)

Although Innocent III was no longer on the scene when Frederick II was crowned Roman emperor in 1220, Innocent's successors were just as determined as he to prevent the union of the north and the south of Italy, with the Papal States helpless in between. Frederick left Germany in 1220 after having his son recognized as king of Germany. But the German problem was one that Frederick II never did resolve, and it would remain unresolved until the nineteenth century. The problem was that Germany had never been brought under strong royal control, although Frederick I Barbarosa had taken steps in that direction. The principle of hereditary succession had never been widely accepted for the kingship, and the German princes, the rulers of the main divisions of the kingdom, held strongly to the principle of election. Consequently, candidates for election had to buy the necessary votes. That practice led to the granting away of titles and properties, thus weakening the economic base of the monarchy. In addition to the secular princes, a number of ecclesiastical princes also claimed the right to vote: the archbishops of Mainz, Trier, and Cologne, all in the Rhineland. Adding to this mixture of claims was the shift in trade routes from the western Alpine passes leading up to the French fairs in the area of Champagne to the eastern Brenner pass leading to towns along the Rhine. Frederick II may well have hoped to organize Germany to form the core of his empire, but his difficulties elsewhere and the resistance of the German princes seemingly forced him to leave the princes much to their own devices while he concentrated on centralizing the kingdom of Sicily and then reasserting the imperial authority over the north Italian towns.

In pursuing his goals, Frederick was constantly at odds with the papacy. The first clash was over Frederick's delay in going on a crusade which he had promised to do at the time of his election. But since Frederick was involved in setting up a regime in Germany and organizing the kingdom of Sicily, he was unable to go until 1227. He left in that year for the Holy Land by sea, only to turn around and come back due to illness. He was promptly excommunicated, and then the following year, while still under excommunication, he went again on crusade and by negotiation married the heiress to the kingdom of Jerusalem and had himself crowned king of Jerusalem by the patriarch of Jerusalem, whereupon he was again excommunicated (see Appendix A). Shortly thereafter, Sicily was well enough organized that he could begin to tackle the north Italian towns. Again the towns banded together to resist the reassertion of the imperial rights, and in the almost constant fighting for the next twenty years, the advantage seesawed back and forth, with Frederick having something of an advantage. Throughout this time the Italian towns were backed by the papacy, providing a good deal of the money that was necessary to pay the mercenaries who formed the core of their armies.

This papal money was obtained by taxing the clergy, especially in England, where Henry III believed he had become king after the death of his father King John through the offices of the pope. This was not strictly true, but a papal legate (official representative of the pope) was in England at the time that the barons accepted Henry as king and the legate participated in establishing a regency to rule England while Henry was a minor. The protests of the English clergy over the exorbitant taxes assessed by the papacy, as well as the increasing papal assertion of the right to name candidates to vacant office in England at the expense of English candidates, were made known to the king, but the king backed the pope.

In the end, Frederick II failed to bring the north Italian towns under imperial control, and his plans for the future of his extended empire came to an end with his death in 1250. The papacy, determined to prevent the continued control of north and south Italy by a single power, declared the kingdom of Sicily escheated (forfeited) to its overlord, the pope, because of the disloyalty of the Hohenstaufen. Pope Innocent IV, seeking a new candidate for the Sicilian throne, opened negotiations with England and France. He concluded an agreement with Henry III of England whereby Henry's second son, Edmund, should become king of Sicily in return for Henry's assuming the papal debt, which was now very high because of the many years of opposing Frederick II. (See Chapter 5 for an analysis of the effects of this agreement in England.) Because of baronial opposition, Henry had to renege on this agreement, and Innocent IV turned to France where Louis IX (St. Louis) had initially turned down the offer on behalf of his younger brother, Charles of Anjou. Now Innocent played on Louis' desire to go on another crusade to point out the desirability of having a French prince in command of such a strategic place as Sicily. The agreement was made, and Charles established an Angevin dynasty (not related to the English Angevins) in Sicily in return for recognizing the overlordship of the papacy, assuming a portion of the papal debt, and agreeing to make a substantial annual payment to the papacy. In return, Louis IX obtained a safe place for launching his second crusade in 1270 against Tunisia, from where he expected to move eastward to the Holy Land. Instead Louis died in Tunisia, and Charles shortly thereafter (1282) lost the island of Sicily to an Aragonese ruler.

The island had rebelled against the Angevins and their heavy exactions to support Charles' ambitions to create a Mediterranean empire. Thereafter, the kingdom of Sicily was confined to the island; the Angevins retained southern Italy, which now came to be known as the kingdom of Naples.

As for the German part of Frederick II's empire, papal interference after 1250 prevented not only the election of a Hohenstaufen but also the election of a German prince. In effect, there was no central authority until 1272 when Rudolf of Hapsburg, a minor German prince, was elected. By that time, the individual princes were virtually independent and imperial authority was but a shadow.

This summary helps explain events in Europe in the thirteenth century, but it does not do justice to Frederick. Although Frederick's political ambitions were eventually defeated, those ambitions were only one aspect of his career. He achieved an important bureaucratic and legal reorganization of the kingdom of Sicily. He was important in the revival of learning and was an accomplished poet and observer of nature, as well as a patron of the arts. His court at Palermo, Sicily, was an intellectual center where the learned of all western faiths (Christian, Jew, and Muslim) lived in harmony in association with the emperor. It was for these other aspects of his life that he is sometimes called the first Renaissance man.

Henry II

Henry II (1133–89) was the first of three sons of Geoffrey, count of Anjou (1128–51), and Matilda, daughter and heiress (after 1120) of Henry I, king of England (1100–35) and duke of Normandy (1106–35). His dynasty is known as Angevin (from the county of Anjou) or Plantagenet (from the French word for the broom plant, a sprig of which his father wore in his hat).

Henry's quarrel with the Church about secular jurisdiction over criminous clerks and the resulting standoff with Thomas Becket, first Henry's chancellor and later his archbishop of Canterbury, has been covered in Chapter 1 and in the biography, "Thomas Becket (St. Thomas)." Henry's contributions to the causes of the baronial revolt of 1215–16 have been covered in Chapter 3. And his role in guiding the crown's activities in developing the English common law has been covered in Chapter 4. His relations with his family have been covered in the biographies "Eleanor of Aquitaine" and "Sons of Henry II."

Henry of Anjou was already count of Anjou and Maine, duke of Normandy, and (in right of his wife) duke of Aquitaine, when he became king of England in 1154 on the death of King Stephen. (He had become Stephen's heir in 1153 in the Treaty of Winchester.) He and his wife, Eleanor of Aquitaine, married in 1152, already had a son. Henry was twenty-one when he became king of England. He had been trained in the administration of territory by his father, Geoffrey of Anjou, who had conquered Normandy for him as his mother's heir and provided him with tutors to give him sufficient education for his needs. He could speak and read French and Latin, although he probably could not write (it was more efficient to use clerks who could both read and write).

Henry was a man of tremendous energy, always on the move from one part of his realm to another. His lands stretched from the border of Scotland in the north to the Pyrenees Mountains between France and Spain in the south. He was supremely self-confident and inherited marked impatience and easy anger from the Normans on his mother's side and from the Angevins on his father's. His many political successes doomed him to failure in personal conflicts with Thomas Becket and his four sons.

Sons of Henry II: Henry, Richard, Geoffrey, John

Henry II Plantagenet of England, Normandy, Anjou, and Aquitaine and his queen, Eleanor, countess of Poitou and duchess of Aquitaine, had four sons who grew to maturity: Henry (1155–83; the young king, 1170–83), Richard (1157–99; count of Poitou, 1172–99; Richard I, king of England, 1189–99), and John (1167–1216; lord of Ireland, 1177–1216; king of England, 1199–1216).

Little is known about the lives of these sons before 1170 when Henry II decided to have his oldest son crowned king in order to insure the succession, a practice that the Capetians of France had been following for some time. The young Henry was duly crowned, though by the archbishop of York rather than the archbishop of Canterbury as had become the custom, since Thomas Becket was in exile. (The coronation was directly related to the murder of Becket in December 1170.) Becket had prohibited York from officiating and excommunicated him for performing it. It was Becket's excommunication of York and all the other bishops involved that led to Henry's outburst of rage that resulted in the murder of Becket. After the coronation, the elder Henry set up a household for his son the young Henry and assigned an experienced knight, William Marshal, to be his tutor in chivalry, his guardian, companion, and friend. With the exception of a couple of years when he was out of favor, Marshal followed the young king Henry loyally until Henry's death in 1183.

Richard first appears by the side of his mother Eleanor in 1167 when she was assigned to set up court at Poitiers (in Poitou) to try to control the unruly barons of Henry's and her southern dominions. Eleanor and Henry were estranged by this time. Richard was installed as count of Poitou in 1172, although between 1167 and 1173 Eleanor issued all major acts under her seal or in her or Richard's name. Henry retained control over financial and military matters. In 1170 Henry II indicated a future division of his territory. Henry the young king would have England, Normandy, and Anjou; Richard would have Aquitaine; and Geoffrey, betrothed to the heiress to Brittany, would have Brittany. John, the youngest son, only three at the time, was assigned no land. His father would make him lord of Ireland in 1177 following a partial pacification of that island.

The three oldest sons (Henry, Richard, and Geoffrey) were dissatisfied with the division and with their lack of real power. At the time Henry and Richard were at the court of Louis VII where they were knighted and the French king was deliberately encouraging the young men to revolt against their father. The French king was seeking to reduce the power of Henry II, who was so much stronger than Louis VII, his overlord, the king of France. The boys' mother, Eleanor of Aquitaine, also encouraged the revolt. The revolt (1173–74) was a serious one, but Henry II had little trouble bringing the situation under control. He captured Eleanor, who had encouraged the rebellion, and sent her back to England where she had little independence of movement until Henry's death in 1189. Henry dealt lightly with his sons. Henry the young king was given an enlarged household and a significantly increased monetary allowance. However, he was given no real authority, and he lived the rest of his life in France where he spent his time in knightly activity, enjoying the French court (he was married to a daughter of Louis VII and of Louis' second wife), and traveling around eastern France participating in tournaments.

In 1174 Richard received half the revenues of Poitou and two residences. In 1175 he received command of the army of Poitou and became his father's agent in Aquitaine and Gascony. In the following years Richard gained an enviable military reputation in attempting to establish control over the southern barons. In these efforts, he relied heavily on mercenaries since southern France had not developed what is usually described as feudalism. In Aquitaine and Gascony, the tie between lord and man implied little more than loyalty and frequently not even that. Knight service was unknown, centralized courts and exchequers were unknown, feudal aids were unknown. The barons could be kept under control only through military effort. Some income was produced from the ports—La Rochelle and Bordeaux—and from the count's own domain, but Richard always had to have financial support from Henry II. In 1182 Richard was so hard pressed in his efforts that Henry II himself had to intervene, and somehow the situation escalated into a struggle between Richard and his brother Henry, and then Geoffrey entered the plot against Richard. Henry II's efforts to pacify the young Henry by having Richard do homage to him ended with Richard flatly refusing to do so. The struggle continued with Philip II, who succeeded his father Louis VII in 1180, sending aid to the young Henry. Even so the young Henry ran out of money and began ravishing the countryside, plundering the monastery of Saint-Martial at Limoges and the shrine of Rocamadour. In the midst of these activities, the young Henry became ill and died (1183).

Henry II refused to name Richard as his heir and increasingly interfered in Richard's actions in Aquitaine. Richard feared more and more that in the long run Henry would turn to his younger brother John. (Geoffrey had been killed in a tournament in 1186, and his son was born posthumously.) Philip II of France encouraged Richard, joined also by John, to take up arms against the old king. Henry II now faced the combined forces of Richard and Philip II Augustus of France and was forced to capitulate as he lay dying (1189).

Richard I the Lionheart

Henry II died on July 6, 1189, whereupon Richard was installed as duke of Normandy on July 20, crossed to England on August 13, and was crowned by Archbishop of Canterbury Baldwin in Westminster Abbey in early September. Even before he left France, Richard had sent ahead to have his mother Eleanor released from her confinement, and she was at his side during the coronation celebration.

Richard's first priority was participation in a crusade which he had vowed to undertake following the fall of Jerusalem to the Turks in 1187. In making his dispositions with a view to his absence, he thought to keep John under control by granting him enough properties to satisfy him. In Anjou John became count of Mortain, the title by which he was usually known until Richard's death; he was married to Isabel of Gloucester, heiress to the earldom of Gloucester; and he was given the counties of Somerset, Dorset, Devon, and Cornwall, representing a solid block of land in the southwest, Nottinghamshire and Derbyshire, and the honors of Lancaster and Wallingford, in which the royal power hardly penetrated. But John was not satisfied and plotted to replace Richard.

Continental records do not indicate what arrangements Richard made for the government of the individual parts of the French property, but in making these dispositions the question of his marriage did arise. It was decided that a marriage would be arranged with Berengaria, daughter of the king of Navarre, a mountainous kingdom in northern Spain adjoining the southern border of Gascony. This arrangement did bring the king of Navarre north of the Pyrenees on at least one occasion to subdue a baronial uprising against Richard's government while Richard was gone.

English records provide a good picture of the arrangements made for England. For the most part, he selected administrators who had had long service in England or Normandy. Chief of these was the Norman William Longchamp, who was named chancellor of England, elected bishop of Ely, named co-justiciar (which he soon converted into chief justiciar), and designated papal legate in the absence of Archbishop of Canterbury Baldwin, who was going on the crusade. A number of associate justiciars were named. Most of them were men of long experience in the service of Henry II, who mostly came from the lesser baronage trained in the households of the king or of the justiciar (Ranulf Glanville) and not at one of the newly organized universities. An exception to these experienced men was William Marshal. He was named one of these associate justiciars even though he had had little, if any, administrative experience. But he was a renowed fighting man, served loyally, and learned much. This experience would serve him well when he became regent of England following John's death in 1216.

Longchamp was an effective justiciar who generally kept John in check, but he was extremely ambitious and took advantage of his position of power to increase his income and to defeat his enemies. By June 1191, Richard was in Sicily, where the queen-mother Eleanor would bring Berengaria, and here were brought reports about what was going on in England. Richard sent Walter, archbishop of Rouen, who was with him, back to England with instructions to warn Longchamp to amend his ways. By the time Walter arrived in England, a serious conflict between Longchamp and John was under way, but Walter's intervention avoided war. Still, Longchamp refused to heed Walter's warnings, and his mistreatment of Geoffrey, archbishop of York, Richard's half-brother, brought on a crisis to which Walter replied by producing a letter of deposition that Richard had provided him with should Longchamp fail to improve his ways. Walter of Coutance, archbishop of Rouen, another Norman, served as chief justiciar until December 1193 when Hubert Walter, an Englishman, was named to succeed.

Richard the Lionheart was out of England from December 1189 until February 1194, during which time, his appointed government worked well at all levels. However, John continued to plot to take the crown for himself, and it seemed possible that a French invasion of England might take place. By the summer of 1192, word was sent to Richard advising that he should return even though he had not yet driven the Turks from Jerusalem. The port city Acre had fallen to the crusaders in July 1191. Richard concluded that he must return and accordingly entered into negotiations with Saladin, whereby Christians would be able to visit Jerusalem.

On the return to England, Richard tried to avoid possible capture in France (he and Philip Augustus of France had become bitter enemies while on crusade) by traveling up the Adriatic Sea and crossing Germany incognito. He was recognized in Austria, however, and sold by the duke of Austria to another enemy of Richard, the German emperor Henry VI. Although Philip Augustus of France, supported by John, urged Emperor Henry to keep Richard in custody indefinitely, Henry VI's need of money for a campaign in Sicily to insure his wife's inheritance was too pressing to agree. Instead he negotiated to release Richard on the payment of an enormous ransom.

Richard returned to England in February 1194. He had been preceded by Hubert Walter, bishop of Salisbury, who had been in the Holy Land and had participated in the siege of Acre and in the negotiations with Saladin. Returning from the east, Walter had landed in Sicily where he learned of Richard's capture. He therefore proceeded to Germany where he received instructions from Richard about raising the ransom money and instructions for those in charge of the government in England with regard to certain changes. Walter and the queen-mother Eleanor were largely responsible for raising the ransom money, and they would both go to Germany with the first installment to be present when Richard was released in February 1194. In the meantime, in accordance with Richard's instructions, Hubert Walter was elected archbishop of Canterbury, succeeding Archbishop Baldwin who had died in the Holy Land; Walter was also named chief justiciar.

Richard remained in England only long enough to come to terms with his brother John (John would accompany him to France to join Richard's campaign against Philip II, John's previous co-conspirator), and to raise money, supplies, and soldiers for the military expedition. Richard would never return; he died in April 1199.

Richard vigorously attempted to recover the land he had lost to Philip Augustus, and in general Richard had the better of the struggle, partly because he usually had the backing of the count of Flanders and other magnates in the Low Countries. By 1197 Philip was ready to negotiate, but he was not willing to give up certain castles on the border between Normandy and the royal lands in the Isle de France. So the war continued desultorily on until April 1199 when Richard had turned southward to bring his own rebellious vassals under control in Poitou. While preparing to lay siege to the castle of Chalus, he received a bolt from a crossbow launched from a rampart on the castle. He died from the blow; he was only forty-one. The death of Richard without an heir of his own threw the situation into the hands of John who proved no match for Philip Augustus. Richard's death gave Philip Augustus a decisive advantage.

Any analysis of Richard as king must take into account the fact that his popularity in his own day depended on his military prowess on the

Second Crusade and his continued military successes after his return. On the other hand, from the English standpoint, he was an absentee king who paid little heed to the needs of the kingdom. Although Richard had had little administrative experience before his accession, he was sufficiently familiar with the governments of England and Normandy to know that his father's reforms had provided both of those provinces with a well-ordered government that was capable of working in the absence of the king. Certainly, Richard provided England with able and loyal administrators (with the exception of Longchamp), who carried on the government with some long-distance direction from Richard. In one aspect, however, Richard's reign set the scene for rebellion against his brother John. Richard's needs to keep his military campaign going forced him to demand much greater financial support from England than his father Henry II had required. He basically relied on England to provide the means for the reconquest of the continental territory lost to Philip Augustus. How long could England afford to support this cause?

John

John was the youngest son of Henry II and Eleanor. Between the ages of two and six, John lived with the nuns at the abbey of Fontevrault, together with his slightly older sister Joan. After the end of the rebellion by Henry's older sons in 1174, Henry took John back to England with him. He then placed John in the household of the young King Henry, where John would remain until just before the young king's death in 1183. It was in the young king's household that John came to know William Marshal.

Between 1182 and 1185, John was placed in the household of the justiciar Ranulf Glanville, and it was presumably there that John learned many of the intricacies of the English bureaucracy, especially as it related to law and the administration of justice. Hubert Walter, later to be John's chancellor, was in Glanville's household at the same time.

In 1185–86 Henry sent John to Ireland to assume the lordship of Ireland, a position that had been created for John in 1177. Accompanying John were a number of experienced counselors, also from the household of Glanville.

All of Henry II's sons had a good basic education for the time, including a knowledge of reading Latin. John's education, however, appears to have been better than that of the others, and he apparently had a real interest in books and in building up a significant library. He also had more sophisticated tastes than his brothers, showing a particular interest in jewels and finer clothing. It was the very considerable treasure John had built up in such items that would provide the means whereby William Marshal was able to defeat the baronial rebels and run the government in the years immediately following John's death.

At Richard's accession in 1189, John had received not only the county of Mortain in Anjou but also sufficient lands in England to elevate him to a position as one of the magnates of the land. Although John's position was important through the resources that he controlled, he was not given any administrative position in Richard's government either in England or on the Continent. Nonetheless, he did serve Richard loyally during Richard's attempt to regain his continental territory between 1194 and 1199, and Richard almost certainly intended John to succeed him should he die without heirs.

John succeeded Richard in 1189 without great difficulty, although there was another possible heir to whom Philip Augustus naturally threw his support. This was Arthur of Brittany, posthumous son of Geoffrey, an older brother of John and countess Constance of Brittany, who was violently antagonistic to the Angevins. Eventually, John captured Arthur in battle, after which Arthur disappeared (he was removed either by John himself or at John's command), and succeeded in gaining enough support to obtain Philip Augustus' acceptance in the northern as well as the southern lands, where Eleanor had rushed on Richard's death to ensure the loyalty of the south. John paid heavily for this acceptance, but he was freed from the constant warfare in which Richard had been engaged.

John may have been one of the more intelligent of the Angevins, but he had little political sense. He almost immediately gave Philip Augustus the excuse to call him before the French royal court to answer a charge that John had not respected the rights of one of his vassals, Hugh de Lusignan. When John refused to appear, the court declared John a contumacious (rebellious) vassal and declared his French fiefs forfeit. By 1204 John had lost Normandy, Anjou, Maine, and Touraine, but he never abandoned his intention to regain them. To this end he stored up money and other resources, looking to the day when he would wage a military campaign to regain his land. It was this goal that lay behind John's increasingly high demands for scutages and other payments from his barons, payments that went beyond feudal custom and into the realm of tyranny. John's troubles with the papacy over the election to the archbishopric of Canterbury probably did not contribute to the rising baronial resistance, but John's submission to Pope Innocent III in 1213 and his decision to turn England and Ireland over to the papacy as fiefs may well have done so. But the crisis was primarily the result of John's unrelenting efforts to prepare for the day that he could launch an attack on Philip Augustus to regain his lost fiefs, and so he drew larger and larger amounts from England. This customarily meant assessing the barons, selling wardships and marriages for higher and higher prices, demanding fines (payments) for office, and using the legal system (which John knew well) to extract larger and larger amounts from his kingdom. Of course, he was also active in selling privileges to the towns although this source of income was not as well developed as income from land.

John did not launch his invasion of France until 1214, when he proceeded in concert with an invasion from the east by his ally, Otto IV of the German Empire. That year John's force was unable to join up with Otto IV at the decisive battle of Bouvines, and Otto's defeat at Bouvines meant the end of John's hopes to recover his French land, although his successors as kings of England did not give up hope. Bouvines meant that baronial opposition that had been building since 1212 now increased rapidly until the episode of Magna Carta in 1215 (see Chapter 3).

It is hard to judge John's handling of the crisis of 1215–16. He underestimated the eagerness of a number of younger barons to gain a share in the making of decisions at the expense of the older barons and the experienced royal councilors of long standing. He was determined to exercise the rights and privileges enjoyed by his father and grandfather, Henry II and Henry I, before him. He was not an absentee king but resided in England for most of his reign, and he participated in the activities of government, especially judicial activities. He had had much better training for the kingship than Richard (which perhaps inspired Richard's fear that he would be replaced by John in their father's succession plans). But he was heir to the Angevin temper, to its egotism, and to its failure to consider the opinions of others; moreover, he was lethargic and unable to act when things were pressing. Perhaps the best thing he could do for England was to die in 1216, leaving a nine-year-old son as heir.

Innocent III

   Innocent III was born Lotario dei Conti of Segni (c. 1160–1216) and was elected Pope Innocent III in 1198 at the age of thirty-seven. He succeeded the elderly Celestine III (1191–98), who had been confined to Rome by the overwhelming power in Italy and Sicily of the German Roman emperor Henry VI, married to Constance of Sicily. After Henry VI died unexpectedly in 1197, the cardinals probably were looking for younger leadership to face the imperial crisis, and in Lotario found a candidate with education and the support of one of the lesser aristocratic Roman families.

   Lotario had received his primary education in Rome and had gone to Paris when he was about fifteen. He may have remained at Paris as long as ten years, studying and teaching the liberal arts and theology. Paris was not yet organized as a university (that would not come until 1200), but scholars were welcomed there and the kings, Louis VII and Philip II, maintained good peace and order in contrast to the turbulent conditions that reigned in Rome. From Paris Lotario went to Bologna in northern Italy where a university had been organized, receiving privileges from the Roman emperor and the pope. Bologna was in the papal territory but close to the border of imperial Italy on the main road from Germany to Rome. Both emperor and pope had need of the legally trained clerks who were turned out at Bologna to staff their increasingly centralized and bureaucratized governments. Students at Bologna studied both civil (Roman) law and canon law and were much in demand.

   Lotario entered the papal curia (court) in about 1189, being appointed cardinal deacon of the church of Sts. Sergio and Bacco by a relative, Clement III. This was a period of growing legal activity by the Roman church; through its increasing influence utilizing the recently codified canon law (the *Decretum* of Gratian, 1143) many cases were attracted to Rome. Lotario was a very active member of the curia, participating as judge delegate or auditor in the many cases being appealed to Rome and witnessing documents. During his tenure before election, Lotario must have been building a body of support among the cardinals.

   After his election, Innocent III was required to enter the priesthood before he could be enthroned as pope. He immediately became a very active pope, not hesitant to assert the superiority of the spiritual power over the secular. Henry VI, Roman emperor and king of Sicily (in right of his wife Constance), died in 1197, leaving Sicily in Constance's hands. Constance of Sicily died in 1198 having turned over her three-year-old son Frederick to Innocent as his ward (the kingdom of Sicily had been created as a fief of the papacy in 1130). Innocent declared a crusade against the German administrators of the island who were very unpopular with the natives, although the papal representatives were not particularly popular either. Sicily remained a turbulent kingdom until Frederick was of an age to assert himself as ruler of that kingdom (about 1208). One of Innocent's earliest and longest lasting policies was to prevent the union of Sicily and the empire under a single ruler.

At the same time that Innocent III was trying to drive the Germans out of Sicily, he was trying to oust them from the many positions they had secured in the Papal States. In this effort Innocent was quite successful, for the Italians were just as eager as the Sicilians to get rid of the Germans. Innocent was ready to see that papal appointees or those approved of by the papacy got these fiefs. And this was another important goal: to bring the Papal States back under papal control—and more, to reacquire territories that had been long lost. In attaining this goal, Innocent III was remarkably successful. But it should be noted that both the Sicilian and Papal States actions were very costly inasmuch as mercenary troops had to be hired. These actions, combined with Innocent's widespread activities elsewhere, forced him to devise ways of taxing the clergy. Eventually, a kind of income tax was imposed on the clergy.

Another of Innocent's goals involved expanding the Christian world under the headship of Rome. This meant urging crusades against the infidel Turks who had recently captured Jerusalem and had reduced the area of Christian control to a narrow strip of Palestinian coastline. He had urged the crusade that ended up as the Fourth Crusade, which, out of papal control, captured the Christian city of Zara on the Dalmatian coastline for Venice and finally overthrew the East Roman (Byzantine) Empire, named a Frankish emperor, and designated a Roman Christian to succeed the patriarch of Constantinople. Innocent III condemned the action but welcomed the opportunity to reunite the eastern and western churches under the leadership of Rome. But the Greek clergy refused to accept the clerics installed by Rome and retreated to the remnants of Byzantine power in western Asia Minor, known as the kingdom of Nicaea. When the East Roman Empire was restored in 1261, relations between the eastern and western churches were worse than ever.

In Spain, Innocent encouraged the continuation of Christian expansion at the expense of the Muslim kingdom of Granada, and in northeastern Europe he supported crusaders and missionaries in conquering and converting to Christianity the areas of Pomerania, Prussia, Livonia, Estonia, and Finland. He was active in encouraging monarchs to surrender their kingdoms to the papacy and to receive them back as papal fiefs. The first of the papal fiefs had been Hungary, created in 1000 when Stephen was crowned king and important for spreading Rome's influence in central eastern Europe. The next papal fief was the kingdom of Sicily, created in 1130 by the papacy in anticipation of the Norman conquest of southern Italy and Sicily, thus providing a protector in the south. Portugal came into the papal fold in 1179. In 1201 the Christian kingdom of Armenia, in Asia east of Asia Minor, accepted papal leadership, and in 1203, Innocent accepted the empire of Johannitsa of Bulgaria, much to the discomfiture of Hungary which had a claim to part of the land claimed by Johannitsa. But to Innocent this was all extending the leadership of Rome and thus preventing the spread of the Greek church. In 1203 Peter of Aragon approached Rome requesting acceptance of Aragon as a fief of the papacy and was received. Apparently, Peter feared that the actions of the Albigensian Crusade against the heretical Cathars of Languedoc in southern France might spill over into some of his neighboring lands. And in 1213 John of England turned over the kingdoms of England and Ireland to the papacy and received them back as papal fiefs (see Chapter 3). In his voluminous correspondence, Innocent was in constant contact with all of these states, often dictating policy, using the threat of interdict and excommunication to achieve his ends.

In his attempt to protect Christians against heresy, Innocent investigated a number of movements that seemed to deviate from the usual Christian position as approved by Rome. He was remarkably flexible in working out an acceptable practice (e.g., with the Humiliati, Francis of Assisi, and Dominic). The Franciscans and Dominicans would become the chief preaching orders of the thirteenth century. But the Cathars of Languedoc with their dualistic conception of the universe had strayed too far from orthodox doctrine. Innocent therefore preached a crusade (the Albigensian Crusade) against them and provided rules for examining them about their beliefs, rules that would form the background of the procedure used by the later Inquisition. The Albigensian Crusade would end in the massacre of many believers and unbelievers, advance the career of Simon de Montfort the elder (father of the English baron Simon de Montfort, leader of the baronial opposition to Henry III of England), and lead to the absorption of Languedoc into the realm of France under Louis VIII.

From the standpoint of England and Magna Carta, Innocent III's importance lies in the quarrel between King John and Innocent III over the disputed election to the see (province) of Canterbury and John's refusal to accept the papal candidate, Stephen Langdon. Innocent III used his spiritual weapons to force acceptance, with the result that England lay under an interdict between 1207 and 1213 and John was excommunicated during the later part of this period. Innocent was ready to release the English from their oaths of allegiance to their king and authorized Philip II Augustus of France to invade England and overthrow John. It was this threat, combined with a baronial plot against him, that caused John to turn over England and Ireland to the papacy and receive them back as papal fiefs. As a result, Innocent changed sides and forbade Philip to invade England, threatening excommunication if he did. In the baronial rebellion to come, Innocent did back John against the barons and even declared Magna Carta invalid.

Innocent's interference in the German imperial election following the death of Henry VI (and the continuing interference of Innocent's successors in imperial affairs) doomed to defeat any move toward centralization in Germany and guaranteed that the German empire would remain a collection of virtually independent principalities.

All of these essentially political activities brought Innocent and his policies to the attention of the English king and his baronial council in the early thirteenth century. But other aspects of Innocent's reign were more favorable to the image of the Roman church. He was an accomplished canon lawyer and spent much time in adjudicating the increasing number of suits brought before the papal court. (The court had come to have both original and appellate jurisdiction.) The papal registers that begin during this reign have preserved much of this activity. In addition, Innocent was an indefatigable letter writer giving legal advice on a wide variety of canon law problems. Gregory IX collected and published many of Innocent's decisions or recommendations in a new official collection of canon laws in 1234.

Stephen Langton

   Stephen Langton was born in Lincolnshire at an undetermined date, perhaps in about 1165, the son of a well-to-do freeman or a minor baron. He received a good education of the kind that was then available in a cathedral school and went to Paris at probably the usual age of fifteen. There he completed the basic liberal arts course and went on to become a master of theology. He remained for some years teaching theology at Paris where he was interested in a number of theological problems such as the social function of the secular clergy—those who work in the world rather than live in a monastery under a rule (the regular clergy). He decried the tendency to have chapters of monks associated with cathedrals claiming the right to elect the bishop because monks almost always chose a monk and he did not think that the unworldly goals of a monk were suitable for a bishop who worked in the world. He also pondered the limits of obedience to the papacy (obedience vs. conscience). It was in Paris that Stephen Langton met Lotario dei Conti, a few years older than he. When Lotario was elected pope as Innocent III in 1198, he invited Stephen Langton to Rome and in 1206 made him cardinal priest of St. Chrysogonus.

   In 1206 the monks of Christ Church Cathedral, Canterbury, were in Rome attending to the business of a disputed election to the see of Canterbury following the death of the archbishop Hubert Walter in 1205. Innocent III declared both elections invalid and presented Stephen Langton to the monks with the recommendation that they elect him archbishop. The monks proceeded to do so, but King John of England refused to accept him and kept him out of England; he also exiled the monks of Canterbury.

   The standoff between king and pope lasted from 1207 to 1213, during which time Innocent used his spiritual weapons to force compliance. England was laid under an interdict, during which church services could not be performed, and later John was excommunicated. When all else had failed, Innocent III resorted to the expedient of releasing John's subjects from their oaths of obedience, thus deposing him. At a church council in Paris in 1213 the papal legate Pandulf authorized Philip II to attack England in a holy war on behalf of "suffering church." In the interval between his election to the archbishopric in 1207 and his arrival in England in 1213, Langton lived most of the time at the monastery of

Pontigny in the territory of Auxerre in France. Becket had lived here during part of his earlier exile, and Langton may have thought that he was following Becket in the struggle to free the Church.

Threatened with a French invasion in 1213, John capitulated and agreed to accept Langton and to reimburse the Church for its damages. In addition, John handed England and Ireland over to the pope, as feudal lord, and received them back as fiefs of the papacy. Innocent accepted and withdrew his support for Philip. Langton sailed for England but was accompanied by the papal legate (representative of the pope) Nicholas, who interfered in church elections to favor John's candidates whom Langton did not think worthy. Nicholas also favored John in disputes between Church and king over amounts owed in recompense to the Church. The legate reported Langton's protests to Rome, and as a result Langton's reputation there began to decline.

In England, as a member of the baronial great council, Langton met with the king and barons on a number of occasions. He seems to have been sympathetic with some of the baronial demands and tried to negotiate some compromise between them and the king. Someone, perhaps Langton, brought forward the coronation oath of Henry I and its "charter of liberties," which the barons wanted John to accept as a basis of negotiation. John refused. And things escalated toward rebellion on the part of the baronage. Stephen Langton, William Marshal, and other king's men met with the barons and worked out the charter that came to be known as Magna Carta. Threatened by armed defiance, John capitulated and signed, but immediately wrote to Innocent III asking to be released from his oath to observe the charter since he had signed under the threat of force. Innocent III indeed released John from his oath, declared Magna Carta invalid, and ordered Stephen Langton to excommunicate the barons. By the time Innocent's orders arrived, however, events had moved rapidly in England. Clearly, neither John nor the rebellious barons were going to accept Magna Carta, and so civil war broke out. The crisis was compounded by a baronial invitation to Louis, heir to Philip II, to invade and join them in deposing John. Louis was led to believe that he would become king.

Stephen Langton, believing that excommunication of the barons was no way to restore peace in the kingdom, refused to carry out the papal order. For this defiance he was suspended from office and recalled to Rome in the summer of 1215; he was there when the Lateran Council of 1215 began in November. Langton was therefore absent from England during the civil war, the death of John, the coronation of Henry III, and the defeat of the barons and Prince Louis in 1216 and 1217.

Langton's suspension was lifted by Innocent's successor Honorious III. Langton returned to England in 1218 and became very active as archbishop of Canterbury and adviser to the king, achieving a number of triumphs. In 1220 he successfully guided the process that resulted in the canonization of St. Hugh of Lincoln. The year 1220 also marked the fiftieth anniversary of the martyrdom of St. Thomas, and in an impressive ceremony the saint's body was translated (moved) to a specially prepared shrine in the new choir of the cathedral church. And in 1220, too, Langton made his last visit to Rome where he was received with honor. He later reported that health had been restored to the English church and that a papal legate was no longer needed there. The papal legate Pandulf was recalled to Rome. Langton died in 1228.

Louis IX (St. Louis)

Louis IX (1214–70), king of France (1226–70), was the son of Louis VIII (1223–26) and Blanche of Castile, granddaughter of Henry II and Eleanor. He was twelve years old when his father died and named Blanche as guardian of the boy and the kingdom. For the first ten years by herself and for the next ten years in concert with her son Louis IX, the two resisted the efforts of the nobles of France to rebel and place someone else on the throne, or to rebel against the centralizing power of the crown built up over the preceding century. All these troubles were aided and abetted by Henry III of England who hoped to take advantage of the minority to regain some of the lands lost to Philip II in 1204 and 1214. All resistance was finally overcome, and Louis could turn his attention to furthering the growth of the royal power that his father and grandfather had established.

Influenced by his mother, Louis IX was deeply religious as demonstrated by his interest in ecclesiastical building (the Sainte Chapelle in Paris is an example) and his many charitable gifts. But it was also demonstrated by his determination to go on crusade. After several years of preparation, including the building of a new port, Aigues Mortes, on the Mediterranean from which he and his expedition sailed, he headed for Egypt intending to approach Jerusalem from the south. Louis IX remained in the east from 1248 to 1254. His mother Blanche of Castile was again regent until her death in 1252. From Blanche's death until Louis' return in 1254 the king's younger brothers Alfonso of Poitiers and Charles of Anjou were in charge, but were mostly ineffective except to promote their own interests.

Louis was not a very successful crusader. His army captured the city of Damietta on one of the eastern mouths of the Nile River, but he and his army were captured in trying to cross the Nile. As the price for his own and his men's release, he was forced to surrender Damietta. He remained in the east until 1254 when reports from France indicated that his presence was necessary to prevent serious disorder.

Louis returned to France even more committed to Christian rule than before. He became austere in his own devotions and increased his gifts to ecclesiastical institutions. He came to be the model Christian prince. All the same, in all his commitments to the Church, he kept his own royal prerogatives in mind. He objected to papal nomination of foreigners to office in France and the expansion of the jurisdiction of the church courts at the expense of the state courts. He avoided taking sides in the contest between the papacy and the Hohenstaufen emperor Frederick II, and he initially refused to allow his brother Charles of Anjou to accept the throne of Sicily as a papal fief. He reorganized royal officials at the local level in order to make them more responsive to the needs of the people, and he issued the first important legislation for the kingdom of France. He had the reputation of peacemaker.

But important as his work was for France and for furthering the image of French royalty, Louis continued to regard the crusade as the right goal for a Christian king. After several years of preparation, he left France in 1270 but, already ill, allowed himself to be persuaded to attack Tunisia in north Africa. There before the town of Tunis he became sick and died. But his work and his reputation for saintliness led to his canonization in 1297. He was succeeded by his son Philip III (1270–85).

William Marshal

William Marshal (c. 1147–1219) was the fourth son of John Marshal, a member of the lesser baronage, who acknowledged Stephen as king following the death of Henry I in 1135. In about 1140 the older Marshal became disillusioned with Stephen and shifted his loyalty to Matilda, daughter of Henry I. When her son Henry of Anjou (Henry Plantagenet) took over her cause and became king of England a few years later, he gave his loyalty to him.

When William was about thirteen, an announced disposition of the family properties among the three elder sons left William, the fourth son, with nothing. He was sent to a relative, William of Tankerville in Normandy, to live in his household. There he learned little or nothing of "letters," but much of the knightly activities of fighting, hawking, and the tournament. Tankerville knighted him in 1167 after William had demonstrated his prowess in a number of tournaments. Hereafter defeating opposing knights and claiming their armor and horses became a way for William to support himself.

In 1167 or 1168 Tankerville reduced the size of his retinue, and William Marshal returned to England where he was taken into the service of his uncle Patrick, earl of Salisbury. Patrick was being sent to Poitou to help Queen Eleanor in her new task of trying to rule Aquitaine. Poitou was very turbulent, and Patrick's escort of Eleanor was ambushed by rebels. He was cut down from behind, and William Marshal, fighting valiantly without his helmet, was wounded and taken prisoner and held for ransom. Marshal could not pay the ransom, but unexpectedly Eleanor paid it and took him into her service. Marshal would remain with her until 1170. He was on the way to becoming a perfect courtier.

In 1170 Henry II had his oldest son, Henry, crowned during his lifetime, a device intended to insure the succession. Henry the younger was crowned by the archbishop of York since Thomas Becket, archbishop of Canterbury, was in exile. When Becket and Henry were reconciled later in the year, Becket would use the excuse of York and his fellow bishops disobeying him to excommunicate all who participated in the coronation. The furor over this excommunication and Becket's refusal to lift it was an immediate cause of Becket's murder. After the coronation of the young king, Henry II assigned William Marshal to the young king's household. He became Henry's tutor in chivalry, his guardian, and his companion. When Henry, joined by his brothers Richard and Geoffrey, rebelled against their father in 1173–74 (encouraged by their mother Eleanor and Louis VII of France), William Marshal followed his young lord and does not as a result seem to have fallen out of favor with Henry II. Due to an intrigue against him by some jealous members of the young Henry's court, Marshal was out of favor with the young king between

1180 and 1183; he was recalled in that year because his fighting prowess was needed. The young king Henry and his brother Geoffrey had become involved in an Angevin family feud and now faced Richard and Henry II. However, this campaign became too much for the young Henry; he grew ill and died in 1183. Marshal was at Henry's bedside as he lay dying when he asked Marshal to take his place in his vow to go on a crusade.

After Henry II gave William Marshal permission to leave the country, Marshal made his way east where he remained for several years. Virtually nothing is known about this period in his life, but he must certainly have learned much about warfare and the new castles being built by the crusading orders of knights.

Back in England in 1186, Marshal was taken into Henry II's household and was given a fief as well as custody of the heiress of William de Lancaster. But fighting between Henry II and Philip II, who had become king of France in 1180, was almost constant in the next three years. Accordingly, Marshal did not remain in England but followed Henry to France where his fighting skills were in demand. Again the jealousies of Henry's sons compounded the problems: Henry refused to declare Richard his heir and have his barons swear loyalty to him. And since he frequently had John with him, Richard thought Henry would leave everything to John. Therefore Richard did homage to Philip II for all the continental fiefs, joined Philip II against Henry II, and finally, since John was also uncertain about Henry's intentions, John joined Philip and Richard (the third son Geoffrey died in 1186). Both Philip II and his father Louis VII had always been prompt to take advantage of quarrels in the Angevin household, quarrels stemming from Henry's refusal to give up any of his power even now that he was growing old and weary and the alliance against him stronger than he could overcome. Henry, dying, was forced to sign a treaty that was very advantageous to Philip recognizing Richard as heir to England as well as to the Angevin territories in France, and ceding to France some very strategic territory in the Loire Valley between the Angevin holdings in Normandy and Greater Anjou to the north and the southern territory in Poitou and Aquitaine. Neither Richard nor John made his way to his deathbed (1189). Henry was attended by a number of courtiers, including John Marshal. Marshal was forced to borrow money to make preparations for Henry's burial at the abbey of Fontevrault.

William Marshal presented himself to Richard who repaid the money borrowed and took him into his service presumably because of his reputation for loyalty to his lord, first to the young king Henry and then to King Henry II. Richard even carried out a pledge made by Henry to marry him to the heiress to the lordship of Striguil. Marshal thereby became a marcher lord (the Welsh marches were frontier counties between England and Wales). But Richard was not interested in remaining in England; he was interested only in going on the Third Crusade. He stayed in England only long enough to raise financial support for his campaign and to name a regency to rule England in his absence. Strangely, considering Marshal's lack of administrative and judicial experience, Marshal was named an associate justiciar in the regency and was fully occupied in going out on eyres (judicial circuits) with other justices and attending business in London and Westminster. However, he had no independent authority, and neither did his fellow justiciars; all real power was wielded by the man whom Richard had named chancellor, William de Longchamp. Longchamp made so many enemies by his arbitrary ways that Richard removed him and replaced him with Hubert Walter who had been with him in the Holy Land; Walter would have the title of chief justiciar. He was also elected archbishop of Canterbury to replace Archbishop Baldwin who had died on the crusade.

Marshal remained a member of the regency, although his activities were overshadowed by Hubert Walter and the queen mother Eleanor, who led the effort to raise the ransom for the release of Richard who had been captured on his way home from the crusade and sold to the German emperor Henry VI. But the entire regency was involved in preventing John from claiming the throne through the use of force. Nonetheless, when Richard arrived in 1194, John's rebellion dissolved fast enough, and Richard turned his attention to raising money to challenge Philip II of France. Philip had returned early from the crusade and in the absence of the militant Richard was in the process of capturing some of the English territories in France.

When Richard crossed to France later in 1194, William Marshal went with him and spent the years until Richard's death in 1199 in doing what he did best, fighting. Richard had some success in freeing southwestern Normandy and Anjou-Maine from Capetian (French) control, until 1199 when he was diverted into the Limousin by rebellion in Poitou and was reconnoitering a siege of the castle of Chalus without full armor when he took a crossbow bolt in his shoulder. It was a terrible wound and in eleven days Richard died. Before Richard's death, however, he alerted his mother Eleanor, William Marshal, and Archbishop Walter, who were all in Normandy, of his approaching death and requested that they throw their influence to John as his heir.

The question of John as heir was an important one. It could be argued whether a brother's right took precedence over that of the son of an older brother (Geoffrey had left a young son, Arthur). Richard's advisers considered John's character as not promising, but he was an adult with a great deal of experience. John was known in England; Arthur was not. Arthur was a child in the guardianship of Philip II who pushed Arthur's claims. John was presented to the barons of England and crowned king by the archbishop of Canterbury.

John inherited from his brother a war with Philip II, but he was not in a hurry to pursue it. Instead he sought a truce with Philip on terms that were favorable to Philip: Louis, heir to the French throne, would marry Blanche of Castile, granddaughter of Henry II and Eleanor of Aquitaine; John would pay a relief of 20,000 marks for the continental fiefs; and Philip gained the Norman Vexin and part of the county of Evreux, which were very strategically placed in northeastern Normandy adjoining Philip's own land. John thus secured several years of peace during which he would get into trouble with his French overlord over his marriage to Isabelle of Angouleme, and by 1204 John had lost Normandy, Maine, Anjou, and Touraine. Although he intended to fight to regain them, conditions were not right until 1214, when he lost them for good.

In the meantime, William Marshal entered John's service and was amply rewarded. He was given many grants, including the earldom of Pembroke in Wales and the lordship of Leinster in Ireland. He had become one of the greatest of the English barons. But in 1205 he lost John's favor. John regarded him as disloyal when Marshall refused to participate in a campaign against Philip of France. Marshal, thinking that John would not succeed in regaining Normandy, feared the loss of his holdings in Normandy—he had a major one in Longueville in eastern Normandy. He asked John's permission to do homage to Philip for these holdings since John would continue to be his liege lord; that is, Marshall would owe first loyalty to John. But in France Philip refused to receive Marshal's homage unless it were liege homage, and a man could not fight against his liege lord. Marshal did the liege homage and as a result fell out of favor. He remained in Ireland (where he led the opposition to John's policies) until he was recalled to court in 1210 when John's suspicions of other barons became greater than his suspicions of Marshal.

In the meantime, since 1207 John had been embroiled in a conflict with Innocent III over the election of Stephen Langton to the archbishopric of Canterbury. Since neither interdict nor excommunication had brought John to heel, Innocent III now decided to use the strategy of releasing John's subjects from their allegiance to the king. He sent letters to Philip II of France deposing John, and the papal legate Pandulf ordered Philip to attack England in a holy war on behalf of "suffering church." After William Marshal recommended that the king make peace with Innocent III, John proceeded to do so, agreeing to accept Langton as archbishop, to indemnify the Church for its losses, and to hand England and Ireland over to the papacy and receive them back as fiefs of the papacy. Marshal was right; Innocent immediately ordered Philip not to invade England, threatening excommunication if he did.

Between 1210 and 1215, Marshal negotiated between John and the barons, but when civil war broke out in 1215, Marshal remained loyal to the king and was prominent in the king's resistance to the barons, who had invited Prince Louis of France to join them in the war against John, promising the crown of England to him if John were defeated. Louis and his men were excommunicated for their role in the civil war, but Philip II was not since he had carefully not authorized the invasion. When John died unexpectedly in October 1216, Marshal joined the other barons in recognizing John's son, Henry III. It was William who knighted the young king before his coronation by the bishop of Winchester. (Stephen Langton had been suspended and recalled to Rome for his refusal to carry out the papal command to excommunicate the rebel barons.)

Between 1216 and his death in 1219, William Marshal served as the guardian of the young king and head, with papal legate Gualo, of a regency that governed in Henry III's name. In this role he led an army that defeated Louis of France, recommended and carried a policy of admitting the defeated barons back into civil society with little if any penalty, and somehow managed to find (with great difficulty) the money to pay off the royal mercenaries and to restore the administrative and judicial machinery of the government. He died in May 1219, in the presence of his family (he and his countess, Isabelle, had five sons and five daughters), his most important advisers, and members of the court. He was buried in the church of the New Temple, London.

Simon de Montfort

Simon de Montfort (c. 1208–65) was the son of Simon de Montfort the elder from one of the great aristocratic families of France. The main family residence was located about thirty miles west of Paris and about equidistant from the border of Normandy. The elder Simon de Montfort was the son of Amicia, sister and co-heiress of Robert de Beaumont, earl of Leicester in England. The elder de Montfort thus had a claim through his mother to land in England. The younger Simon de Montfort was the third of four sons, so his claim to land in either France or England after his father was subordinate to the claims of his two older brothers.

The older Simon de Montfort responded to Innocent III's call for a crusade against the heretical Cathars in Languedoc in southern France, known as the Albigensian Crusade. He was a man of narrow piety and regarded it as his role to extirpate any evidence of heresy in this land. He won two major victories: one in 1211 at Castelnaudary against Count Raymond of Toulouse, and another in 1213 at Muret against Peter, king of Aragon. He laid siege to Toulouse in 1217 but died in 1218 before the city fell. During his time in southern France, the older Simon was accompanied by his wife who shared his piety and dedication to the cause. It is usually assumed that her sons were with her and may have been influenced by the intense religious feeling of the time.

In 1230 the younger Simon de Montfort went to England to try to obtain his English grandmother's inheritance. His father was dead, and he had come to terms with his older brothers whereby they would sell to him any rights they might have in the English property and he in turn released any claim he might have to property in France. The land was in the possession of the king, Henry III, who had granted it as a life estate to Ranulf, earl of Chester. Montfort applied to the king who, planning a first campaign to recapture the land in France that had been surrendered by his father John, took Montfort into his service, perhaps influenced by the military reputation of Montfort's father. With the approval of the elderly and heirless Ranulf of Chester, he was given the honor of Leicester (not the much larger earldom). Although the expedition did not take place, Montfort remained at court, and he and Henry III seem to have become friends.

In January 1138 Montfort was allowed to marry Henry's sister Eleanor in a very quiet ceremony about which Henry did not consult his barons. Eleanor was an extremely important pawn (her sister had married the emperor Frederick II), and Montfort was at the time a very impecunious Frenchman. So there were baronial protests about this marriage, and the Church had its doubts because Eleanor had taken a vow of chastity (a vow not to remarry) on the death of her first husband in 1231. But Henry remained firm, as did Montfort and Eleanor, and the marriage was a re-markably compatible one. In November 1138 their first son Henry was born, and in February 1139 Montfort received the earldom of Leicester (but still without a major land grant).

But Montfort's relative poverty and his mounting debts (he still owed on the money he promised his brothers upon release of their claims to the English property to him) forced him to increase his attempts to ob-tain a larger holding from Henry III. His own financial problems were compounded by Eleanor's problems in dealing with the family of her first husband over her dower rights in the Pembroke inheritance. She had been married to William Marshal, earl of Pembroke, who died in 1231 (the son of William Marshal who served Henry II, Richard, and John). Montfort had to borrow money using Henry III as a reference, and as a result Montfort lost Henry's favor in August 1239 and went into exile in France. But he was back in favor in April 1240 and was given permis-sion to participate in a crusade. Nothing is known of his activities on this crusade, but he was back in the fall of 1141, staying with the duke of Burgundy in eastern France.

In the meantime, Henry III called a parliament of his barons and asked for an aid (money grant) for a campaign in Poitou to recover that part of the county that had been lost to the French. Henry was refused the aid, but Henry went to Poitou anyway and called Montfort to serve in his army. The campaign was so poorly organized and underfunded that the English were soundly defeated and the rest of the county was surrendered to the French. The English were left with the rest of the duchy of Aquitaine, which included the county of Gascony. The county of Poitou would later be granted as an appanage to his brother Alphonse by Louis IX (St. Louis) of France. Alphonse would be known as Alphonse of Poitiers.

In the fall of 1243, Montfort and Eleanor were back in England, and Montfort was richly rewarded for his services in France. Many of his debts were forgiven, a marriage portion was provided for Eleanor, it was arranged that the Marshals make dower payments to Eleanor (they were difficult to collect), and Montfort was given custody of the castle of Kenilworth, which became his principal seat (residence). Montfort was now one of the great barons of England.

Montfort was in England between 1243 and 1248, a time of increasing baronial discontent with Henry III's government. The discontent at this time centered in the lesser baronage and the country gentry. Montfort as earl of Leicester was frequently at court and was not involved in the protests against Henry's policies, but he does seem to have drifted from the center of the court to its periphery. However, the real split between Montfort and Henry came from Henry's appointing Montfort as his lieutenant in Gascony in 1248. The appointment was to be for seven years, and Henry was to bear the cost of the military actions, castle building, and other necessary expenses. The province was exceptionally unruly, and Montfort went to work to restore order by force if necessary. Complaints against Montfort's forceful actions and his requests for money (which Henry could not supply) brought Montfort back to England in 1152 to face charges about his conduct in Gascony. In the trial Montfort and Henry threw charges back and forth against each other, but in the end the magnates (the earls of Cornwall, Gloucester, Norfolk, and Hereford) supported Montfort, the earl of Leicester. Henry decided to pacify Gascony himself and went to Gascony, accompanied by Montfort, between 1252 and 1254. This was Henry's only successful campaign, and it was fought in the way that Montfort had demonstrated earlier was the only way to quell the rebels.

Between 1254 and 1258 discontent with Henry's foreign policy increased because it was unwise and very costly. At the same time, Henry's half-brothers, the Lusignans, were at court where they received money and favors from the king at the expense of the English barons. Montfort was among the barons who opposed the foreign Lusignans (they were the sons of Henry III's mother Isabelle and her second husband, Hugh de Lusignan). His quarrel was primarily with William de Valence who had been given the Pembroke lands in the Welsh marches. Each accused the other of trespassing on his lands, and they came to blows on several occasions in Parliament. By 1258 the barons were ready to force Henry to accept baronial guidance in the making of policy and in the naming of the chief advisers of the crown. (For the course of the rebellion against Henry and Montfort's role in it, see Chapter 5.)

Montfort died on the battlefield of Evesham in 1265 facing a royalist army under the command of Edward, Henry III's heir, with a baronial army that was just lukewarm in its support of Montfort since Montfort's "rule" had been as arbitrary and oppressive as Henry's. His lands were confiscated, and his family was forced into exile. But the battlefield became virtually a shrine to Montfort, and there was much feeling that he died in a good cause and should be regarded as a martyr. On the other hand, his failure to establish baronial reform tarnished the reform movement, and future baronial reform movements were less revolutionary until the monarchy was overthrown in 1645.

Philip II Augustus

Philip II Augustus (1165–1223), king of France (1180–1223), was the son of Louis VII (1137–80) and his third wife, Adela of Champagne whom Louis had married after the divorce of his first wife, Eleanor of Aquitaine (from whom he had two daughters), and the death of his second wife (from whom he had had two daughters). Adela was married in 1160 and amid great rejoicing gave birth in 1165 to a son, Philip.

Philip II became king of France at a time when western European politics were dominated by Henry II of England, Normandy, greater Anjou, Poitou, and Aquitaine. Although Henry was a completely independent ruler only in England and for the other territories he was nominally subordinate to the king of France, his real political and economic power gave him a decided advantage in dealings with France. Nor was Henry the only French vassal who was strong enough to defy the French king. The princes who ruled Flanders, Champagne, Blois, Toulouse, and the other great fiefs overshadowed the king whose own territory included the Isle de France (the territory around Paris) and a rather narrow area reaching from Amiens in the northeast to Orleans on the Loire River in the south; on the central western frontier, the royal lands had a common boundary with the duchy of Normandy.

The Capetians belonged to a relatively new dynasty (ruling family) that had succeeded the Carolingian dynasty in 987 with the recognition of Hugh Capet, count of Paris, as king of the west Franks. The Carolingian dynasty got its name from Charles the Great (Charlemagne), king of the Franks (768–814), king of the Lombards (774–814), and Roman emperor (800–814). Charlemagne's successors drew great prestige from his reputation as a warrior, conqueror, ruler, and patron of learning, but in fact the empire to which they succeeded almost immediately was in the process of breaking up. The Frankish kings had traditionally followed the practice of dividing their kingdom among male heirs, with the usual result that warfare followed among the successor kings until only one ruler was left. After the death of Louis the Pious, Charlemagne's only surviving son, the pattern continued until what had been Charlemagne's empire fell into three major parts; the kingdom of the west Franks (Francia), the kingdom of the east Franks (Germany), and a middle kingdom that included Italy and the imperial title. In the tenth century, Italy and the imperial title would go to the German ruler, and at approximately the same time the Carolingian rulers of west Francia had so declined in power and authority that the election of Hugh Capet was possible. Nonetheless, the power of the Capetians was not very great. They had none of the prestige and glamor of the Carolingians, and they suffered from the fact that the ninth and tenth centuries had seen Francia invaded from north, south, and east (by the Vikings, Saracens, and Hungarians, respectively), the central authority had declined as protection fell to local leaders, and these local leaders gradually absorbed the king's military and judicial responsibilities.

Philip II Augustus is credited with reversing this situation. He greatly increased the territory over which he exercised direct authority, or had established recognition of the king as feudal lord, that by the end of the Middle Ages the foundations were laid for the emergence of a very strong monarchy in France. Philip was not the first Capetian king to recognize the problem and to try to resolve it, but he was the central figure in reducing the power of the Angevin rulers of England and subordinating them to the French king for the lands they still held in France. Philip was capitalizing on the progress made in overcoming his own unruly barons by his father and grandfather, Louis VII and Louis VI (1108–37). In this effort, Suger, abbot of St. Denis, a monastery just outside Paris, advised both kings. Suger envisioned a revival not only of monastic power (symbolized by the new church he built at St. Denis with its architectural innovations presaging Gothic), but also of royal power. In the advice he gave the kings and in his writings he always emphasized the dignity of the royal power and worked with the king to overcome the local castellans (holders of castles) in the Isle de France.

In the struggle with the Angevins in western France, Philip was following the strategy of his father, Louis VII, which was to offset his lack of the power and resources of the king of England by taking advantage of the quarrels in Henry's family revolving around the domestic troubles between Henry and his queen (Eleanor of Aquitaine) and their sons, Henry, Richard, Geoffrey, and John. In Henry, Richard, and Geoffrey's rebellion against their father in 1173–74, they were encouraged not only by their mother but also by Louis VII. In the last rebellion by Richard and John in 1189 (the young Henry and Geoffrey had died earlier), Philip II had actively participated in defeating and humiliating the old king.

Following the death of Henry II, Richard I became king of England and ruler of the Angevin lands in France (1189–99). At first the friendship that had developed between Richard and Philip during the days of opposition to Henry II continued, and both prepared to go on the Third Crusade together. But on the crusade it became apparent that the interests of the two were adversarial, not cooperative. When Acre in Palestine had fallen to the crusaders, Philip immediately went home, determined to take advantage of Richard's absence to occupy those of Richard's French lands which he could obtain by encouraging holders of strategic points to desert Richard or those he could occupy by military force. In this endeavor he obtained the support of Richard's brother John, who was anxious to gain the English throne for himself. Again it was the same policy of taking advantage of the ambitions of members of the Angevin family. In pursuing these policies, Philip now seemed for the first time to have resources that were at least equal to those of the Angevins; considering Richard's extra expenditures for the crusade and for raising the money for his ransom from the German emperor, Philip probably had more. At any rate, Philip could afford to remain on a war footing for a longer time than he and his predecessors could previously.

When Richard returned from the crusade and captivity in Germany in 1194, he spent only two months in England, long enough just to see that his new government organization under Hubert Walter was working well (it was) and to raise money for a campaign against Philip Augustus to recover those territories that the French had occupied. At this time, Philip was concentrating on two areas: (1) the northeastern part of Normandy closest to Paris, and (2) the salient between greater Anjou (Anjou, Maine, and Touraine) and the northeastern part of the county of Poitou. Richard remained in France without returning to England; John was also in France and seems to have served Richard loyally since he would almost certainly succeed to the throne if Richard and his queen Berengaria had no children. There was another candidate in the person of a young son of John's older brother, Geoffrey, dead since 1186.

Between 1194 and his death in battle in 1199, Richard had recovered most of the land occupied by Philip Augustus while Richard was absent in the east and in Germany. Not all of it had been won back, however, especially some of the most strategic points for the defense of the duchy of Normandy. What would have happened if he had not been killed in the siege of a castle held by a rebel in Poitou is impossible to say. Whatever may be said about Richard as an absentee king in England, there is no doubt about his inspired military leadership. Even so, his military expenditures were enormous, especially the building of an up-to-date new-style castle, Chateau Gaillard, at Les Andelys on the Seine River near the border between Normandy and the French royal lands. He had been taking large sums out of England to pay for this castle and his military expeditions, and as a result the English barons were already beginning to grumble. Whether they would have supported Richard if he had continued to require such sums for years into the future is impossible to tell. As it was, John inherited the situation, and John was no match for the wily Philip Augustus.

With Richard's death, Philip threw his support to Arthur of Brittany, son of the older brother Geoffrey, against John. But the barons of England and Normandy were persuaded to support John, and changing allegiances among a number of crucial subordinates convinced Philip to accept John in 1200. According to the terms of the agreement, John held all of Richard's former fiefs from Philip in return for a very large payment in relief; part of the county of Evreux in northeastern Normandy was ceded to Philip; and John's niece Blanche of Castile (daughter of a daughter of Henry II and Eleanor) was to marry the future Louis VIII and was given lands in Poitou as a dowry. Philip definitely came out ahead in this agreement, but John was given time to regroup his resources. The fact that Philip was willing to make peace on these terms was probably due to problems he was having over his second marriage to Ingeborg of Denmark. Philip's first marriage had been to Isabella of Hainault who became the mother of Philip's son and heir, Louis, before her death in 1189. Philip then married Ingeborg of Denmark whom he immediately repudiated and then married Agnes of Meran. Innocent III refused to recognize the divorce from Ingeborg and demanded that Philip restore her as queen.

When Philip refused, he suffered excommunication and an interdict on France. Although these ecclesiastical penalties do not seem to have upset the French king and his advisers very much, there were those who would all too willingly use them against the king. Philip finally capitulated and agreed to receive Ingeborg back (in name only). Fortunately for Philip, Agnes died shortly after this capitulation, and Philip was able to induce the pope to legitimize her children (a girl and a boy). Philip thus would have another potential male heir should Prince Louis not live.

In the meantime, John involved himself in a marital adventure by marrying Isabelle of Angouleme with her father's consent. From the standpoint of John's holdings in Poitou, the alliance with Angouleme was a wise move. Unfortunately, John neglected to come to terms with one of his vassals to whom Isabelle had been betrothed. Emerging feudal custom demanded that John give Hugh of Lusignan some form of compensation. When John refused it, Hugh appealed to John's overlord, the king of France, and King Philip agreed to hear the case in his own court in Paris. John was cited to appear before the court, but he refused to come. After several summonses, the French court in 1202 found John a rebellious vassal and declared his French fiefs forfeit. Philip and Arthur of Brittany immediately moved into Normandy, Philip from the east and Arthur from the west. John enjoyed only one success in the west: the capture of Arthur. This capture led to one of John's reprehensible acts—the elimination of his rival for the throne by murder. Other than this, Philip was successful in the east, and by 1204, John, no longer able to defend Normandy, withdrew to England. In the coming months, Philip would occupy Anjou, Maine, and Touraine as well and would confirm holding some of the lands to the east of Poitou. The Angevin domination was ended, although John did not acknowledge this; he would spend the rest of his reign planning to return to France and recover his lands that Philip had occupied.

John was unable to wage his campaign against Philip Augustus to regain his lost lands until 1214, when he was defeated. This defeat contributed to the baronial rebellion that pressed Magna Carta upon John.

Meanwhile, Philip Augustus concentrated on making royal French rule acceptable in the considerable territory he had obtained from the Angevins and as the result of marriages made between members of the Capetian family and heiresses to fiefs in the eastern part of France. In so doing, he adopted many of the practices developed by the Anglo-Norman and Angevin rulers of England and Normandy that extended royal legal and financial control in the provinces and developed centralized institutions staffed by professional administrators trained in civil and canon law. Although the law in northern France was still based on unwritten customary law, that customary law varied significantly from province to province and placed no obstacle on the application of civil (i.e., Roman) law as a bulwark of royal power. This, combined with elaborate royal ceremonials, especially on the occasion of coronations, and the steady propaganda of royalist apologists created a strong myth emphasizing the French royal power. This was in great contrast to what was happening in England.

Although England and France were not at war between 1204 and 1214, the rulers of both countries were preparing for war throughout that time. Philip Augustus expected to invade England to defeat John for a final time, and John constantly planned and stored up treasure to build an alliance on the Continent (his cousin Otto IV of Brunswick was German Roman emperor) that would allow a pincer movement against Philip Augustus from two directions. This plan was put in effect in 1214, leading to the decisive battle of Bouvines whereby John's plan was defeated and the English were left with only part of Poitou, Aquitaine, and Gascony. All of these areas were so unruly that the French kings were not ready to try to incorporate them into the royal domain.

Philip Augustus, however, did not wait until 1214 for war and its unknown outcome. By 1213 he was ready to invade England. He had the necessary resources to hire a largely mercenary army, he had a potentially able commander in his son Louis, heir to the throne, and he had the blessing of Pope Innocent III, who urged him to undertake a crusade to bring the English church back to obedience to the papacy. This last element in Philip Augustus' preparedness was the result of conflict between John and Innocent over the archbishopric of Canterbury. Innocent refused to accept John's candidate to succeed Hubert Walter as archbishop of Canterbury and obtained the election of his own candidate, Stephen Langton, whom John refused to allow to land in England. The struggle had begun in 1207 and as John refused to give in, Innocent put England under an interdict. Then later when John still did not move, he excommunicated John. But as in the earlier case of Philip Augustus and his excommunication, John and England were not intimidated. Stephen Langton was kept out of the country, and those bishops who obeyed the pope were exiled, leaving their episcopal lands in the hand of the king, thus increasing John's income. There was no popular protest, and some clerical opinion favored the king.

By 1213 John faced an imminent French invasion, and on this occasion he outmaneuvered Philip Augustus. He came to terms with Innocent III and even turned over to Innocent England and Ireland, which John would hold as fiefs of the papacy. Innocent immediately withdrew his approval of a French invasion of England and threatened interdict and excommunication if Philip proceeded. Philip Augustus could do nothing except disband his army, although he had not given up on the project.

In 1216, after civil war had broken out in England between the rebel barons and John, Philip Augustus could not take advantage of the situation to intervene. (Innocent III had excommunicated the barons who rebelled against his vassal John.) However, when the rebel barons invited his heir, Louis, to invade England on their behalf and held out the prospect of the English throne as enticement, Philip Augustus made no official move to support the invasion and thus avoided excommunication. Louis invaded England and was excommunicated. The rebel barons of England, reinforced by Louis' army, captured a number of royal castles and succeeded in controlling much of the southeast of England and East Anglia. Whether Louis could have eventually prevailed and whether Philip Augustus could have an acquired kingdom to bestow on his second son do not seem likely because of the increasing confidence of the majority of the English barons as Englishmen. As it happened, John's unexpected death in October 1216 removed the greatest stumbling block to an increase in royal resistance in the name of the nine-year-old king Henry III. Prince Louis had no choice but to withdraw.

In France, Philip Augustus continued to take advantage of every opportunity to expand the royal domain, and in Prince Louis he had the instrument to do so. Languedoc had not yet been brought completely under royal control when Philip died in 1223, but by the time of his son Louis VIII's death in 1226 it had become so. That Philip Augustus' reforms in government had been effective was proved during the reign of his grandson, Louis IX, who came to the throne as a minor under the regency of his mother, Blanche of Castile. Since Blanche was a woman and not a Frenchman, a number of the French barons revolted, but the movement was not coordinated. At his majority Blanche turned over to her

son a France undiminished in territory and power. On the basis of the
work of Louis VI, Louis VII, Philip II Augustus, and Louis VIII, Louis IX,
to be canonized as St. Louis, would continue to build a strong and effective royal government in a France that now seemed to dominate western Europe.

Hubert Walter

Hubert Walter (c. 1150–1205), archbishop of Canterbury (1193–1205),
was born in Norfolk, one of five sons of a lesser baron. Thus neither was
Walter destined to inherit, nor was the family wealthy enough to send
him to university. Instead, he was placed as a clerk with his uncle Ranulf Glanville, who became chief justiciar in 1180. Walter's financial and
legal education was confined to the practical experience he received in
Glanville's household.

By 1184 Walter was a baron of the exchequer and was made dean of
the cathedral of York, a position of some importance since the archbishop
had died in 1181 and the archbishopric was left vacant until after the
death of Henry II in 1189. At that time Geoffrey, illegitimate son of
Henry II, was elected archbishop. At the same time, Hubert Walter was
elected bishop of Salisbury. At this time he was one of King Richard's
men, worked in the collection of men and money for the Third Crusade,
and in 1190 sailed for the Holy Land in company with Archbishop of
Canterbury Baldwin and the justiciar, Ranulf Glanville. This group of
crusaders joined in the siege of Acre where in the fall of 1190 both
Glanville and Baldwin died, leaving Hubert Walter in command of the
English contingent then present.

In April 1191, Philip II Augustus of France arrived with the French
crusaders and joined the siege, and in June Richard arrived. The siege,
which had not been going well because of illness among the crusaders,
now came under the command of Richard who, though ill, directed the
actions that led to the fall of Acre in July. Philip II of France immediately went home. For the next year, Richard continued to fight toward
Jerusalem, but his opponent, Saladin, was a commander of about equal
ability as Richard, and their triumphs and defeats were about the same.

In mid-1192 Richard was urged to return to England because of trea-
sonable activity by his brother John. In September 1192 Hubert Walter
was sent to negotiate with Saladin, and a truce was arranged whereby

Christians held a strip of coastland that had been reconquered from Tyre to Jaffa and Christian pilgrims could visit Palestine, including Jerusalem. Richard did not go as a pilgrim to Jerusalem but sent Hubert Walter instead. Richard and a royal party left Palestine before Hubert Walter. Avoiding a return through France where Philip II, now Richard's enemy, was fighting to acquire some of Richard's territories, Richard instead went up the Adriatic Sea, hoping to travel incognito through the German lands. When Hubert Walter reached Sicily on his way home, he was met with the news that Richard had been captured and had been turned over to the German emperor Henry VI, another crusading enemy of Richard's. Walter went to Germany, saw Richard, and returned to England as Richard's representative to raise the enormous ransom demanded by the emperor.

Walter returned to England in April 1193 and made a truce with Richard's brother, John, who in concert with Philip II had planned to fight Richard for the throne. Walter joined with the queen mother Eleanor of Aquitaine and the justiciars Richard had appointed to rule England in his absence in raising the ransom. In accordance with Richard's wishes, Hubert Walter was elected archbishop of Canterbury later in 1193 and at almost the same time, was named chief justiciar, that is, regent in the absence of the king.

Richard returned to England in early 1194 but remained there only two months to collect men and money for a campaign in France to recover those territories that the French had taken. Richard died in 1199, still fighting, having never returned to England. Until 1198, Hubert Walter headed the government as justiciar, and when he resigned in 1198, he continued to be an active supporter of the king. He had been called to France in 1199 to negotiate a peace with Philip II, the terms of which Richard refused to accept, and he was there when Richard was killed in April. He and William Marshal were sent ahead to England to smooth the way for the succession of John, youngest son of Henry II.

John, who was in Normandy at the time of Richard's death, came to England in May 1199 and was crowned by Hubert Walter acting in his right as archbishop of Canterbury. Immediately thereafter, John named Walter chancellor, and in this position he initiated the practice of enrolling (that is, making copies on rolls of parchment) the charters, writs, and letters issued by the chancery. These important records joined those earlier started in the exchequer (treasury) and royal courts, placing England at the forefront of European governing entities keeping complete government records. As chancellor Walter worked well with John's justiciar, Geoffrey fitz Peter. Under these two experienced administrators, it might be said that the administrative innovations of Henry II were perfected. Unfortunately, this tended to be at the expense of those greater secular barons who had previously attended the king's large council in an advisory role. Meetings of the council now tended to rely heavily on the professional servants of the crown.

Hubert Walter was an effective and loyal secular and ecclesiastical administrator. Although he was criticized for his lavish lifestyle, his interest in accumulating wealth, and his nonuniversity Latin, he symbolized the new professionalism in both church and state. Although he obtained his education through experience, he gathered around him clerks who had some training in civil and canon law. These men staffed the courts of Henry III, and their knowledge of both canon and common law systems allowed the vast expansion of the common law that occurred in the thirteenth century.

William the Conqueror

William the Conqueror, also known as William the Bastard, was duke of Normandy (1035–87) and King William I of England (1066–87). The name "William the Bastard" comes from the irregular union between Duke Robert I of Normandy (1027–35) and Herleva, daughter of a burgher of the town of Falaise in Normandy. As duke of Normandy, Robert always referred to William as his son, and when he was preparing to go on pilgrimage to the Holy Land in 1035, he had the great Norman barons take oath to accept William as his heir. King Henry I of France (1031–60) as overlord confirmed this arrangement.

William's status as a bastard heir was not all that unusual for the tenth and early eleventh centuries. In those years, the western church as a whole had little direction since the centralizing papacy, under the control of a number of noble Roman families, was very weak, and local churches were effectively under the control of local rulers (in this case the duke of Normandy). In any event it was sometimes Germanic custom that bastards could be heirs, although later in the early twelfth century the Church would have put in effect a number of reforms, among them reforms dealing with marriage and bastardy. Therefore, when Henry

I of England neared death a hundred years later in 1135, there was little chance that he could be followed by one of his bastard sons, even though his single legitimate son had predeceased him. This shift in social attitudes threw England into a civil war over the succession.

Pilgrimages to the Holy Land were very popular in the tenth and eleventh centuries partly because of an increase in population, the restless energy of a warrior aristocracy, and an increase in trade between east and west. In addition, there was a great deal of curiosity about what was going on in the Asiatic Muslim world as the decline in the universal power of the Abbasid caliphate (the caliphs were the successors to Muhammed) at Bagdad allowed the Seljuk Turks to acquire effective political-military control. With Turkish control extended also to the Asia Minor provinces of the Byzantine Empire in 1071 following the battle of Manazkert, the background for the First Crusade was set. But for the moment the Crusades were in the future, and the big adventure was pilgrimage. A number of the northern French comital (i.e., the counts from the plural *comites* or companions) rulers, in addition to the duke of Normandy, were tempted. Robert, duke of Normandy, father of William the Bastard, did not return from his pilgrimage to Jerusalem, although he sent back a holy relic, one of the fingers of St. Stephen. It was to house this relic that William later built the abbey of St. Étienne for men at Caen in western Normandy, where his wife built La Trinité for women.

The oaths of the Norman baronage to recognize William as the heir had little restraining effect on events once Duke Robert had left for the east in 1035. At the time William was only seven or eight, and there were many older relatives ready to take advantage of his weakness. He first received some protection from a great uncle, the elderly Archbishop Robert of Rouen, but Robert died in 1037. Thereafter William was usually in hiding with one or two of his father's loyal staff. He also received some support from his mother Herleva, whom Duke Robert before his departure had married to a minor baron, Herluin de Conteville. This marriage would provide William with two half-brothers, Odo and Robert, who would be closely associated with William in his conquest of England. (All—Herleva, Herluin, Odo, and Robert—would be richly rewarded after the conquest.) In addition to this Norman support, when all seemed lost, William appealed to his overlord, Henry I of France. And survive William did. Gradually as he passed his mid-teen years, he began to gain control over his duchy, subduing the unruly baronage by military action. By 1054 he had defeated the last attempt to replace him as duke by one of his relatives, but he still remained vigilant. Normandy itself was turbulent—this was the period of Norman emigration to southern Italy—and Normandy's neighbors, the French king to the northeast and the Angevin count to the southwest, were trying to improve their frontiers with Normandy, as William was trying to improve his against them.

The eleventh century in general was a period of constant warfare throughout France as regional counts and dukes and even the king tried to regain control from local leaders who had provided what peace and protection were available in the breakup of the Carolingian Empire caused by dynastic weakness and invasions from without (Northmen in the north, Muslims in the south, Hungarians from the east). In effect, they were trying to overcome political disintegration by utilizing the ubiquitous lord–man relationship to obtain military service and gradually, in small increments, were building up a number of "feudal incidents" that would foster the relationship and provide some income for the lord. The dukes of Normandy had moved along this road with considerable success before the disasters associated with Robert and the early years of William. Before 1066, however, William had Normandy under control and well enough organized to provide the resources to attract and sustain a considerable army of adventurers to invade England that year. The county of Anjou had made some progress in this direction under Count Fulk Nerra (987–1040) and Count Geoffrey Martel (1040–60), but then a disputed succession threw the county into chaos again. In the twelfth century the baronage of Anjou would have to be overcome again by Count Geoffrey (1128–51), father of Henry of Anjou who would become King Henry II of England. The kings of France lagged behind the rulers of both Normandy and Anjou in subduing their baronage, but in the twelfth century, beginning with Louis VI (1108–37), the French kings would begin the process of establishing closer relations with their own baronage. Recognition by their own baronage would give the kings of France the strength to increase their control over the regional rulers of other parts of France.

In building up his strength in Normandy, William had a number of assets, including a thorough grounding in medieval warfare and his ability as a horse warrior. He was a realist about his position and could be very cruel to his defeated enemies. On the other hand, he understood well what his loyal followers expected: they expected to be rewarded for their services, and since land was the main form of wealth among the military aristocracy, William was generous with gifts from his own land (his demesne). He was also generous with land confiscated from followers who were disloyal or slow to come to William's aid. William, though ruthless, was also generous. That William's reputation was promising is indicated by the fact that some time between 1050 and 1052 he married Matilda, daughter of Count Baldwin V of the well-organized and increasingly wealthy county of Flanders in northeastern France. William's lack of formal education seems to have been of little import relative to the power he had acquired.

The story of William's claims as heir of the English king, Edward the Confessor, and his successful military invasion of England in 1066 to obtain the English throne has been told in Chapter 1. It is sufficient here to emphasize that William not only had to fight the battle of Hastings to gain his throne, but he had to remain or return to England almost constantly between 1067 and 1071 because of rebellions, especially in the north. These rebellions were ruthlessly put down, but they had the added advantage that widespread confiscation of property of rebels provided William with much land to distribute among his followers. Essentially this is the way William treated England, as a source of wealth to be returned to Normandy and those other provinces that had provided support. He was also extremely generous in his gifts to churches.

Although William regarded England as primarily an adjunct to his home province of Normandy, he did institute strong Norman rule based on respecting English legal institutions but providing for his own followers to enjoy their own customs—a formula that allowed gradual fusion of the two. He did not foresee a union of Normandy and England under his successors, and he provided that his eldest son Robert should inherit Normandy (as was beginning to be the custom on the Continent in the case of inherited land), his second son should inherit the acquired territory, England, and the youngest son would inherit only treasure. But as in the case of his great grandson, Henry II in the late twelfth century, William failed to grasp the nature of the hopes and ambitions of his sons; Normandy and England would be united by his youngest son, Henry I.

PRIMARY DOCUMENTS

The five documents that follow are closely associated with the making of Magna Carta and its establishment as law of the land. The first document is "The Coronation Charter" of Henry I, issued in the year 1100. It is sometimes referred to as a blueprint for Magna Carta because it outlines the grievances that the barons of England had voiced against the rule of Henry's predecessor, William II. Many of these grievances were the same as those held by the barons of 1215 against King John. It is interesting to note how the customs governing the holding of land from the king had developed during the century that intervened between the earlier document and Magna Carta issued in 1215.

For the meaning of technical words, see the Glossary.

DOCUMENT 1
"The Coronation Charter" of Henry I (August 5, 1100)

This charter was issued by Henry I (third of the Norman kings of England) in 1100 as an addition to the usual English coronation oath promising peace and security to the people of the realm. It was in response to complaints made against his brother, William II, who had collected more income from the tenants who held land from him than had become customary. Henry was evidently appealing for support of these men. It should be noted, however, that contrary to the promises made here, Henry continued many of the practices of his predecessors.

Henry, king of the English, to Samson the bishop, and Urse of Abbe-tot, and to all his barons and faithful vassals, both French and English, in Worchestershire, greeting.

1. Know that by the mercy of God and by the common counsel of the barons of the whole kingdom of England I have been crowned king of this realm. And because the kingdom has been oppressed by unjust ex-actions, I now, being moved by reverence towards God and by the love I bear you all, make free the Church of God so that I will neither sell nor lease its property; nor on the death of an archbishop or bishop or an abbot will I take anything from the demesne of the Church or from its vassals during the period which elapses before a successor is installed. I abolish all the evil customs by which the kingdom of England has been unjustly oppressed. Some of those evil customs are here set forth.

2. If any of my barons or of my earls or of any other of my tenants shall die, his heir shall not redeem his land as he was wont to do in the time of my brother, but he shall henceforth redeem it by means of a just and lawful "relief." Similarly the men of my barons shall redeem their lands from their lords by means of a just and lawful "relief."

3. If any of my barons or of my tenants shall wish to give in marriage his daughter or his sister or his niece or his cousin, he shall consult me about the matter; but I will neither seek payment for my consent, nor will I refuse my permission, unless he wishes to give her in marriage to one of my enemies. And if, on the death of one of my barons or of one of my tenants a daughter should be his heir, I will dispose of her in mar-riage and of her lands according to the counsel given me by my barons. And if the wife of one of my tenants shall survive her husband and be without children, she shall have her dower and her marriage portion, and I will not give her in marriage unless she herself consents.

4. If a widow survives with children under age, she shall have her dower and her marriage portion, so long as she keeps her body chaste; and I will not give her in marriage except with her consent. And the guardian of the land, and of the children, shall be either the widow or another of their relations, as may seem more proper. And I order that my barons shall act likewise towards the sons and daughters and widows of their men.

5. I utterly forbid that the common mintage, which has been taken from the towns and shires, shall henceforth be levied, since it was not so

levied in the time of King Edward. If any moneyer or other person be taken with false money in his possession, let true justice be visited upon him.

6. I forgive all pleas and all debts which were owing to my brother, except my own proper dues, and except those things which were agreed to belong to the inheritance of others, or to concern the property which justly belonged to others. And if anyone had promised anything for his heritage, I remit it, and I also remit all "reliefs" which were promised for direct inheritance.

7. If any of my barons or of my men, being ill, shall give away or bequeath his movable property, I will allow that it shall be bestowed according to his desires. But if, prevented either by violence or through sickness, he shall die intestate as far as concerns his movable property, his widow or his children or his relatives or one of his true men shall make such division for the sake of his soul, as may seem best to them.

8. If any of my barons or of my men shall incur a forfeit, he shall not be compelled to pledge his movable property to an unlimited amount, as was done in the time of my father and my brother; but he shall only make payment according to the extent of his legal forfeiture, as was done before the time of my father and in the time of my earlier predecessors. Nevertheless, if he be convicted of breach of faith or of crime, he shall suffer such penalty as is just.

9. I remit all murder-fines which were incurred before the day on which I was crowned king; and such murder-fines as shall now be incurred shall be paid justly according to the law of King Edward.

10. By the common counsel of my barons I have retained the forests in my own hands as my father did before me.

11. The knights, who in return for their estates perform military service equipped with a hauberk of mail, shall hold their demesne lands quit of all gelds and all work; I make this concession as my own free gift in order that, being thus relieved of so great a burden, they may furnish themselves so well with horses and arms that they may be properly equipped and prepared to discharge my service and to defend my kingdom.

12. I establish a firm peace in all my kingdom, and I order that this peace shall henceforth be kept.

13. I restore to you the law of King Edward together with emendations to it as my father made with the counsel of his barons.

14. If since the death of my brother, King William, anyone shall have seized any of my property or the property of any other man, let him speedily return the whole of it. If he does this no penalty will be exacted, but if he retains any part of it he shall, when discovered, pay a heavy penalty to me.

Witness: Maurice, bishop of London; William, bishop-elect of Winchester; Gerard, bishop of Hereford; Henry the earl; Simon the earl; Walter Giffard; Robert of Montfort-sur-Risle; Roger Bigot; Eudo the steward; Robert, son of Haimo; and Robert Malet.
At Westminister when I was crowned. Farewell.

This translation is taken from David C. Douglas and George W. Greenaway, eds., *English Historical Documents, 1042–1189*, 2nd ed. (London: Eyre Methuen, and New York: Oxford University Press, 1981), pp. 432–434.

DOCUMENT 2
Magna Carta, 1215

Four copies of this charter survive: two in the British Museum and one each in the cathedrals of Lincoln and Salisbury. The original of the document, as well as the copies, was not divided into separate articles, but for ease of reading and understanding, all recent editors and translators have retained the division into paragraphs followed here.

John, by the grace of God, king of England, lord of Ireland, duke of Normandy and Aquitaine, and count of Anjou, to the archbishops, bishops, abbots, earls, barons, justiciars, foresters, sheriffs, stewards, servants, and to all his bailiffs and faithful subjects, greeting. Know that we, out of reverence for God and for the salvation of our soul and those of all our ancestors and heirs, for the honour of God and the exaltation of holy church, and for the reform of our realm, on the advice of our venerable fathers, Stephen archbishop of Canterbury, primate of all England and cardinal of the holy Roman church, Henry archbishop of Dublin, William of London, Peter of Winchester, Jocelyn of Bath and Glastonbury, Hugh of Lincoln, Walter of Worcester, William of Coventry and Benedict of Rochester, bishops, of master Pandulf, subdeacon and member of the household of the lord pope [i.e., papal legate], of brother Aymeric, master of the order of Knights Templar in England, and of the noble men William Marshal earl of Pembroke, William earl of Salisbury, William earl of Warenne, William earl of Arundel, Alan of Galloway constable of Scotland, Warin fitz Gerold, Peter fitz Herbert, Hubert de Burgh seneschal of Poitou, Hugh de Neville, Matthew fitz Herbert, Thomas Basset, Alan Basset, Philip de Aubeney, Robert of Ropsley, John Marshal, John fitz Hugh, and others, our faithful subjects:

1. In the first place have granted to God and by this our present charter confirmed for us and our heirs for ever that the English church shall be free, and shall have its rights undiminished and its liberties unimpaired; and it is our will that it be thus observed; which is evident from the fact that, before the quarrel between us and our barons began, we willingly and spontaneously granted and by our charter confirmed the freedom of elections which is reckoned most important and very essential to the English church, and obtained confirmation of it from the lord pope Innocent III; the which we will observe and we wish our heirs to observe it in good faith for ever. We have also granted to all free men of our kingdom, for ourselves and our heirs for ever, all the liberties written below, to be had and held by them and their heirs of us and our heirs.

2. If any of our earls or barons or others holding of us in chief by knight service dies, and at his death his heir be of full age and owe relief he shall have his inheritance on payment of the old relief, namely the heir or heirs of an earl £100 for a whole earl's barony, the heir or heirs of a baron £100 for a whole barony, the heir or heirs of a knight 100s, at most, for the whole knight's fee; and he who owes less shall give less according to the ancient usage of fiefs.

3. If, however, the heir of any such be under age and a ward, he shall have his inheritance when he comes of age without paying relief and without making fine.

4. The guardian of the land of such an heir who is under age shall take from the land of the heir no more than reasonable revenues, reasonable customary dues and reasonable services, and that without destruction and waste of men or goods; and if we commit the wardship of the land of any such to a sheriff, or to any other who is answerable to us for its revenues, and he destroys or wastes what he has wardship of, we will take compensation from him and the land shall be committed to two

lawful and discreet men of that fief, who shall be answerable for the revenues to us or to him to whom we have assigned them; and if we give or sell to anyone the wardship of any such land and he causes destruction or waste therein, he shall lose that wardship, and it shall be transferred to two lawful and discreet men of that fief, who shall similarly be answerable to us as is aforesaid.

5. Moreover, so long as he has the wardship of the land, the guardian shall keep in repair the houses, parks, preserves, ponds, mills and other things pertaining to the land out of the revenues from it; and he shall restore to the heir when he comes of age his land fully stocked with ploughs and the means of husbandry according to what the season of husbandry requires and the revenues of the land can reasonably bear.

6. Heirs shall be married without disparagement, yet so that before the marriage is contracted those nearest in blood to the heir shall have notice.

7. A widow shall have her marriage portion and inheritance forthwith and without difficulty after the death of her husband; nor shall she pay anything to have her dower or her marriage portion or the inheritance which she and her husband held on the day of her husband's death; and she may remain in her husband's house for forty days after his death, within which time her dower shall be assigned to her.

8. No widow shall be forced to marry so long as she wishes to live without a husband, provided that she gives security not to marry without our consent if she holds of us, or without the consent of her lord of whom she holds, if she holds of another.

9. Neither we nor our bailiffs will seize for any debt any land or rent, so long as the chattels of the debtor are sufficient to repay the debt; nor will those who have gone surety for the debtor be distrained so long as the principal debtor is himself able to pay the debt; and if the principal debtor fails to pay the debt, having nothing wherewith to pay it, then shall the sureties answer for the debt; and they shall, if they wish, have the lands and rents of the debtor until they are reimbursed for the debt which they have paid for him, unless the principal debtor can show that he has discharged his obligation in the matter to the said sureties.

10. If anyone who has borrowed from the Jews any sum, great or small, dies before it is repaid, the debt shall not bear interest as long as the heir is under age, of whomsoever he holds; and if the debt falls into our hands, we will not take anything except the principal mentioned in the bond.

11. And if anyone dies indebted to the Jews, his wife shall have her dower and pay nothing of that debt; and if the dead man leaves children who are under age, they shall be provided with necessaries befitting the holding of the deceased; and the debt shall be paid out of the residue, reserving, however, service due to lords of the land; debts owing to others than Jews shall be dealt with in like manner.

12. No scutage or aid shall be imposed in our kingdom unless by common counsel of our kingdom, except for ransoming our person, for making our eldest son a knight, and for once marrying our eldest daughter; and for these only a reasonable aid shall be levied. Be it done in like manner concerning aids from the city of London.

13. And the city of London shall have all its ancient liberties and free customs as well by land as by water. Furthermore, we will and grant that all other cities, boroughs, towns, and ports shall have all their liberties and free customs.

14. And to obtain the common counsel of the kingdom about the assessing of an aid (except in the three cases aforesaid) or of a scutage, we will cause to be summoned the archbishops, bishops, abbots, earls and greater barons, individually by our letters—and in addition, we will cause to be summoned generally through our sheriffs and bailiffs all those holding of us in chief—for a fixed date, namely, after the expiry of at least forty days, and to a fixed place; and in all letters of such summons we will specify the reason for the summons. And when the summons has thus been made, the business shall proceed on the day appointed, according to the counsel of those present, though not all have come who were summoned.

15. We will not in future grant any one the right to take an aid from his free men, except for ransoming his person, for making his eldest son a knight and for once marrying his eldest daughter, and for these only a reasonable aid shall be levied.

16. No one shall be compelled to do greater service for a knight's fee or for any other free holding than is due from it.

17. Common pleas shall not follow our court, but shall be held in some fixed place.

18. Recognitions of *novel disseisin,* of *mort d'ancester,* and of *darrein presentment,* shall not be held elsewhere than in the counties to which they relate, and in this manner—we, or, if we should be out of the realm, our chief justiciar, will send two justices through each county four times

a year, who, with four knights of each county chosen by the county, shall hold the said assizes in the county and on the day and in the place of meeting of the county court.

19. And if the said assizes cannot all be held on the day of the county court, there shall stay behind as many of the knights and freeholders who were present at the county court on that day as are necessary for the sufficient making of judgments, according to the amount of business to be done.

20. A free man shall not be amerced for a trivial offence except in accordance with the degree of the offence, and for a grave offence he shall be amerced in accordance with its gravity, yet saving his way of living; and a merchant in the same way, saving his stock-in-trade; and a villein shall be amerced in the same way, saving his means of livelihood—if they have fallen into our mercy: and none of the aforesaid amercements shall be imposed except by the oath of good men of the neighbourhood.

21. Earls and barons shall not be amerced except by their peers, and only in accordance with the degree of the offence.

22. No clerk shall be amerced in respect of his lay holding except after the manner of the others aforesaid and not according to the amount of his ecclesiastical benefice.

23. No vill or individual shall be compelled to make bridges at river banks, except those who from of old are legally bound to do so.

24. No sheriff, constable, coroners, or others of our bailiffs, shall hold pleas of our crown.

25. All counties, hundreds, wapentakes and trithings [mid-size territorial unit in the north] shall be at the old rents without any additional payment, except our demesne manors.

26. If anyone holding a lay fief of us dies and our sheriff or bailiff shows our letters patent of summons for a debt that the deceased owed us, it shall be lawful for our sheriff or bailiff to attach and make a list of chattels of the deceased found upon the lay fief to the value of that debt under the supervision of law-worthy men, provided that none of the chattels shall be removed until the debt which is manifest has been paid to us in full; and the residue shall be left to the executors for carrying out the will of the deceased. And if nothing is owing to us from him, all the chattels shall accrue to the deceased, saving to his wife and children their reasonable shares.

27. If any free man dies without leaving a will, his chattels shall be distributed by his nearest kinsfolk and friends under the supervision of the church, saving to every one debts which the deceased owed him.

28. No constable or other bailiff of ours shall take anyone's corn or other chattels unless he pays on the spot in cash for them or can delay payment by arrangement with the seller.

29. No constable shall compel any knight to give money instead of castle-guard if he is willing to do the guard himself or through another good man, if for some good reason he cannot do it himself; and if we lead or send him on military service, he shall be excused guard in proportion to the time that because of us he has been on service.

30. No sheriff, or bailiff of ours, or anyone else shall take the horses or carts of any free man for transport work save with the agreement of that freeman.

31. Neither we nor our bailiffs will take, for castles or other works of ours, timber which is not ours, except with the agreement of him whose timber it is.

32. We will not hold for more than a year and a day the lands of those convicted of felony, and then the lands shall be handed over to the lords of the fiefs.

33. Henceforth all fish-weirs shall be cleared completely from the Thames and the Medway and throughout all England, except along the sea coast.

34. The writ called *Praecipe* shall not in future be issued to anyone in respect of any holding whereby a free man may lose his court.

35. Let there be one measure for wine throughout our kingdom, and one measure for ale, and one measure for corn, namely "the London quarter"; and one width for cloths whether dyed, russet or halberget, namely two ells within the selvedges. Let it be the same with weights as with measures.

36. Nothing shall be given or taken in future for the writ of inquisition of life or limbs; instead it shall be granted free of charge and not refused.

37. If anyone holds of us by fee-farm, by socage, or by burgage, and holds land of another by knight service, we will not, by reason of that fee-farm, socage, or burgage, have the wardship of his heir or of land of his that is of the fief of the other; nor will we have custody of the fee-farm, socage, or burgage, unless such fee-farm owes knight service. We

will not have custody of anyone's heir or land which he holds of another by knight service by reason of any petty serjeanty which he holds of us by the service of rendering to us knives or arrows or the like.

38. No bailiff shall in future put anyone to trial upon his own bare word, without reliable witnesses produced for this purpose.

39. No free man shall be arrested or imprisoned or disseised or outlawed or exiled or in any way victimized, neither will we attack him or send anyone to attack him, except by the lawful judgment of his peers or by the law of the land.

40. To no one will we sell, to no one will we refuse or delay right or justice.

41. All merchants shall be able to go out of and come into England safely and securely and stay and travel throughout England, as well by land as by water, for buying and selling by the ancient and right customs free from all evil tolls, except in time of war and if they are of the land that is at war with us. And if such are found in our land at the beginning of a war, they shall be attached, without injury to their persons or goods, until we, or our chief justiciar, know how merchants of our land are treated who were found in the land at war with us when war broke out; and if ours are safe there, the others shall be safe in our land.

42. It shall be lawful in future for anyone, without prejudicing the allegiance due to us, to leave our kingdom and return safely and securely by land and water, save, in the public interest, for a short period in time of war—except for those imprisoned or outlawed in accordance with the law of the kingdom and natives of a land that is at war with us and merchants (who shall be treated as aforesaid).

43. If anyone who holds of some escheat such as the honour of Wallingford, Nottingham, Boulogne, Lancaster, or of other escheats which are in our hands and are baronies dies, his heir shall give no other relief and do no other service to us than he would have done to the baron if that barony had been in the baron's hands; and we will hold it in the same manner in which the baron held it.

44. Men who live outside the forest need not henceforth come before our justices of the forest upon a general summons, unless they are impleaded or are sureties for any person or persons who are attached for forest offences.

45. We will not make justices, constables, sheriffs or bailiffs save of such as know the law of the kingdom and mean to serve it well.

46. All barons who have founded abbeys for which they have char-ters of the kings of England or ancient tenure shall have the custody of them during vacancies, as they ought to have.

47. All forests that have been made forest in our time shall be im-mediately disafforested; and so be it done with river-banks that have been made preserves by us in our time.

48. All evil customs connected with forests and warrens, foresters and warreners, sheriffs and their officials, river-banks and their wardens shall immediately be inquired into in each county by twelve sworn knights of the same county who are to be chosen by good men of the same county, and within forty days of the completion of the inquiry shall be utterly abolished by them so as never to be restored, provided that we, or our justiciar if we are not in England, know of it first.

49. We will immediately return all hostages and charters given to us by Englishmen, as security for peace or faithful service.

50. We will remove completely from office the relations of Gerard de Athee so that in future they shall have no office in England, namely En-gelard de Cigogne, Peter and Guy and Andrew de Chanceaux, Guy de Cigogne, Geoffrey de Martigny and his brothers, Philip Marc and his brothers and his nephew Geoffrey, and all their following.

51. As soon as peace is restored, we will remove from the kingdom all foreign knights, cross-bowmen, serjeants, and mercenaries, who have come with horses and arms to the detriment of the kingdom.

52. If anyone has been disseised of or kept out of his lands, castles, franchises or his right by us without the legal judgment of his peers, we will immediately restore them to him: and if a dispute arises over this, then let it be decided by the judgment of the twenty-five barons who are mentioned below in the clause for securing the peace: for all the things, however, which anyone has been disseised or kept out of without the law-ful judgment of his peers by king Henry, our father, or by king Richard, our brother, which we have in our hand or are held by others, to whom we are bound to warrant them, we will have the usual period of respite of crusaders, excepting those things about which a plea was started or an inquest made by our command before we took the cross; when however we return from our pilgrimage, or if by any chance we do not go on it, we will at once do full justice therein.

53. We will have the same respite, and in the same manner, in the doing of justice in the matter of the disafforesting or retaining of the

forests which Henry our father or Richard our brother afforested, and in the matter of the wardship of lands which are of the fief of another, wardships of which sort we have hitherto had by reason of a fief which anyone held of us by knight service, and in the matter of abbeys founded on the fief of another, not on a fief of our own, in which the lord of the fief claims he has a right; and when we have returned, of if we do not set out on our pilgrimage, we will at once do full justice to those who complain of these things.

54. No one shall be arrested or imprisoned upon the appeal of a woman for the death of anyone except her husband.

55. All fines made with us unjustly and against the law of the land, and all amercements imposed unjustly and against the law of the land, shall be entirely remitted, or else let them be settled by the judgment of the twenty-five barons who are mentioned below in the clause for securing the peace, or by judgment of the majority of the same, along with the aforesaid Stephen, archbishop of Canterbury, if he can be present, and such others as he may wish to associate with himself for this purpose, and if he cannot be present the business shall nevertheless proceed without him, provided that if any one or more of the aforesaid twenty-five barons are in a like suit, they shall be removed from the judgment of the case in question, and others chosen, sworn and put in their place by the rest of the twenty-five for this case only.

56. If we have disseised or kept out Welshmen from lands or liberties or other things without the legal judgment of their peers in England or in Wales, they shall be immediately restored to them; and if a dispute arises over this, then let it be decided in the March by the judgment of their peers—for holdings in England according to the law of England, for holdings in Wales according to the law of Wales, and for holdings in the March according to the law of the March. Welshmen shall do the same to us and ours.

57. For all things, however, which any Welshman was disseised of or kept out of without the lawful judgment of his peers by king Henry, our father, or king Richard, our brother, which we have in our hand or which are held by others, to whom we are bound to warrant them, we will have the usual period of respite of crusaders, excepting those things about which a plea was started or an inquest made by our command before we took the cross; when however we return, or if by any chance we do not

set out on our pilgrimage, we will at once do full justice to them in accordance with the laws of the Welsh and the aforesaid regions.

58. We will give back at once the son of Llywelyn and all the hostages from Wales and the charters that were handed over to us as security for peace.

59. We will act toward Alexander, king of the Scots, concerning the return in the same manner in which we act towards our other barons of England, unless it ought to be otherwise by the charters which we have from William his father, formerly king of the Scots, and this shall be determined by his peers in our court.

60. All these aforesaid customs and liberties which we have granted to be observed in our kingdom as far as it pertains to us towards our men, all of our kingdom, clerks as well as laymen, shall observe as far as it pertains to them towards their men.

61. Since, moreover, for God and the betterment of our kingdom and for the better allaying of the discord that has arisen between us and our barons we have granted all these things aforesaid, wishing them to enjoy the use of them unimpaired and unshaken for ever, we give and grant them the under-written security, namely, that the barons shall choose any twenty-five barons of the kingdom they wish, who must with all their might observe, hold and cause to be observed, the peace and liberties which we have granted and confirmed to them by this present charter of ours, so that if we, or our justiciar, or our bailiffs or any one of our servants offend in any way against anyone or transgress any of the articles of the peace or the security and the offence be notified to four of the aforesaid twenty-five barons, those four barons shall come to us, or to our justiciar if we are out of the kingdom, and, laying the transgression before us, shall petition us to have that transgression corrected without delay. And if we do not correct the transgression, or if we are out of the kingdom, if our justiciar does not correct it, within forty days, reckoning from the time it was brought to our notice or to that of our justiciar if we were out of the kingdom, the aforesaid four barons shall refer that case to the rest of the twenty-five barons and those twenty-five barons together with the community of the whole land shall distrain and distress us in every way they can, namely, by seizing castles, lands, possessions, and in such other ways as they can, saving our person and the persons of our queen and our children, until, in their opinion, amends

have been made; and when amends have been made, they shall obey us as they did before. And let anyone in the land who wishes take an oath to obey the orders of the said twenty-five for the execution of all the aforesaid matters, and with them to distress us as much as he can, and we publicly and freely give anyone leave to take the oath who wishes to take it and we will never prohibit anyone from taking it. Indeed, all those in the land who are unwilling of themselves and of their own accord to take an oath to the twenty-five barons to help them to distrain and dis-tress us, we will make them take the oath as aforesaid at our command. And if any of the twenty-five barons dies or leaves the country or is in any other way prevented from carrying out the things aforesaid, the rest of the aforesaid twenty-five barons shall choose as they think fit another one in his place, and he shall take the oath like the rest. In all matters the execution of which is committed to these twenty-five barons, if it should happen that these twenty-five are present yet disagree among themselves about anything, or if some of those summoned will not or cannot be present, that shall be held as fixed and established which the majority of those present ordained or commanded, exactly as if all the twenty-five had consented to it; and the said twenty-five shall swear that they will faithfully observe all the things aforesaid and will do all they can to get them observed. And we will procure nothing from anyone, ei-ther personally or through anyone else, whereby any of these concessions and liberties might be revoked or diminished; and if any such thing is procured, let it be void and null, and we will never use it either person-ally or through another.

62. And we have fully remitted and pardoned to everyone all the ill-will, indignation and rancour that have arisen between us and our men, clergy and laity, from the time of the quarrel. Furthermore, we have fully remitted to all, clergy and laity, and as far as pertains to us have com-pletely forgiven, all trespasses occasioned by the same quarrel between Easter in the sixteenth year of our reign and the restoration of peace. And, besides, we have caused to be made for them letters testimonial patent of the lord Stephen archbishop of Canterbury, of the lord Henry archbishop of Dublin and of the aforementioned bishops and of master Pandulf about this security and the aforementioned concessions.

63. Wherefore we wish and firmly enjoin that the English church shall be free, and that the men in our kingdom shall have and hold all the aforesaid liberties, rights and concessions well and peacefully, freely and

quietly, fully and completely, for themselves and their heirs from us and our heirs, in all matters and in all places for ever, as is aforesaid. An oath, moreover, has been taken, as well on our part as on the part of the barons, that all these things aforesaid shall be observed in good faith and without evil disposition. Witness the above-mentioned and many others. Given by our hand in the meadow which is called Runnymede between Windsor and Staines on the fifteenth day of June, in seventeenth year of our reign.

This translation is taken from Harry Rothwell, ed., *English Historical Documents 1189–1327* (New York: Oxford University Press, 1975), pp. 316–324.

DOCUMENT 3
Magna Carta, 1225

This is the "final" revision of Magna Carta after the original issue in 1215, the revised reissue of 1216 following John's death, and another reissue of 1217. All of the reissues dropped the articles (10 and 11) dealing with debts to the Jews and dropped those articles declaring that no scutage or aid should be assessed except with the consent of the common counsel of the realm and those dealing with summonses to meetings of the common counsel (12 and 14). The articles dealing with removal of foreigners (50), with Wales and Scotland (56–59), and with enforcement of the terms of the charter by a baronial council of twenty-five (55–61) were dropped. Also, the articles dealing with forests and preserves and with the forest law (44, 47, and 48) were omitted in the reissues of Magna Carta but were covered in another document, the Charter of the Forest, accompanying Magna Carta in 1217. The Charter of the Forest of 1225 follows the 1225 version of Magna Carta given here. From 1225 on, the two charters (Magna Carta and the Charter of the Forest) were always issued together.

Henry by the grace of God, king of England, lord of Ireland, duke of Normandy, Aquitaine, and count of Anjou, to the archbishops, bishops, abbots, priors, earls, barons, sheriffs, stewards, servants and to all his bailiffs and faithful subjects who shall look at the present charter, greeting. Know that we out of reverence for God and for the salvation of our soul and the souls of our ancestors and successors, for the exaltation of holy church and the reform of our realm, have of our own spontaneous goodwill given and granted to the archbishops, bishops, abbots, priors, earls, barons and all of our realm these liberties written below to be held in our kingdom of England for ever.

1. In the first place we have granted to God, and by this our present charter confirmed for us and our heirs for ever, that the English church shall be free and shall have all its rights undiminished and its liberties unimpaired. We have also granted to all free men of our kingdom, for ourselves and our heirs for ever, all the liberties written below to be had and held by them and their heirs of us and our heirs for ever.

2. If any of our earls or barons or others holding of us in chief by knight service dies, and at his death his heir be of full age and owe relief he shall have his inheritance on payment of the old relief, namely the heir or heirs of an earl £100 for a whole earl's barony, the heir or heirs of a baron £100 for a whole barony, the heir or heirs of a knight s100, at most, for a whole knight's fee; and he who owes less shall give less according to the ancient usage of fiefs.

3. If, however, the heir of any such be under age, his lord shall not have wardship of him, nor of his land, before he has received his homage; and after being a ward such an heir shall have his inheritance when he comes of age, that is of twenty-one years, without paying relief and without making fine, so, however, that if he is made a knight while still under age, the land nevertheless shall remain in the wardship of his lord for the full term.

4. The guardian of the land of such an heir who is under age shall take from the land of the heir no more than reasonable revenues, reasonable customary dues and reasonable services, and that without destruction and waste of men or goods; and if we commit the wardship of the land of any such to a sheriff, or to any other who is answerable to us for the revenues of that land, and he destroys or wastes what he has wardship of, we will take compensation from him and the land shall be committed to two lawful and discreet men of that fief, who shall be answerable for the revenues to us or to him to whom we have assigned them; and if we give or sell to anyone the wardship of any such land and he causes destruction or waste therein, he shall lose that wardship and it shall be transferred to two lawful and discreet men of that fief, who shall similarly be answerable to us as is aforesaid.

5. Moreover, so long as he has the wardship of the land, the guardian shall keep in repair the houses, parks, preserves, ponds, mills and other things pertaining to the land out of the revenues from it; and he shall restore to the heir when he comes of age his land fully stocked with ploughs and all other things in at least the measure he received. All these things shall be observed in the case of wardships of vacant archbishops, bishoprics, abbeys, priories, churches and dignities that pertain to us except that wardships of this kind may not be sold.

6. Heirs shall be married without disparagement.

7. A widow shall have her marriage portion and inheritance forthwith and without any difficulty after the death of her husband, nor shall she pay anything to have her dower or her marriage portion or the inheritance which she and her husband held on the day of her husband's death; and she may remain in the chief house of her husband for forty days after his death, within which time her dower shall be assigned to her, unless it has already been assigned to her or unless the house is a castle; and if she leaves the castle, a suitable house shall be immediately provided for her in which she can stay honourably until her dower is assigned to her in accordance with what is aforesaid, and she shall have meanwhile her reasonable estover of common. There shall be assigned to her for her dower a third of all her husband's land which was his in his lifetime, unless a smaller share was given her at the church door. No widow shall be forced to marry so long as she wishes to live without a husband, provided that she gives security not to marry without our consent if she holds of us, or without the consent of her lord if she holds of another.

8. We or our bailiffs will not seize for any debt any land or rent, so long as the available chattels of the debtor are sufficient to repay the debt and the debtor himself is prepared to have it paid therefrom; nor will those who have gone surety for the debtor be distrained so long as the principal debtor is himself able to pay the debt; and if the principal debtor fails to pay the debt, having nothing wherewith to pay it or is able but unwilling to pay, then shall the sureties answer for the debt; and they shall, if they wish, have the lands and rents of the debtor until they are reimbursed for the debt which they have paid for him, unless the principal debtor can show that he has discharged his obligation in the matter to the said sureties.

9. The city of London shall have all its ancient liberties and free cus-

toms. Furthermore, we will and grant that all other cities, boroughs, towns, the barons of the Cinque Ports, and all ports shall have all their liberties and free customs.

10. No one shall be compelled to do greater service for a knight's fee or for any other free holding than is due from it.

11. Common pleas shall not follow our court, but shall be held in some fixed place.

12. Recognitions of novel disseisin and of mort d'ancestor shall not be held elsewhere than in the counties to which they relate, and in this manner—we, or, if we should be out of the realm, our chief justiciar, will send justices through each county once a year, who with knights of the counties shall hold the said assizes in the counties, and those which cannot on that visit be determined in the county to which they relate by the said justices sent to hold the said assizes shall be determined by them elsewhere on their circuit, and those which cannot be determined by them because of difficulty over certain articles shall be referred to our justices of the bench and determined there.

13. Assizes of darrein presentment shall always be held before the justices of the bench and determined there.

14. A free man shall not be amerced for a trivial offence except in accordance with the degree of the offence and for a grave offence in accordance with its gravity, yet saving his way of living; and a merchant in the same way, saving his stock-in-trade; and a villein other than one of our own shall be amerced in the same way, saving his means of livelihood; if he has fallen into our mercy: and none of the aforesaid amercements shall be imposed except by the oath of good and law-worthy men of the neighbourhood. Earls and barons shall not be amerced except by their peers, and only in accordance with the degree of the offence. No ecclesiastical person shall be amerced according to the amount of his ecclesiastical benefice but in accordance with his lay holding and in accordance with the degree of the offence.

15. No vill or individual shall be compelled to make bridges at river banks, except one who from of old is legally bound to do so.

16. No river bank shall henceforth be made a preserve, except those which were preserves in the time of king Henry, our grandfather, in the same places and for the same periods as they used to be in his day.

17. No sheriff, constable, coroners, or others of our bailiffs shall hold pleas of our crown.

18. If anyone holding a lay fief of us dies and our sheriff or bailiff shows our letters patent of summons for a debt that the deceased owed us, it shall be lawful for our sheriff or bailiff to attach and make a list of chattels of the deceased found upon the lay fief to the value of that debt under the supervision of law-worthy men, provided that none of the chattels shall be removed until the debt which is manifest has been paid to us in full; and the residue shall be left to the executors for carrying out the will of the deceased, saving to his wife and his children their reasonable shares.

19. No constable or his bailiff shall take the corn or other chattels of anyone who is not of the vill where the castle is situated unless he pays on the spot in cash for them or can delay payment by arrangement with the seller; if the seller is of that vill he shall pay within forty days.

20. No constable shall compel any knight to give money instead of castle-guard if he is willing to do it himself or through another good man, if for some good reason he cannot do it himself; and if we lead or send him on military service, he shall be excused guard in respect of the fief for which he did service in the army in proportion to the time that because of us he has been on service.

21. No sheriff, or bailiff of ours, or other person shall take anyone's horses or carts for transport work unless he pays for them at the old-established rates, namely at ten pence a day for a cart with two horses and fourteen pence a day for a cart with three horses. No demesne cart of any ecclesiastical person or knight or of any lady shall be taken by the aforesaid bailiffs. Neither we nor our bailiffs nor others will take, for castles or other works of ours, timber which is not ours, except with the agreement of him whose timber it is.

22. We will not hold for more than a year and a day the lands of those convicted of felony, and then the lands shall be handed over to the lords of the fiefs.

23. Henceforth all fish-weirs shall be cleared completely from the Thames and the Medway and throughout all England, except along the sea coast.

24. The writ called Praecipe shall not in future be issued to anyone in respect of any holding whereby a free man may lose his court.

25. Let there be one measure for wine throughout our kingdom, and one measure for ale, and one measure for corn, namely "the London quarter"; and one width for cloths whether dyed, russet or halberget, namely

two ells within the selvedges. Let it be the same with weights and measures.

26. Nothing shall be given in future for the writ of inquisition by him who seeks an inquisition of life or limbs: instead, it shall be granted free of charge and not refused.

27. If anyone holds of us by fee-farm, by socage, or by burgage, and holds land of another by knight service, we will not, by reason of that fee-farm, socage or burgage have the wardship of his heir or of land of his that is of the fief of the other; nor will we have custody of the fee-farm, socage, or burgage, unless such fee-farm owes knight service. We will not have custody of anyone's heir or land which he holds of another by knight service by reason of any petty serjeanty which he holds of us by the service of rendering to us knives or arrows or the like.

28. No bailiff shall in future put anyone to manifest trial or to oath upon his own bare word without reliable witnesses produced for this purpose.

29. No free man shall in future be arrested or imprisoned or disseised of his freehold, liberties or free customs, or outlawed or exiled or victimized in any other way, neither will we attack him or send anyone to attack him, except by the lawful judgment of his peers or by the law of the land. To no one will we sell, to no one will we refuse or delay right or justice.

30. All merchants, unless they have been publicly prohibited beforehand, shall be able to go out of and come into England safely and securely and stay and travel throughout England, as well by land as by water, for buying and selling by the ancient and right customs free from all evil tolls, except in time of war and if they are of the land that is at war with us. And if such are found in our land at the beginning of a war, they shall be attached without injury to their persons or goods, until we, or our chief justiciar, know how merchants of our land are treated who were found in the land at war with us when war broke out; and if ours are safe there, the others shall be safe in our land.

31. If anyone who holds of some escheat such as the honour of Wallingford, Boulogne, Nottingham, Lancaster, or of other escheats which are in our hands and are baronies dies, his heir shall give no other relief and do no other service to us than he would have done to the baron if that had been in the baron's hands; and we will hold it in the same manner in which the baron held it. Nor will we by reason of such a

barony or escheat have any escheat or wardship of any men of ours unless he who held the barony or escheat held in chief of us elsewhere.

32. No free man shall henceforth give or sell to anyone more of his
land than will leave enough for the full service due from the fief to be
rendered to the lord of the fief.

33. All patrons of abbeys who have charters of advowson of the kings
of England or ancient tenure or possession shall have the custody of them
during vacancies, as they ought to have and as is made clear above.

34. No one shall be arrested or imprisoned upon the appeal of a
woman for the death of anyone except her husband.

35. No county [court] shall in future be held more often than once a
month and where a greater interval has been customary let it be greater.
Nor shall any sheriff or bailiff make his tourn through the hundred save
twice a year (and then only in the due and accustomed place), that is to
say, once after Easter and again after Michaelmas. And view of
frankpledge shall be held then at the Michaelmas term without interference, that is to say, so that each has his liberties which he had and was
accustomed to have in the time of king Henry our grandfather or which
he has since acquired. View of frankpledge shall be held in this manner,
namely, that our peace be kept, that a tithing be kept full as it used to
be, and that the sheriff shall not look for opportunities for exactions but
be satisfied with what a sheriff used to get from holding his view in the
time of king Henry our grandfather.

36. It shall not in future be lawful for anyone to give land of his to
any religious house in such a way that he gets it back again as a tenant
of that house. Nor shall it be lawful for any religious house to receive
anyone's land to hand it back to him as a tenant. And if in future anyone does give land of his in this way to any religious house and he is convicted of it, his gift shall be utterly quashed and the land shall be forfeit
to the lord of the fief concerned.

37. Scutage shall be taken in future as it used to be taken in the time
of king Henry our grandfather. And let there be saved to archbishops,
bishops, abbots, priors, Templars, Hospitallers, earls, barons and all other
persons, ecclesiastical and secular, the liberties and free customs they had
previously. All these aforesaid customs and liberties which we have
granted to be observed in our kingdom as far as it pertains to us towards
our men, all of our kingdom, clerks as well as laymen, shall observe as
far as it pertains to them towards their men. In return for this grant and

gift of these liberties and of the other liberties contained in our charter on the liberties of the forest, the archbishops, bishops, abbots, priors, earls, barons, knights, freeholders and all of our realm have given us a fifteenth part of all their movables. We have also granted to them for us and our heirs that neither we nor our heirs will procure anything whereby the liberties contained in this charter shall be infringed or weakened; and if anything contrary to this is procured from anyone, it shall avail nothing and be held for nought. These being witness: the lord S. archbishop of Canterbury, E. of London, J. of Bath, P. of Winchester, H. of Lincoln, R. of Salisbury, B. of Rochester, W. of Worcester, J. of Ely, H. of Hereford, R. of Chichester and W. of Exeter, bishops; the abbot of St. Albans, the abbot of Bury St. Edmunds, the abbot of Battle, the abbot of Peterborough, the abbot of Reading, the abbot of Abingdon, the abbot of Malmesbury, the abbot of Winchcombe, the abbot of Hyde, the abbot of Chertsey, the abbot of Sherborne, the abbot of Cerne, the abbot of Abbotsbury, the abbot of Milton, the abbot of Selby, the abbot of Whitby, the abbot of Cirencester, H. de Burgh the justiciar, R. earl of Chester and Lincoln, W. earl of Salisbury, W. earl of Warenne, G. de Clare earl of Gloucester and Hertford, W. de Ferrers earl of Derby, W. de Mandeville earl of Essex, H. le Bigod earl of Norfolk, W. count of Aumale, H. earl of Hereford, John the constable of Chester, Robert de Ros, Robert fitz Walter, Robert de Vipont, William Brewer, Richard de Munfichet, Peter fitz Herbert, Matthew fitz Herbert, William de Aubeney, Robert Grelley, Reginald de Braose, John of Monmouth, John fitz Alan, Hugh de Mortimer, Walter de Beauchamp, William of St. John, Peter de Maulay, Brian de Lisle, Thomas of Moulton, Richard de Argentein, Geoffrey de Neville, William Mauduit, John de Balun. Given at Westminster on the eleventh day of February in the ninth year of our reign.

This translation is taken from Harry Rothwell, ed., *English Historical Documents 1189–1327* (New York: Oxford University Press, 1975), pp. 342–346.

DOCUMENT 4
Charter of the Forest, 1225

The first Charter of the Forest was issued in 1217 at the same time that the 1217 version of Magna Carta was issued. It represented an adap-

*tation of and expansion of those articles in Magna Carta 1215 dealing
with royal forest issues (44, 47, and 48). From 1217 on, Magna Carta
and the Charter of the Forest were always issued together.*

Henry by the grace of God, king of England, lord of Ireland, duke of Normandy, Aquitaine, and count of Anjou, to the archbishops, bishops, abbots, priors, earls, barons, justices, foresters, sheriffs, stewards, servants and to all his bailiffs and faithful subjects who shall look at the present charter, greeting. Know that we, out of reverence for God and for the salvation of our soul and the souls of our ancestors and successors, for the exaltation of holy church and the reform of our realm, have of our own spontaneous goodwill given and granted to the archbishops, bishops, earls, barons and all of our realm these liberties written below to be held in our kingdom of England for ever.

1. In the first place, all the forests which king Henry our grandfather made forest shall be viewed by good and law-worthy men, and if he made forest any wood that was not his demesne to the injury of him whose wood it was, it shall be disafforested. And if he made his own wood forest, it shall remain forest, saving common of pasture and other things in that forest to those who were accustomed to have them previously.

2. Men who live outside the forest need not henceforth come before our justices of the forest upon a general summons, unless they are impleaded or are sureties for any person or persons who are attached for forest offences.

3. All woods made forest by king Richard our uncle, or by king John our father, up to the time of our first coronation shall be immediately disafforested unless it be our demesne wood.

4. Archbishops, bishops, abbots, priors, earls, barons, knights and freeholders who have woods within forests shall have them as they had them at the time of the first coronation of king Henry our grandfather, so that they shall be quit forever in respect of all purprestures, wastes and assarts made in those woods between that time and the beginning of the second year of our coronation. And those who in future make waste, purpresture or assart in them without licence from us shall answer for wastes, purprestures and assarts.

5. Our regarders shall go through the forests making the regard as it

used to be made at the time of the first coronation of king Henry our grandfather, and not otherwise.

6. The inquest or view of the expeditating of dogs in the forest shall henceforth be made when the regard ought to be made, namely every third year, and then made by the view and testimony of law-worthy men and not otherwise. And he whose dog is then found not expeditated shall give as amercement three shillings, and in future no ox shall be seized for failure to expeditate. The manner, moreover, of expeditating by the assize shall generally be that three claws of the forefoot are to be cut off, but not the ball. Nor shall dogs henceforth be expeditated except in places where it was customary to expeditate them at the time of the first coronation of the aforesaid king Henry our grandfather.

7. No forester or beadle shall henceforth make *scotales* or levy sheaves of corn, or oats or other grain or lambs or piglets or make any other levy. And by the view and oath of twelve regarders when they make the regard as many foresters are to be set to keep the forests as shall seem to them reasonably sufficient for keeping them.

8. No swanimote shall henceforth be held in our kingdom except three times a year, namely a fortnight before the feast of St. Michael, when our agisters meet to agist our demesne woods, and about the feast of St. Martin, when our agisters ought to receive our pannage-dues; and at these two swanimotes foresters, verderers and agisters shall appear but no others shall be compelled to do so; and the third swanimote shall be held a fortnight before the feast of St. John the Baptist for the fawning of our beasts, and for holding this swanimote foresters and verderers shall come but others shall not be compelled to do so. And in addition every forty days throughout the year the foresters and verderers shall meet to view attachments of the forest both of the vert and of the venison on the presentment of those foresters and with the attached present. The aforesaid swanimotes however shall only be held in counties in which they were wont to be held.

9. Every free man shall agist his wood which he has in the forest as he wishes and have his pannage. We grant also that every free man can conduct his pigs through our demesne wood freely and without impediment to agist them in his own woods or anywhere else he wishes. And if the pigs of any free man shall spend one night in our forest he shall not on that account be so prosecuted that he loses anything of his own.

10. No one shall henceforth lose life or limb because of our venison,

but if anyone has been arrested and convicted of taking venison he shall be fined heavily if he has the means; but if he has not the means, he shall lie in our prison for a year and a day; and if after a year and a day he can find pledges he may leave prison; but if not, he shall abjure the realm of England.

11. Any archbishop, bishop, earl or baron whatever who passes through our forest on his way to us at our command shall be allowed to take one or two beasts under supervision of the forester, if he is to hand; but if not, let him have the horn blown, lest he seem to be doing it furtively. They shall be allowed to do the same as is aforesaid on their return journey.

12. Every free man may henceforth without being prosecuted make in his wood or in land he has in the forest a mill, a preserve, a pond, a marl-pit, a ditch, or arable outside the covert in arable land, on condition that it does not harm any neighbour.

13. Every free man shall have the eyries of hawks, sparrowhawks, falcons, eagles and herons in his woods, and likewise honey found in his woods.

14. No forester henceforth who is not a forester-in-fee rendering us a farm for his bailiwick may exact any chiminage in his bailiwick; but a forester-in-fee rendering us a farm for his bailiwick may exact chiminage, namely for a cart for half a year 2*d* and for the other half year 2*d*, and for a horse with a load for half a year 1/2*d* and for the other half year 1/2*d*, and only from those who come from outside his bailiwick as merchants with his permission into his bailiwick to buy wood, timber, bark or charcoal and take them elsewhere to sell where they wish; and from no other cart or any load shall chiminage be exacted, and chiminage shall only be exacted in places where it used to be exacted of old and ought to have been exacted. Those, on the other hand, who carry wood, bark, or charcoal on their backs for sale, although they get their living by it, shall not in future pay chiminage.

15. All who from the time of king Henry our grandfather up to our first coronation have been outlawed for a forest offence only shall be released from their outlawry without legal proceedings and shall find reliable pledges that they will not do wrong to us in the future in respect of our forest.

16. No castellan may hold forest pleas and be determined before him.

17. These liberties concerning the forests we have granted to every-

body, saving to archbishops, bishops, abbots, priors, earls, barons, knights, and other persons, ecclesiastical and secular, Templars and Hospitallers, the liberties and free customs in forests and outside, in warrens and other things, which they had previously. All these aforesaid customs and liberties which we have granted to be observed in our kingdom as far as it pertains to us towards our men, all of our kingdom shall observe as far as it pertains to them towards their men. In return for this grant and gift of these liberties and of the other liberties contained in our greater charter on other liberties, the archbishops, bishops, abbots, priors, earls, barons, knights, freeholders and all of our realm have given us a fifteenth part of all their movables. We have also granted to them for us and our heirs that neither we nor our heirs will procure anything whereby the liberties contained in this charter shall be infringed or weakened; and if anything contrary to this is procured from anyone, it shall avail nothing and be held for nought. These being witness [the list of witnesses is the same as in Magna Carta 1225]. Given at Westminster on the eleventh day of February in the ninth year of our reign.

This translation is taken from Harry Rothwell, ed., *English Historical Documents 1189–1327* (New York: Oxford University Press, 1975), pp. 347–349.

DOCUMENT 5
The Confirmation of the Charters, 1297

This document was issued by Edward I in 1297. Edward had engaged in a costly war and castle building in Wales early in his reign and then become involved in a long-drawn-out war in Scotland because as overlord of Scotland he claimed the right to determine who should be king in the event of a disputed succession. The Scots did not agree and in the long run Edward did not prove his point, although the issue had not been finally decided at his death in 1307. In the meantime, England and France had been preparing for a renewal of warfare over the English fiefs in France. Edward had requested an additional aid (money grant) from Parliament to allay his expenses, but it was not enough. Therefore he arbitrarily sought from a meeting of a few of his followers a grant of an eighth of movables to apply to all of his barons, lay and clerical alike. This grant brought strong protests from the greater barons on behalf of all. After attempts to collect the aid failed, Edward granted the document known as

the Confirmation of the Charters. It became the basis for the parliamen-
tary claim that no taxation could be assessed without the consent of Par-
liament.

1. Edward, by the grace of God king of England, lord of Ireland and
duke of Aqutaine, to all those who see or hear these present letters, greeting. Know that we, to the honour of God and of holy church and for the
benefit of our whole realm, have granted for us and our heirs that the
great charter of liberties and the forest charter which were made by common assent of all the realm in the time of king Henry, our father, be kept
in all their points without any impediment to their working. And we will
that these same charters be sent under our seal to our justices (to those
of the forest as well as to the others), to all sheriffs of counties, and to
all our other officials, and to all our cities throughout the land, together
with our writs, in which it shall be contained that they cause the aforesaid charters to be published and have it declared to the people that we
have granted they be kept in all their points; and to our justices, sheriffs, mayors and other officials, who have to administer under us and for
us the law of the land, to have these same charters allowed in all their
points in pleadings before them and in judgments—the great charter of
liberties, that is, as common law and the forest charter in accordance
with the assize of the forest—for the betterment of our people.

2. And we will that if any judgments are given henceforth contrary
to the points of the aforesaid charters by justices or by other officials of
ours who hold pleas before them contrary to the points of the charters,
they shall be undone and held for nought.

3. And we will that these same charters be sent under our seal to
cathedral churches throughout our realm and remain there, and be read
before the people twice a year.

4. And that archbishops and bishops pronounce sentences of greater
excommunication against all those who contravene the aforesaid charters (whether of their own doing or by assisting or advising) or infringe
or contravene any point of them. And that these sentences be pronounced and published twice a year by the aforesaid prelates. And if the
same prelates, the bishops, or any of them are negligent over making the
abovesaid denunciation, let them be reprimanded by the archbishops of
Canterbury and York for the time being, as is proper, and be compelled
to make this same denunciation in the form aforesaid.

5. And because some people of our realm fear that the aids and contributions they have furnished us with of their own granting and their goodwill before now for our wars and other needs in whatever way they were done could lead to bondage for them and their heirs because another time they might be found enrolled, and likewise the prises which have been taken throughout the realm by our officials in our name, we have granted for us and our heirs that henceforth we will not make a precedent of such aids, mises or prises for anything that may have been done or that could be found out from the roll or in any other way.

6. And we have likewise granted for us and our heirs to the archbishops, bishops, abbots, priors and other folk of holy church, and to the earls and barons and all the community of the land that for no need will we take such manner of aids, mises or prises from our realm henceforth except with the common assent of all the realm and for the common profit of the same realm, saving the ancient aids and prises due and accustomed.

7. And because by far the greater part of the community of the realm feel themselves greatly burdened by the maltote on wool, namely 40 shillings on each sack of wool, and have entreated us to be good enough to relieve them, we at their request have completely relieved them and have granted that we will not take this or any other in future without their common assent and their goodwill, saving for us and our heirs the custom on wool, skins and leathers granted earlier by the community of the aforesaid realm. In witness of which things we have had these our letters patent made. Given at Ghent [in the county of Flanders], the fifth day of November in the twenty-fifth year of our reign [1297].

This translation is taken from Harry Rothwell, ed., *English Historical Documents 1189–1327* (New York: Oxford University Press, 1975), pp. 485–486.

APPENDIX A:
THE CRUSADES AND CRUSADING STATES OF THE EAST

The Crusades were a series of military encounters between armies made up of contingents from various of the western Christian states of Europe and armies under the leadership of a Muslim commander whether he were a descendant of one of the Arabic dynasties (Abbasid or Fatimite) or was a Seljuk Turk. These Christian expeditions that took thousands of European warriors to the eastern Mediterranean began in the late eleventh century and continued until the late thirteenth century. There were later Crusades into the seventeenth century that followed the replacement of the Seljuk Turks by the Ottoman Turks. The Ottoman Turks overthrew the East Roman (Byzantine) Empire in the fifteenth century and expanded into the Balkan peninsula and up the Danube Valley, threatening central Europe.

We are concerned here with the earlier of these conflicts that covered the two hundred years from the late eleventh to the late thirteenth century. One of the most important causes was religious-political—the absorption of the Christian territories along the Syrian-Palestinian coastline into an expanding Arabic Muslim Empire by the middle of the seventh century. The occupation of this territory was at the expense of the East Roman or Byzantine Empire. Shortly afterward, Byzantine territory in Egypt and along the north African coast to the Atlantic Ocean would also become Muslim. Beginning in the early eighth century, Muslim armies crossed the Straits of Gibraltar, overthrew the Visigothic kingdom, and eventually controlled almost all of the Spanish peninsula. With the conquest of Spain, Islamic power controlled much (but never all) of the

Mediterranean Sea. At the same time, Islam advanced to the east, creating a land empire that stretched from the Mediterranean to the borders of India and beyond. Although this immense "empire" early began to break up into more regional political-religious powers called caliphates (Abbasid in Baghdad, Ommyiad in Cordova [Spain], and Fatimite in Egypt), it developed a common culture based on the Muslim religion, inheritance of the luxury trade between East and West, an advanced degree of learning and industrial skills, and a considerable amount of religious tolerance. This was a sophisticated culture with an appreciation for literary and visual arts far in advance of western Europe at the time.

As the Islamic world expanded, western Europe broke up into a number of Germanic states, the most important in the seventh century being the Lombard kingdom in Italy, the Visigothic kingdom in Spain, the Frankish kingdom in Gaul (modern France), and the various Anglo-Saxon kingdoms in Britain. These kingdoms had emerged in the breakup of the western Roman Empire, a breakup due largely to the inability of the empire to sustain the enormous military forces needed to protect a very long frontier in Europe. With the collapse of the empire, trade (both external and internal) declined, population decreased, and town life contracted and disappeared unless the town were important enough to justify the construction of defensive walls around it. Life in Europe seemed poor in comparison with the riches and splendor of the east.

After the eastern, southern, and far western shores of the Mediterranean had been conquered for Islam, communication between West and East gradually revived, encouraged by the general religious tolerance of the Muslims for Christians and Jews, subject to some restrictions. So pilgrims were allowed to travel to the holy places in western Asia, and in the late tenth and early eleventh centuries the flow of travelers increased significantly.

By the end of the tenth century, the new barbarian invasions of Europe (Viking in the north, Hungarian in the Danube Valley, and Saracen [Muslim] in the south) had been contained. With more stable conditions and possibly an improved climate, food production increased followed by an increase in population, and increased population led to an expansion of cultivation into areas that had been forested before this time and finally into marginal land. With the stable conditions and rapidly increasing population, there was a growth of towns and markets where surplus food could be sold, growing towns encouraged further trade, and by the eleventh century Europe had an expanding economy. These changes infected all levels of society with a land hunger that would make invitations to participate in adventures that promised wealth (in land or trade) attractive.

To such socioeconomic factors there was added a catalyst for expansion: religion. During the eleventh century, the Roman church was undergoing reform aimed at removing secular control of the Church. To this end, the papacy became the central motivator of reform designed to improve the education, morals, and administration of the clergy and to remove secular interference in church affairs, and reform that would encompass recognition of the leadership of the Roman papacy by the Greek church under the patriarch of Constantinople. An embassy sent to Constantinople (1054) to negotiate a compromise between the two positions ended in failure, the western representative (Cardinal Humbert) excommunicating the patriarch of Constantinople and the patriarch excommunicating the pope (Leo IX). Until this time there was not apparently any great concern about the breach between the two churches that had begun in the eighth century, when the popes concluded that they could not continue to obtain protection from the east emperor and sought protection from the Franks instead. Now with the formal breach, working for the reunion of the eastern and western churches became one of the tenets of the reform movement.

A number of unrelated events in the eleventh century provided the immediate background for the Crusades. The power of the Abbasid caliphate at Bagdad gradually declined and was replaced by the Seljuk Turks who had come out of the interior of Asia and been converted to Islam (the Muslim faith). The Seljuks continued conquering westward and in 1071 at the battle of Manazkert defeated the East Roman (Byzantine) army and thereafter held Asia Minor (Anatolia). From this time on, the Byzantine emperor sought allies to help recover this lost land since Asia Minor was a major recruiting ground for the Byzantine army and a major economic mainstay. Also in the eleventh century a number of rising maritime states in Italy—Pisa and Genoa in the northwest and Venice in the northeast—began to challenge the Muslim naval power and sought entry into the Muslim ports in north Africa and along the east Mediterranean seaboard. They were seeking the carrying trade for the luxury items that found their way from the far east to the Syrian and Egyptian ports by way of land caravan routes and by sea from the Indian

Ocean. Their ships became available for the increasing numbers of pilgrims and by the time of the First Crusade were available not only to supply Christians in the east but also to transport crusaders. And finally, it should be noted that, although the Seljuk Turks had suppressed the Abbasids, they had little experience in ruling a large state and tended to break up into quarreling groups that fought with the Fatimids of Egypt, who held the southern Syrian coastline where Jerusalem was located, or fought among themselves. The Seljuks' lack of cohesion under a single ruler would make the successes of the First Crusade possible.

In seeking help in recovering his provinces in Asia Minor, the Byzantine emperor Alexius I Comnenus (1081–1118) appealed to Pope Urban II in 1095 for mercenary troops. Instead of sending a contingent of mercenary troops to reinforce the Byzantine army, Urban at the Council of Clermont (in central France) in 1095 urged that the forces of western Christendom under papal leadership unite in bringing together the Eastern and Western churches and recovering the holy places from the infidel Turks. Pope Urban definitely held out the prospect of gaining land in the east, that "land of milk and honey."

In response to this appeal spread throughout western Europe by papal representatives and by popular preachers, a great deal of enthusiasm developed among both the warrior aristocracy and the peasantry. In fact, several peasant groups were organized before the actual armies were ready and generally headed up the Rhine River and down the Danube toward Constantinople. All of these peasant armies were lost along the way to Constantinople or in near Asia Minor itself.

The First Crusade (1096–99) broke up into four main groups. One came from northeast France (Flanders) and the lower Rhineland (Lorraine) and was under the leadership of Godfrey of Bouillon (duke of Lower Lorraine) and his brother, Baldwin of Flanders. This group took the Rhine-Danube route to Constantinople where the four contingents planned to meet. The second group came from the north-central part of France and was led by Robert, duke of Normandy (oldest son of William the Conqueror). These northern Normans traveled through eastern France, over the Alps into Italy where they joined with the third group, the Normans of Sicily under Bohemund, who was accompanied by his nephew Tancred. The fourth group of crusaders came from southwest France and was under the leadership of Raymond IV of the county of Toulouse. This group also traveled a southern route.

All four groups met in Constantinople where it was very difficult without a single leadership to come to terms with the emperor; it was almost impossible to supply four different armies. But eventually the crusaders crossed over into Asia Minor and owing to the lack of unity among the Turks enjoyed a number of successes (as well as great hardships)—successes that restored much of Asia Minor to Byzantine rule. As the crusading army came to the Syrian coastline, the army split, with one contingent under Baldwin headed eastward and succeeding in establishing the county of Edessa, the first of the crusader states. Along the coast, the next state established was the Principality of Antioch, the third was the Latin Kingdom of Jerusalem, and the fourth was between Antioch and Jerusalem, the county of Tripoli.

The establishment of the four Christian States of the Levant, the highpoint of the crusading movement, was made possible by the fervor and military expertise of the westerners, the disunity of the Turks, and the crusaders' ability to receive supplies by naval support from the Italians. There had been great rivalry among the crusaders to obtain the newly established states. Baldwin of Flanders and his followers had conquered Edessa and claimed the county as theirs. Bohemond of Taranto won out over Raymond of Toulouse in acquiring Antioch. Godfrey of Bouillon, who led the assault on Jerusalem, had been the strongest leader in keeping the crusade on course to capture the city. Jerusalem fell to the crusaders in June 1099; much of the population was massacred. Raymond of Toulouse finally got the county of Tripoli in 1109; Robert of Normandy returned home as did many, if not most, of the other crusaders—after all, most of the holy places were once again under Christian control.

Establishing four Christian states along the Syrian coastline was one thing, but keeping them was another. Almost immediately difficulties arose. The Turks learned from their defeats and began a slow consolidation of power. With the return of many crusaders to Europe, defense became increasingly difficult for the four Christian states, although they received significant help from the two religious military orders: the Knights of the Hospital of Saint John of Jerusalem, known as the Hospitallers, established in 1099; and the Poor Knights of Christ and of the Temple of Solomon, established in about 1119, known as the Knights Templar. Although fresh appeals for help were sent out from time to time, no major action was taken before the fall of Edessa in 1144.

The Second Crusade (1147–49) followed. There were two main contingents in this effort: a German one under the leadership of the emperor Conrad III and a French one under the leadership of King Louis VII, accompanied by his wife Eleanor of Aquitaine. This crusade accomplished nothing in the face of the reorganized Turkish resistance, although it was important in future relations between Louis VII and his queen.

After the Second Crusade, interest in Europe died down in spite of further appeals for help. In the meantime, further Turkish consolidation took place. The previous consolidation had involved the Turkish forces in the north. Concentration now was on the Muslim Fatimite caliphate headquartered in Egypt, which controlled the southern frontier of the Latin Kingdom of Jerusalem; this caliphate was now in decline. The move toward Turkish control came to be under the leadership of a man by the name of Saladin who abolished the Fatimite caliphate in 1171. He also gained control of the northern area on the death of Nur al-Din in 1174. Saladin then spent the next twelve years overcoming rivals to his position but was then ready to move against the remaining Christian territory in what had already been called a jihad (holy war).

Jerusalem fell to the Turks in 1187, and much of the remaining Christian land fell to Saladin by 1189. It was the fall of Jerusalem that led to the Third Crusade (1189–92), the best known of the Crusades. It was to have consisted of three contingents: a German one under the command of the elderly German Roman emperor, Frederick I Barbarossa; a French contingent under the command of King Philip II Augustus; and an English one under the command of King Richard I the Lionheart. The German contingent went by land and got as far as eastern Asia Minor where their leader, Frederick I, drowned in a river accident; the Germans went home. The French and English armies went separately but were in close contact along the way, mostly by sea. But long before reaching Acre (the port at which the assault was aimed), relations between the two kings had become very strained, and as soon as Acre fell to the combined Christian armies, Philip pled illness and went home. Richard, who had been responsible for most of the military success so far, remained in the east and continued to strive toward Jerusalem.

Although Richard and Saladin both enjoyed military successes and failures, Richard did not succeed in taking Jerusalem. However, he was able to obtain entry into Jerusalem for Christian pilgrims in 1192 before returning home. The Christians retained only a short strip of coastline between Jaffa and Tyre. Richard was captured by Christians in the German Roman Empire on his way back and held for ransom; although the event is important in history and legend, it is not directly related to the Crusades.

Innocent III had become pope in 1198, one of the strongest medieval popes and extremely ambitious to extend the power of the papacy. Sponsoring a crusade was important to him, and at his urging a number of knights, mostly French, took the cross. However, Innocent III did not have much control over the following events. The crusaders sent representatives to Venice to arrange transportation to Egypt, the goal of this crusade, for it was assumed that it would be easy to launch an attack against Jerusalem from Egypt as a base. Egypt would be the goal of all later Crusades—none of them succeeded in using it as a launching place. The representatives of the leaders of the Fourth Crusade came to an agreement with the Venetians. The contract called for the Venetians to provide transport for over thirty thousand crusaders.

When the crusaders assembled at Venice in 1202, it was found that only about one-third of the anticipated number had arrived. The Venetians had invested heavily in providing ships to transport the expected number of men and could not afford to reduce the price. It was suggested, however, that part of the price could be forgiven if the crusaders would undertake the conquest of the Christian Adriatic city of Zara (modern Zadar) to add to the growing Venetian naval empire. Since there was no other way to pay to get to the east, the crusaders took the town. Innocent III was faced with an accomplished fact, and although he condemned the taking of a Christian town, he imposed no spiritual penalties. Since it was already late in the fall, the crusaders had to wait for another sailing season before starting further.

Enthusiasm for the crusade had been fading for some time, and there were numerous defections; perhaps some less difficult goal could be substituted for Egypt. The earlier appeal of a pretender to the Byzantine (East Roman) throne, Prince Alexios, son of deposed Emperor Isaac II, was now recalled. Restoring Alexios to his throne would provide the crusaders with a powerful ally for their anticipated attack on Egypt. And so the Fourth Crusade was diverted to Constantinople where the Byzantine people did not receive Alexios with joy but resisted every effort of the crusaders to introduce him into the city. Eventually there seemed to be no recourse except to take the city by force, but before that action was taken, the Venetians and the crusaders came to an agreement about how the territory of the empire should be divided. The crusaders did take the city, looted it of much of its wealth, and founded what is called the Latin Empire of Constantinople (1204–61). The Byzantine Empire would be reestablished in 1261 with the aid of Venice's rival, Genoa, but the empire, which was already declining in 1204, was now very weak and would barely hold out against the Ottoman Turks until 1453.

There were other Crusades in the thirteenth century. One involved Frederick II of the German Roman Empire and Sicily, who under excommunication for delaying to launch a promised crusade, now in 1228 led a crusading army to Palestine. The sultan offered to negotiate, and a treaty was signed whereby the Muslims surrendered Jerusalem, Bethlehem, Nazareth, part of Sidon, and Toron to the crusaders; Frederick had himself crowned king of Jerusalem—for which he was excommunicated again.

With the arrival of several additional crusading armies, Jerusalem remained under Christian control until 1244 when it was recaptured by Muslims. It would remain Muslim until the twentieth century, although a few Christian outposts on the coast, including Acre, would remain under Christian control until 1291 when the presence of crusaders in the Near East came to an end.

There would be two further Crusades led by king Louis IX (St. Louis) of France, one in 1248–54, which ultimately accomplished nothing, and one in 1270 on which the king died while laying siege to Tunis in Tunisia. Although these later Crusades had important results for the internal organization of France and England (for Prince Edward of England joined the crusade after the death of Louis), the remaining Christian lands in the east were already doomed. It was remarkable that they lasted as long as they did in a totally alien environment.

APPENDIX B:
THE MEDIEVAL TRIAL
BY ORDEAL

Medieval trials by ordeal were often referred to as judgments of God (*iudicia dei*) inasmuch as the rationale behind this practice was to submit the judicial decision at issue to the intervention of God on the side of truth. The concept—appeal to a higher authority—was not confined to western Europe in the Middle Ages but is a practice found in many places at very different times. However, the specific trial by ordeal that is of concern here is the form that seems to be associated with the Germanic invaders of the Roman Empire as a heritage from their pagan past. At any rate, the first appearance of the trial by hot water (where the hand was plunged into a cauldron of hot water) appears in the first issue of laws for the Franks in the very early sixth century (about 510) when the Franks had only recently accepted Christianity. It was the combination of laws issued by and enforced by kings and the acceptance of a role in the administration of ordeals by the Church that accounts for the use of the ordeal in Europe from the sixth to the early thirteenth century, and even thereafter in areas of weak central authority or in special cases such as in the witchcraft trials between the fifteenth and eighteenth centuries.

The emergence of the ordeal in Europe goes back to a time when the state was weak or nonexistent and the peace and security of individuals depended on belonging to a strong family or other associated group. Protection of individual members relied on the threat of the blood-feud or retaliation, the taking of an eye for an eye. Unrestricted use of the blood-feud meant unrelenting warfare and social chaos unless one individual achieved such a reputation for wisdom that he could act as an arbiter between the contending parties. Partly as a result of natural evolution among the loosely organized Germanic peoples themselves and partly as a result of the influence of the political institutions of the Roman Empire with which the Germanic peoples had extensive contacts from the second century B.C.E. on, the leadership of the various groups began to move in the direction of kingship. For trade and diplomatic contacts, the Romans found it easier to deal with one chieftain rather than with the heads of many family groups and encouraged the emergence of a single figure with whom to negotiate, whether his functions were primarily those of a judge or a military leader, or some combination of the two. The ordeal emerges only when the organization of the group is sufficiently developed to provide a court before which complaints can be brought and with sufficient prestige to expect its decisions to be honored.

In the numerous law codes issued in the early Germanic kingdoms (about 500–800), references to the ordeal are few, but those few are so casual as to imply an institution so well known as not needing description. Sometimes the ordeal is limited to the nonfree, as among the Lombards, and sometimes, as in the case of the Visigoths, it is replaced by the use of torture for the unfree. In both cases—the Lombards in Italy and the Visigoths in Spain—settlement was in an area where Roman law influences were strong. The use of the ordeal in Roman law had disappeared centuries before contact between the Roman state and the Germans; it was unknown in the Roman law of the empire, although torture was used especially in the case of lesser persons or slaves. Customs in the more northerly Germanic kingdoms were more purely Germanic, including the use of the ordeal.

Trial by ordeal was never the most used method of proof in early medieval law. The customary proof—in what we would call both criminal and civil suits—was by compurgation. Compurgation was proof by oathtaking. The use of oathtaking was normally effective because social groups were small and men of the community tended to know what was going on around them. The role of the court was to determine which of the parties, or both, should provide proof, what the mode of that proof should be, and how strong it should be. The factors to be considered in making these decisions were first, the status and reputation of the party (whether accuser or defendant), and second, the seriousness of the accusation. Persons of very high status such as the king or pope, could accuse or defend by their own oath alone. Other high-ranking individuals were allowed to take oath by themselves supported by an additional number of oathhelpers, depending on rank and the seriousness of the case.

Persons of lesser rank or poor reputation had to take oath themselves plus an even larger number of oathhelpers. Persons of servile status were represented by their lords (only the free could be oathhelpers). If the lord refused, guilt was established, and punishment (usually monetary compensation but sometimes death) was exacted. The lord of the slave normally responded in accordance with the value of his slave.

Compurgation was effective because it was a highly regulated and ritualized procedure relying on close cooperation between secular and religious authorities. The rituals were very formal, and it was important that the oathhelpers respond strictly according to a formula—any hesitation to take the oath or any mistake in stating the oath meant loss of the suit. In highly formal procedures in circumstances where the objects on which the oath was taken had been blessed by the priest, an oathhelper needed to be confident in the party for whom he was taking oath. For the oathhelper was not a witness—if there had been witnesses to the act it would not have been necessary to resort to compurgation; the oathhelper was swearing to the value of his party's oath. Much depended on an individual's standing in the community and the strength of the kin group or the lordship to which he belonged. The man without family or lord would not have access to the very large number of oathhelpers needed in very serious cases.

The ordeal was a fallback mode of proof. It was often the accepted mode of proof in the case of slaves, and in the case of someone who could not produce the required number of oathhelpers or who failed the proof by compurgation, that individual would be sent to the ordeal or might ask for the ordeal to prove his innocence. Many different forms of ordeal were developed in the various states of Europe, but in England only three were used by the Anglo-Saxons: the ordeals of hot water, cold water, and hot iron. To these, the Normans of William I added trial by combat. The most explicit description of the various Anglo-Saxon ordeals is dated from the reign of King Athelstan (925–939). For three days before the ordeal, the person being sent to the ordeal was to eat only bread, water, salt, and herbs, and attend mass each day. The ordeals were to be carried out in a church where the fire for the iron or hot water ordeal had been lighted in the presence of the accused and the priest. When the fire was ready, two men from each of the parties to the suit went into the church to determine that the fire was as hot as it should be. Then an equal number of men (up to twelve) from each party entered and one-half stood along each side of the church where the ordeal was being administered. And "all these shall be fasting and shall have abstained from their wives during the night; and the mass-priest shall sprinkle holy water over them all, and each of them shall taste the holy water. And the mass-priest shall give them all the book and the symbol of Christ's cross to kiss. And no one shall continue to make up the fire after the consecration has begun, but the iron shall lie upon the embers" until the conclusion of the ritual (Athelstan II, 23, in Attenborough, p. 139). The accused then took up the iron and carried it for nine feet after which his hand was bound up. After three days it was inspected by the priest to ascertain whether it had become inflamed or remained clean; the priest declared the result of his inspection. If the accused had been sentenced to a single ordeal, the iron to be carried weighed one pound; if the sentence was a triple ordeal, the iron weighed three pounds.

If the ordeal was by hot water, the same procedure was involved but a cauldron of water was placed on the fire and brought to a boil in the presence of the accused and the priest. After that, two men from each party entered and observed that the water was ready and thereafter an equal number of men from each party (up to twelve) entered and took their places on each side of the church to observe the ordeal. The priest then went through his ritual. Afterward, if the trial was by the single ordeal, the accused plunged his hand up to his wrist in the water and removed a stone from the bottom of the cauldron; if it was the triple ordeal, he plunged his arm in up to the elbow. Afterward the wound was bound up and the decision as to the result followed that observed in the case of the hot iron (Athelstan II, in Attenborough, pp. 171–173). If the trial was by cold water, much the same above ritual was observed. However, a pit was dug in the church and filled with water, the accused was bound hand and foot, a rope was attached to him, and he was thrown into the water. If the water received him, he was innocent; if it rejected him, he was guilty. To be innocent, he had to sink to a depth of one and one-half ells (about four and a half feet) as measured on the rope. He was then pulled out (Athelstan II, 23, nos. 1 and 2, Attenborough, pp. 139–141).

In Norman England the favored ordeals were the hot iron and battle. The Angevins seem to have preferred the cold water ordeal to the hot iron, perhaps because the result was instantaneous and not subject to the priest's interpretation of whether or not the wound was clean.

The ordeal by battle differed considerably from the other ordeals. It first appeared among the Lombards as the preferred ordeal for freemen should it be necessary to resort to the ordeal when other means of proof had failed (witnesses, documents, compurgation). However, it is clear that by the time of King Liutprand (712–744), the king had lost confidence in the likelihood that the trial by battle (the *camfio* in the Lombard laws) would provide justice, but Liutprand continues that "on account of the customs of the Lombards we are unable to abolish this law" (Liutprand 71 and 118 in Drew, pp. 174 and 195).

Trial by battle seems to have been the preferred ordeal in William I's Normandy in the case of disputes over property, although William's laws for England provided that in the event of a dispute over property between an Englishman and a Norman, the English might choose the ordeal instead of trial by battle. In the past, trial by battle could be interpreted as various forms of battle between two opponents—on foot with battle axes, swords, or other weapon, or on horseback with lance and sword. In the eleventh century, a Frenchman would likely expect the combat to be between two horsemen since that was the kind of combat that the warrior class who participated in the conquest of England expected. The Englishman, even if a professional warrior, did not fight on horseback. But social change was taking place rapidly in twelfth-century England, and not every landholder became a horse warrior. Henry II (1154–89) therefore had little trouble in getting the landed classes, whether English or French by descent, to accept a recognition jury made up of landed neighbors in place of ordeal (usually cold water by this time) or trial by battle. However, trial by battle did not disappear with proof by ordeal after the prohibition of ordeals in the decrees of the Lateran Council of 1215. It continued in occasional use but as a special privilege of aristocratic families. It did not finally disappear until the legal reforms of the early nineteenth century.

William the Conqueror's introduction of trial by battle into England caused a curious alteration in the nature of the ordeal. The usual ordeals (hot or cold water, hot iron) were unitary proofs—that is, only one party was put to the proof, usually the defendant but not necessarily. In trial by battle, both parties, in effect, were put to the proof, for both parties (or their representatives) fought until one was killed or otherwise completely overcome. So the better fighter (whether the party himself or his or her champion) had the advantage, and a miracle from God was unlikely to influence the outcome.

Henry II's legal reforms eliminated the use of ordeals in civil suits in the common law courts (that is, the royal courts). In the case of criminal suits, Henry's reforms had the effect of substituting the presentment or indictment jury for the personal appeal that had hitherto been necessary in order to get a suspected criminal before the court. But once an individual had been indicted, the form of trial remained the same: the ordeal. Henry's reforms as carried out by himself and by his sons Richard and John did not look beyond the use of the ordeal to determine innocence or guilt in criminal suits, although in the case of notorious offenders they were required to leave the realm even if they "passed" the ordeal. At any rate, as far as England was concerned, no one in 1215 seems to have contemplated doing away with the ordeal and replacing it with a trial jury. However, responding to the decree of the Lateran Council of 1215, which outlawed the participation of the clergy in the ordeal, the regency government under Henry III forbade the practice in the common law courts in 1219. The government had nothing with which it could immediately replace it, and it would be many years and much experimentation before the modern trial jury was developed.

There had always been some skepticism in both secular and ecclesiastical quarters about the reliability of the answers given by the ordeal in specific cases and, in England at least, other means had been devised for use in noncriminal cases. But the move against any use of the ordeal does not seem to have come primarily from secular sources, but from the intellectuals and the canon lawyers. Certainly not all churchmen embraced the move since organizing and participating in ordeals represented a considerable portion of the Church's judicial power (and some income from fees). From the canon lawyer's standpoint, there was inadequate scriptural basis for the ordeal, and from the theological standpoint, God could not be manipulated into performing miracles at the behest of the court. Innocent III (1198–1216) was both a canon lawyer and a theologian, and he was also a very active pontiff. The Fourth Lateran Council met in 1215 with his agenda before it. Participation in ordeals by the clergy was prohibited, and the Church never went back on this position. The use of torture in canon law courts, especially by the Inquisition, is another story entirely.

GLOSSARY

Abbot: The head of a monastery usually elected by the resident monks who lived in common according to a rule (Latin: *regula*); hence they are called the regular clergy in contrast with the secular clergy who live and work in the world.

Advowson: The right to present (name) a cleric to an endowed church position, for example, a priest or prior.

Afforest: To declare a wooded area to be a forest, that is, a hunting preserve as, for example, to be preserved for the king's hunt. To disafforest—to remove from the king's preserve.

Agisters: Inspectors of a forest, especially of a royal forest.

Aid: (1) An English feudal term, referring to regular payments that could be demanded by a lord from his men. The feudal aids were three: a payment on the knighting of the lord's eldest son, on the marriage of his eldest daughter, and a contribution to ransom if the lord were captured in battle.

Aid: (2) A term that came into use as the growth of a money economy forced the English kings into making requests for additional aids—that is, payments in addition to the regular feudal aids. For additional aids, custom required that consent be obtained.

Aldermen: A name by which the members of a medieval town's elected council (the town council) were called.

Amerce: To assess a fine for breach of a rule.

Appanage: A large fief bestowed upon a younger son of the royal family. In this volume the term applies to France. As the great fiefs were acquired by the French crown, they were bestowed as appanages on second sons. Poitou, acquired from England, was bestowed by Louis IX on his younger brother Alphonse. Later, the duchy of Burgundy was used in the same way. The use of appanages could create a danger when the holder tried to become independent.

Appeal: Before the development of the presentment (indictment) jury, the way to bring a criminal to court was to appeal him (that is, formally charge him) before the court. Appeal remained an alternative means of getting a case of injury or damages before the court after the development of the presentment jury.

Arian Christianity: A schismatic form of Christianity that developed in the early fourth century. It differed from orthodox Christianity in not recognizing the three members of the Trinity as equally God. It was important because many of the Germanic barbarians who invaded the Roman Empire had been converted to Arian Christianity. It had died out by the end of the seventh century.

Assart: To bring under cultivation land that had previously been waste or part of a forest. It was partly the result of and partly the cause of the population explosion of the eleventh through thirteenth centuries.

Assizes: A term with many legal uses. It can refer to the holding of a regular common law court; to a pronouncement of legal rules as in the Assize of Clarendon; or to a legal writ obtained to institute a case in a royal court, as in the possessory assizes.

Attach: A legal term. In case of an unpaid debt, the creditor might "attach" (that is, designate) enough of his debtor's chattels (movable property) to clear the debt. Items so attached could not be disposed of until the debt had been paid. Or, in the case of a forest offense, a man might be attached (designated by a forester) to appear before a forest court.

Bailiff: A minor officer serving as a lord's representative.

Baron: A very common word having many meanings. In the early medieval period it could be used to refer to any free man, but by the eleventh century it had come to refer to a member of the landholding class. By the late Middle Ages, it had become the title of the lowest ranking member of the nobility in England.

Bull: Originally the lead seal attached to a document to authenticate it. In this volume refers to a papal document declaring Rome's position on a controversy. Papal bulls are known by their first one or two words.

Burg (burh): A term used to denote the special fortified places that Alfred of Wessex and his successors built. They were intended to provide refuge from the Danes as well as to hold garrisons for protection. In the long run, they became the nuclei of towns that grew in response to the revival of trade.

Burgage tenure: A type of landholding that came to be associated with towns (burgs, therefore burgage tenure, and the townsmen were called burgers, burgesses). Burgage tenure differed from feudal tenure in that the tenure was held for an annual fee and the holder could mortgage or sell his property.

Canonize: A procedure in the Roman Catholic Church whereby an individual is recognized as a saint. By the eleventh and twelfth centuries, each case was carefully investigated by the papal court before canonization was declared.

Cardinals: Priests and deacons who were assigned to churches in the Patrimony of St. Peter, the territory in which the city of Rome is located. The College of Cardinals was utilized by the eleventh-century reformers as a means of providing election of the pope without secular interference.

Carucage: A tax used in the twelfth century assessed according to the number of plow-teams used on the land. It gradually disappeared in favor of other means of raising money that assessed movables.

Castle-guard: A kind of service that a lord might demand in return for his granting a fief. Generally speaking, the holder of a fief was expected to do either knight service or castle-guard, not both.

Cathars: A term that refers to the heretics of southern France in Languedoc against whom Innocent III preached a crusade in the early thirteenth century. The Cathars believed in a dualistic system in which the powers of good and evil were in conflict, where the life of the spirit was good and the life of the flesh was evil. The Albigensian Crusade and the later Inquisition ended this heresy.

Celibacy: An eleventh-century requirement of the clergy, that is, that they not be married. More loosely, the celibate individual is one who does not engage in sexual relations.

Chancery: The writing office of the English king's household presided over by the chancellor.

Chattels: Movable property, not landed property. Taxation in medieval England shifted from taxes on land to taxes on movables.

Cheminage: A road-tax charged outsiders who came into the king's forest to purchase timber, bark, or charcoal and carry it out on horseback or in a cart. No charge was made if a man carried his purchases out on his back.

Chief justiciar: A royal justice who had been appointed by the king to head the English justice system. He also acted as regent in the absence of the king and was the most powerful of the king's men. Frequently, this official appears as simply "justiciar," but he is called "chief justiciar" in this work to distinguish him from all other royal justices, also called "justiciars."

Cinque Ports: Five ports along the southern shore of Wessex that from the time of Alfred were expected to provide naval service in case of need. These towns came to have a town organization at an early time, and their barons (leading men) were consulted from time to time on matters concerning them.

Clerks: A very loose term referring to anyone who could read and write (and was therefore assumed to be a member of the clergy).

Common pleas: One of the three royal courts that developed in England in the twelfth and thirteenth centuries. It heard cases involving the commons, that is, cases that did not involve royal interest.

Communal movement: A movement that was strongest in northern Italy where towns remained active trading centers throughout the early Middle Ages. By the eleventh century, they were strong enough to demand and receive from the emperor Frederick I the right of virtual self-government. This right was obtained by the inhabitants establishing themselves as a commune and working together for their liberties. The communal movement was also strong in the Low Countries and the Rhineland, but it did not have much influence in England where it was opposed by the kings who preferred to negotiate with the towns for specific rights (in return for money grants) and, in the thirteenth century, preferred to invite the townsmen to send representatives to meetings of Parliament.

Community of the land: A political concept that developed in the late twelfth and early thirteenth centuries. The idea grew first on the Continent where towns sought to establish themselves as communes—the communal interest was a community interest. In England, the idea of common interest was expressed in the term *community of the realm*, or *community of the land*. In practical application, the term *Commons* developed to describe that part of Parliament that contrasted with the "Lords."

Composition: In early medieval law, a term used to apply to the compensation assessed by a court that had to be paid to an injured individual or family.

Compurgation: An early medieval method of proof that the court could demand of an individual of high rank or good reputation. In proof by compurgation, the accused had to offer his own oath (taken on some sacred object) and present the number of additional oath-helpers assigned by the court. The oathhelpers were not swearing to the accused's innocence; they were swearing that his oath was a good one.

Constable: A lesser police officer who served the court.

Contumacious: Guilty of rebellion against one's lord. The penalty was loss of one's property.

Corn: Specifically, wheat but a term used loosely to refer to any grain. (The American grain "corn" was not known.)

Coroner: An unpaid elected official of good reputation in the community (county) who helped prepare for the criminal jurisdiction of the county court. He held inquests over violent or other unusual deaths, and over other acts of violence such as rape or assault; he otherwise prepared for the visit of a royal justice.

County court: Successor to the Anglo-Saxon public shire court. It was the basic court in Norman and Angevin England and, when presided over by a royal justice, became a royal court where the common law was applied.

Courtier: One who lived by invitation at the king's court at the king's expense.

Covert: A thicket providing shelter for game.

Cross-bowmen: The professional bowmen of the twelfth and thirteenth centuries; the backbone of the infantry of this time. Superceded in the English army by the longbowmen of the fourteenth and fifteenth centuries.

Customary law: Unwritten law, custom of the community.

Danelaw: The area in England settled by Danes and Norsemen. It lay to the north and east of a line running from London to Chester.

Darrein presentment: One of the possessory assizes. A writ to determine who last presented (named) a cleric to a vacant position, that is, who held advowson. Used in connection with private endowments of a church or office, usually a lesser person, for example, a priest or prior.

Demesne (also domain): Land retained by a lord to maintain himself, his family, and other dependents.

Dialectic method: A method of argument developed in the twelfth century that relied on logic, set contradictory statements posed against one another, and argued logically to a reconciliation of the differences.

Discreet: To be of good reputation (sometimes lawful and discreet).

Disparagement: In the case of marriage, to be married to someone of lesser status.

Disseise: To deprive of possession (seisin).

Distrain: To seize something valuable in order to force compliance with a demand.

Distress: To cause inconvenience.

Domain: *See* Demesne.

Dower: One-third of a widow's deceased husband's property; not to be confused with dowry.

Dynasty: The family of a line of rulers.

Ell: A measure of cloth, approximately one yard.

Endowment: A gift of property the income from which supports someone or something.

Enfeoffment: The grant (sometimes called a fief) created by a lord when he bestowed property on a loyal follower (sometimes called a vassal).

Enroll: Various bureaus of the English government began to keep records by enrolling copies of documents. The enrollments were on long sheets of parchment which were then rolled up, creating rolls.

Escheat: In general, any grant of land without an heir escheated (went back) to the lord who made the grant. In particular, it applied to large baronies in England in frontier areas where the power of the lord was greater than normal because of his responsibility for defense of the area. When one of these escheated to the crown, it was called an escheat (cf. Wallingford), a particular use of the word.

Estover of common: A provision giving a widow reasonable maintenance from her husband's estate until her dower (one-third of his landed property) was turned over to her.

Exactions: Demands by a lord for goods or services beyond those customary.

Excommunicate: An ecclesiastical penalty that cut an individual off from communion with the Church. To die excommunicate was to die without hope of salvation.

Expeditate: A method of maiming dogs owned by men whose holdings were surrounded by a royal forest, done so that the dogs could not chase the deer or other animals protected for the king's hunt. The method of expeditating was to remove three claws of the front feet but not the ball of the foot. The king's regarders (representatives) were to check the dogs.

Eyre: From the Latin *iter* (journey). Refers to the travel circuits of the royal justices to preside over the county courts, thus converting them into royal courts where the common law applied.

Eyries: Broods (families) of birds of prey (falcons, hawks, sparrowhawks, eagles, herons).

Fair: An organized place for buying and selling by professional merchants. Usually created by royal license.

Falcons (also hawks and sparrowhawks): Raptor birds (birds of prey) used for hunting.

Farm: To pay an agreed price to collect the revenues of a certain place. The sheriff "farmed" the royal lands located in his county.

Fealty: Loyalty. A man owed fealty to his lord.

Fee-farm: A free holding that did not owe knight service. Other free holdings (tenures) that did not owe knight service were socage, burgage, and petty serjeanty (see individual entries).

Felony: A serious criminal act that could be tried in a royal court; an act that broke the "king's peace."

Feudal incidents: Irregular assessments that developed in medieval England against a landholding (a fief) that contributed to a lord's income. *See also* Marriage; Relief; Ward. Irregular incidents contrast with feudal aids, the regular payments; *see also* Aid.

Fidelis: A loyal follower of a lord, the relationship created by an oath of loyalty (homage).

Fief: In England, an inheritable property, usually land (but could be other property as in money fief), held by a man from his lord. Services and payments were owed.

Fifteenth part of movables: A form of taxation. By the thirteenth century, the kings of England had shifted their taxation from types assessed against land to types assessed against movables; thus, they were able to tap the wealth of those men who did not hold land.

Fine: A payment made to retain possession of something or to "buy" an office.

Fish-weirs: Fish traps set across rivers to catch fish and thus a hindrance to navigation.

Forest: A wooded area where hunting rights were reserved. *See also* Afforest.

Forester: An officer who patrolled a forest. The head forester presided over courts trying breaches of the forest law.

Forfeit: To give up possession of.

Franchise: An exclusive right to do something purchased from the crown.

Frankpledge: A means of controlling crime in the countryside. From adolescence on, all men who did not have a lord were assigned to tithing groups (groups of ten), the members of which were mutually responsible for the behavior of the others. The sheriff was responsible for holding the view of frankpledge in the hundreds.

Fyrd: A military unit made up of all freemen in Anglo-Saxon England who were not professional soldiers (thegns). The Normans took over this institution, but changes in medieval warfare reduced its significance.

Good men of the neighborhood: Responsible men utilized to attend the county court in many different capacities.

Guardian: The adult individual appointed to look out for a ward during his minority (i.e., until he came of legal age [Magna Carta said twenty-one, but this was not so in all circumstances]) and could manage his inheritance. Mothers could be guardians unless they remarried.

Habeas corpus: A right that parliamentarians of the seventeenth century claimed was guaranteed by Magna Carta. It was a later concept that a person could not be held in jail indefinitely without a formal charge being brought. It was foreshadowed by Magna Carta 1225, Article 29.

Halberget: Perhaps a cloth to be worn under a hauberk (mail vest).

Hauberk (of mail): The upper part of the chain mail armor in use at this time.

Hold in chief: To hold land directly from the king and to owe knight service for the right of holding that land.

Holding: A general term referring to a particular piece of land or other valuable property held by someone of any free status from a lord.

Homage: The ceremony of swearing loyalty to a lord.

Hospitallers: Members of the crusading order known as the Knights of the Hospital of Saint John of Jerusalem. They offered refuges for travelers and the sick.

Hostage: To hold someone or something as a hostage (quasi-prisoner) to insure loyalty or service from an individual.

Hundred: The local unit of government in medieval England; called wapentake in the Danelaw.

Husbandry: The exercise of a rural occupation related to cultivation of the soil.

Impleaded: To have a suit (plea) brought against oneself.

Incident: *See* Feudal incidents.

Indict: A legal term. A presentment jury presented or indicted a person for a crime for which he was later tried.

Inheritance: The widow's right to retain property she had inherited (usually from her family) and to pass it to her heirs. Compare the widow's other inheritance rights: marriage portion (from her family at the time of marriage) and dower (one-third of her husband's property). Widows could be very powerful when all their property rights were considered, or very valuable if their remarriage were controlled by a lord, especially the king.

Inquest: A judicial procedure for the gathering of information. The men of the community are brought together, placed on oath, and asked questions. This procedure was adapted for use as the presentment jury in the criminal jurisdiction of the royal courts.

Install: A formal process of placing someone in an office.

Interdict: An ecclesiastical penalty applied to a district, such as a kingdom, during which most church services could not be held.

Intestate: To die without having made provision for the disposition of one's properties. In the twelfth and thirteenth centuries, the term applied only to movable properties since the descent of land was governed not by a testament (will) but by customary rules.

Invest: A formal procedure conveying certain rights and privileges upon an individual.

Itinerant justices: Royal justices (justiciars) sent out on circuit (*iter*) to preside over the county courts, which thereby became royal courts.

Justices of the forest: Special justices who heard suits involving breaches of the forest law.

Justiciar: A title applied to any of the royal justices. *See also* Chief justiciar.

Knight service: *See* Service (knight).

Knight's fee: A unit of land (fief) held in return for the military service of one knight.

Knights Templar: Members of the crusading order of the Poor Knights of Christ and of the Temple of Solomon. They offered important banking services.

Law merchant: A body of law developed in the eleventh and twelfth centuries to serve the needs of a new merchant class. It was essentially an international law.

Lay fief: A property held for secular rather than spiritual services.

Lay holding: *See* Lay fief.

Lay investiture: A practice condemned by the church reformers (Gregorians) of the eleventh century. Church officers (archbishops and bishops) were selected by the lord of the land in which the church was situated, and the lord formally bestowed upon the officer the symbols (tokens) of the church's land (fiefs). Then he also formally bestowed the symbols (ring and crozier) of the spiritual office.

Letters close: *See* Letters patent.

Letters patent: A general royal communication (order) on parchment addressed to a local official and left unrolled (i.e., open, patent) with royal seal appended (hanging). Letters close were more specific royal instructions addressed to an individual, rolled up (close) and sealed with the small seal.

Liberties: A very general word in the twelfth and thirteenth centuries referring to customary rights enjoyed by a specific group of individuals (e.g., barons, townsmen, clerks).

Make fine: To pay the amount assessed for something, for example, the amount paid to receive an inheritance or for an office.

Marriage: One of the feudal incidents. A lord controlled the marriage of an heiress or the widow of one of his men.

Marriage portion: The property provided by the bride's family, to be held by her following her husband's death and going to her heirs on her death.

Mercenaries: Soldiers for hire. They could be cavalrymen (knights), mounted bowmen, or various kinds of infantry. They served as long as they were paid.

Mort d'ancestor: One of the possessory assizes. A writ to determine who held a tenure at the time of the death of the last holder.

Movable property: Personal rather than landed property. Disposition on death could be controlled by a will (testament).

Murder-fine: A penalty devised by the Norman rulers of England to protect the minority Normans against the majority Englishmen. If the community could not prove that a murdered man was an Englishman, he was assumed to be Norman and the entire community was responsible for the murder-fine (penalty).

Novel disseisin: One of the possessory assizes. A writ to determine whether the purchaser of the writ had been disseised (dispossessed) of his land.

Oathhelper: Part of the Anglo-Saxon system of proof known as compurgation. If the court decided that an individual could make proof (prove himself innocent) by compurgation (oathtaking), he was allowed to take the oath himself and he had to provide an additional number of oathhelpers prescribed by the court. The oathhelpers did not swear to the innocence of the accused (i.e., they were not witnesses); rather, they swore that his oath was good. *See* Appendix B.

Ordeal: A form of proof in Anglo-Saxon law and used until 1215 when the clergy were forbidden to participate. The ordeal was an appeal to God to demonstrate guilt or innocence. There were many ordeals: cold water, hot water, hot iron, beds of coals, and so on. If after the set number of days the resulting wound was clean, God had demonstrated that the man was innocent; if not, he was guilty. *See* Appendix B.

Original and appellate jurisdiction: A legal term. If a court had original jurisdiction, a case (plea, suit) could be initiated (originated, brought, begun) there. If a court had appellant jurisdiction, it could hear cases on appeal from lower courts.

Outlawed: A formal court penalty. If a court declared a person outlawed, he was placed outside the protection of the law. This was usually the equivalent of exile.

Pannage: A fee paid for allowing one's pigs to run in a forest in search of food.

Papal curia (court): A collective term including the pope himself and all the clergy associated with him in the government of the Church.

Peers: Equals. In Magna Carta, the term is used to assure men of baronial status that they would be judged by their social equals, not by just a number of freemen from the community. Such judgment would have to be in a proprietary court (i.e., a lord's private court) or in the court of the king.

Petty serjeanty: A free holding owing a petty annual rent such as a knife, arrow, or rose.

Plea: A legal suit or case.

Ploughs: Plows.

Port reeve: The lord's representative in a town, that is, an urban center surrounded by a wall entered through a gate (port).

Possessory assizes: Chancery writs issued to initiate suits involving possession of some kind of property, not necessarily landed property. *See also* Darrein presentment; Mort d'ancestor; Novel disseisin.

Praecipe: A writ (royal instruction) devised by Henry II to move disputes over land from feudal courts into a royal court. This writ is denied in Magna Carta so as not to threaten the feudal (proprietary, private) courts. However, the same thing was accomplished by the possessory writs which were recognized in Magna Carta.

Present, presentment: A jury assembled for the purpose of answering questions about criminal behavior in a community. It could offer a presentment against (indict) an individual for a particular crime. He would then be tried at the next court (by ordeal until 1215, after which by experimental means until trial by jury was slowly developed).

Primogeniture: A rule of succession (inheritance) whereby the eldest son inherits.

Proprietary courts: Baronial courts presided over by the lord of the fief. Such courts were very generalized. They were attended by lord's men (vassals) whose functions could be advisory, ceremonial, or judicial.

Purpresture: An unauthorized use of royal land.

Recognition jury: A jury available in a royal (common law) court whereby a jury made up of members of the community could be placed on oath and required to say what they knew about the rights of the parties involved.

Recognitions: Civil suits that could be solved in a royal court by a recognition jury.

Reeve: A local representative of a lord—could be from any rank depending on circumstances.

Regarders: Men sent by the king to make regard in his forest, that is, to view what was going on with regard to the maiming of dogs so that they could not attack the king's venison, or to determine whether the number of foresters was correct for the amount of forest they had to patrol. In other words, they made a kind of inventory of the forest.

Regular clergy: *See* Secular clergy.

Relief: A feudal incident. The sum assessed an heir for the right to inherit his father's property (fief).

Rent: A generalized term to refer to a payment or service owed to a lord in return for holding one's property from him.

Retinue: The group of men surrounding a great lord and retained (maintained) by him. The men might be fighting men (knights) or others rendering nonmilitary service.

Return gift: Early Germanic law. It viewed a gift as valid only if it were followed by a return gift—something like the concept that a sale is valid only if some price (even a token one) has been paid.

River bank: Patrolled by a warden. Much as a woods could be made a forest preserve (usually for the king), so a river bank could be made a preserve for the king's hawking.

Russet: Another word for woolen cloth. Much cloth was produced in England and exported.

Scotales: Levies (assessments) of ale made by keepers of the forest (foresters or beadles) on dwellers in the forest. Could also apply to levies of grain, lambs, or piglets from those whose land was enclosed in a royal forest. Prohibited in Charter of the Forest 1225, Article 7.

Scutage: A commutation (substitution for) knight service, a payment or tax levied against a baron owing knight service for his landed fief. The payment was in lieu of rendering the military service in person.

Seat (such as principal seat): A term that usually refers to a place of residence. For example, Simon de Montfort had his principal seat at Kenilworth Castle.

Secular clergy: Those members of the Christian clergy who worked in the world and did not retire to a monastery to live according to a rule (the regular clergy).

Security: Someone willing to be responsible for another's debt, or one's own property offered as security for a debt.

Seigneurial: Referring to relations arising from the custom of holding land from a lord. The term could refer to relations among members of the baronial class or relations between a lord (seigneur) and his peasants.

Seisin: Possession. Disseisin, dispossession.

Selvedge: The finished edge of a bolt of cloth.

Seneschal (of Poitou): A position in the county of Poitou roughly equiv-alent to the English justiciar—an officer with multiple duties.

Serjeants: Officers of the infantry.

Service (knight): The military responsibility in England associated with fiefs held by feudal tenure.

Share at church door: Part of a marriage ceremony. In the ceremony performed at church door, the husband could publicly announce what portion of his estate would go to his wife on his death (i.e., if he was providing less than the legal dower, which was one-third of his property).

Sheriff: The chief royal official at the county level.

Simony: The purchase of an office.

Socage tenure: A free tenure not held for knight service. It could be held by any free man, of any status.

Subinfeudation: The custom for a lord to retain enough land (domain) for himself and his dependents and to grant the remainder to one or more of his faithful men (followers, tenants), and each of them to retain a domain and grant the rest to subtenants, and so on until the land received was only enough to support the tenant.

Swanimote: Meetings held three times a year in a royal forest attended by the king's men: agisters, foresters, and verderers. At one of these meetings, the agisters collected pannage, the amount due from those who ran their pigs in the royal forest.

Take the cross: To vow to go on a crusade. These vows were usually public acts where the individual taking the vow received a cloak with a special crusading patch sewed to the sleeve.

Templars: *See* Knights Templar.

Tenure: A holding, usually of land, or the kind of terms (tenure) by which one held that land.

Thegn: A professional military man in Anglo-Saxon England. A position not necessarily associated with the holding of land.

Tithing: A group of ten men collectively held responsible for the behavior of every man in the group. Tithing groups did not apply to persons in the baronial classes since their behavior was controlled by oaths of loyalty to a lord. *See also* Frankpledge.

Tourn: Visit. The sheriff visited (made his tourn) through the hundreds of his county. Magna Carta limited these visits to twice a year, during one of which the sheriff took the view of frankpledge. *See also* Frankpledge.

Translate: A clerical term referring to formal movement from one office to another, or the removal of a body or relics from one place to another.

Trial by battle: A form of ordeal introduced into England by the Normans for suits involving disputes over the possession of land. The accused was required to do battle (i.e., to fight on horseback) against his accuser. If either accuser or defendant were weak in age, sex, or health, he could be represented by a champion. Most men by the late twelfth century preferred decision by a recognition jury, a form of proof that could be had only in a royal court. *See* Appendix B.

Trithing: Another term for "riding," the divisions of a large county between the hundred (or wapentake) and the county in size. Best known in the large county of York.

Vacancy: Usually refers to an office that does not have an occupant.

Vassal: A very inexact term. Originally, it referred to someone of servile status, but by the tenth century the status had become more honorable, until by the high Middle Ages (twelfth–sixteenth centuries) it was used to refer to a faithful follower of a lord of baronial status.

Venison: *See* Vert and venison.

Verderers: Men of the knightly class chosen in county court to meet with the royal foresters to observe such acts as agisting and the attachment of persons or things by the foresters for breach of the forest law.

Vert and venison: Forest terms. The vert of the forest was the green wood or growing timber; the venison was the game or hunting rights.

Vill: Village.

Villein: A person of servile status whose position was not very well defined by law. In the early Norman period, the tendency was to emphasize their dependent status under the control of the lord's manorial court, and not responsible to the public (hundred and county) courts. But villeins wanted their landholdings to be protected by the royal common law and eventually they would be treated little differently from freemen. Developments toward freedom were very uneven, depending on economic conditions, and some manorial courts survived until the nineteenth century.

Wales: Parts of northern Wales remained independent until the late thirteenth century when they were conquered by Edward I. Until that time, they were governed by the law of Wales. The southeastern part of Wales was held by Norman lords and their successors. Since they held a very unruly frontier area (called the Welsh March), they enjoyed greater powers than other tenants-in-chief of the king. Suits there were settled according to the law of the March. The barons there were called Marcher Lords.

Wapentake: A term equal to the English "hundred"—applied in the Danelaw.

Ward: A person not legally competent either because he was under age, she was an unmarried female, or either was mentally incompetent.

Warden: The officer who patrolled a river bank preserve.

Warrant: To guarantee, as to warrant the possession of land.

Warren: A preserve for small animals, usually rabbits. Kept by a warrener.

Waste: To reduce something in value. As a noun, the part of a landed estate that was not under cultivation, or a part of a forest where trees did not grow.

Writ: A brief written document developed at the Anglo-Saxon court and adopted by the Norman rulers of England.

Writ of inquisition: A writ secured by a man facing a criminal charge (in the hundred or county court where trial was by ordeal) that claimed some unusual circumstance that justified removal into a royal court where an inquest (inquisition) could be held into those circumstances.

ANNOTATED BIBLIOGRAPHY

The Historiography of Magna Carta

Traditional

Stubbs, William. *The Constitutional History of England, in Its Origin and Development.* Vol. I, 5th ed. Oxford: Clarendon, 1906.

———, ed. *Select Charters and Other Illustrations of English Constitutional History from the Earliest Times to the Reign of Edward the First.* 9th ed. Revised by H.W.C. Davis. Oxford: Clarendon, 1913. The traditional interpretation of Magna Carta based on the claims of the seventeenth-century common lawyers and parliamentarians and culminating in the arguments of the nineteenth-century nationalist historians.

Selfish Barons

McKechnie, William S. *Magna Carta: A Commentary on the Great Charter of King John.* 2nd rev. ed. New York: B. Franklin, 1958. The interpretation of Magna Carta that developed in the late nineteenth and early twentieth centuries based on a more "scientific" reading of the document that emphasized what Magna Carta actually said. McKechnie argued that, instead of being a document offering liberties to all freemen, Magna Carta was a class document offering great benefits only to the baronial class.

Modern Interpretation

Davis, G.R.C. *Magna Carta.* London: The British Library, 1996. This is a brief introduction to the copy of Magna Carta on display in the British Museum.

Holt, J. C. *Magna Carta.* 2nd ed. Cambridge: Cambridge University Press, 1992. This is the indispensable work for understanding the present state of Magna Carta studies.

————. *Magna Carta and Medieval Government.* London: Hambledon Press, 1985.

700th Commemoration (1915) during World War I

Malden, Henry Elliot, ed. *Magna Carta Commemoration Essays.* London: Royal Historical Society, 1917.

750th Commemoration (1965)

Ashley, Maurice. *Magna Carta in the Seventeenth Century.* Charlottesville: University Press of Virginia, 1965.

Howard, A. E. Dick. *The Road from Runnymede: Magna Carta and Constitutionalism in America.* Charlottesville: University of Virginia Press, 1968.

Stenton, Doris Mary. *After Runnymede: Magna Carta in the Middle Ages.* Charlottesville: University Press of Virginia, 1965.

Thorne, Samuel E., William H. Dunham, Jr., Philip B. Kurland, and Sir Ivor Jennings. *The Great Charter: Four Essays on Magna Carta and the History of our Liberty.* New York: Pantheon Books, 1965.

As the titles of these works imply, the "popular" point of view still regards Magna Carta as the "cradle of our liberties."

General Histories

Barlow, Frank. *The Feudal Kingdom of England 1042–1216.* 4th ed. London and New York: Longman, 1988. This is an overview of the period beginning with England in the reign of Edward the Confessor and continuing through the reigns of the Norman and Angevin kings to the death of King John.

Bartlett, Robert. *England under the Norman and Angevin Kings, 1075–1225.* Oxford: Clarendon Press; New York: Oxford University Press, 2000. The most up-to-date and intensive study of this period.

Bates, David, and Ann Curry. *England and Normandy in the Middle Ages.* London and Rio Grande, OH: Hambledon Press, 1994. This is a collection of studies by current scholars on the relations of England and Normandy from the establishment of Normandy in 911 to the final loss of Normandy in the fifteenth century during the Hundred Years' War. Nonetheless, fourteen of the twenty-one articles deal with the relations between England and Normandy to the loss of Normandy to Philip Augustus in 1204. Much attention is given to monastic organization and architectural influences, but also examined is the very difficult problem of how the English and

Norman branches of the aristocracy were closely or not so closely inter-twined.

Brooke, Christopher. *From Alfred to Henry III 871–1272*. New York and London: W. W. Norton, 1961. A general introduction to this rather long period of time; written for the general public but generally reliable.

Crouch, David. *The Image of Aristocracy in Britain, 1000–1300*. London and New York: Routledge, 1992.

———. *The Normans: The History of a Dynasty*. London: Hambledon, 2002. An interesting survey of the Norman kings and the way in which the importance of a ruler's descent influenced succession.

Fleming, Robin. *Kings and Lords in Conquest England*. Cambridge and New York: Cambridge University Press, 1991. A study in the shifts of power in England caused by (1) Cnut's conquest, (2) the readjustments under Edward the Confessor, and (3) the Norman conquest. Cnut's conquest destroyed the old Wessex aristocracy and created a new one dominated by three families, of which the most powerful, that of Earl Godwin of Wessex, continued to dominate during the reign of Edward the Confessor. By this time there was already a considerable Norman presence in England, and the resulting tensions provided a background to the conquest by William of Normandy. The power and influence of the old magnates and the new ones created by William are based on a careful study of Domesday Book.

Harding, Alan. *England in the Thirteenth Century*. Cambridge: Cambridge University Press, 1993. This is primarily a socioeconomic history with a concluding section on the political history of the time.

Harper-Bill, Christopher, and Elisabeth van Houts, eds. *A Companion to the Anglo-Norman World*. Woodbridge, Suffolk, and Rochester, NY: Boydell & Brewer, 2003. A collection of articles by specialists on aspects of Anglo-Norman history but also including other parts of the Norman world in southern Italy and Sicily and the Principality of Antioch in the eastern Mediterranean.

Harvey, Barbara, ed. *The Twelfth and Thirteenth Centuries*. Oxford: Oxford University Press, 2001. A collection of eight essays by current scholars focused on the British Isles with the emphasis on England and its relationship to the other parts.

Haskins, Charles Homer. *Norman Institutions*. Cambridge, MA: Harvard University Press, 1918. An early work by a respected medievalist.

Hoyt, Robert S., and Stanley Chodorow. *Europe in the Middle Ages*. 3rd ed. New York: Harcourt Brace Jovanovich, 1976. A general text.

Kaeuper, Richard W. *Chivalry and Violence in Medieval Europe*. Oxford: Oxford University Press, 1999. A study of chivalry from a nonromantic point of view, stressing its violent side.

Liddiard, Robert, ed. *Anglo-Norman Castles*. Woodbridge, Suffolk, and Rochester, NY: Boydell & Brewer, 2002.

Lyon, Bryce. *A Constitutional and Legal History of Medieval England*. 2nd ed. New York and London: Norton, 1980. An excellent survey.

Poole, Austin Lane. *From Domesday Book to Magna Carta, 1087–1216*. 2nd ed. Oxford: Clarendon Press, 1955. A solid study of all aspects of English government and life reflecting the status of scholarship at the time of publication.

Reynolds, Susan. *Fiefs and Vassals, the Medieval Evidence Reinterpreted*. Oxford: Oxford University Press, 1994. Reynolds argues against the use of the terms *feudal* and *feudalism* because the characteristics of the system vary so widely with place and time.

Richardson, H. R., and G. O. Sayles. *The Governance of Mediaeval England from the Conquest to Magna Carta*. Edinburgh: Edinburgh University Press, 1963. This is an important but controversial work.

Roberts, Clayton, and David Roberts. *A History of England*. Vol. I, 3rd ed. Englewood Cliffs, NJ: Prentice Hall, 1991. A general textbook.

Sawyer, P. H. *From Roman Britain to Norman England*. London: Methuen & Co., 1978. This book is for the general reader but is reliable.

Thompson, Faith. *Magna Carta: Its Role in the Making of the English Constitution, 1300–1629*. Minneapolis: University of Minnesota Press, 1950. A detailed study of the use of Magna Carta to support the royal position (as in the reign of Elizabeth I) and later to support Parliament against the Stuart kings.

Warren, W. L. *The Governance of Norman and Angevin England, 1086–1272*. London: Edward Arnold, 1987. A rather brief survey of English government between the death of William I and that of Henry III, utilizing this author's great familiarity with the reigns of Henry II and his sons. There is also a very perceptive analysis of Magna Carta as a critique of Angevin government.

Economic and Social Background

Latouche, Robert. *The Birth of the Western Economy: Economic Aspects of the Dark Ages.* London: Methuen & Co., 1961. Translated from the French *Les Origines de l'Economie Occidentale* (Paris, 1956). It is a general economic history of the early Middle Ages.

Miller, Edward, and John Hatcher. *Medieval England—Rural Society and Economic Change 1086–1348.* London and New York: Longman, 1978. This is an economic history that covers much more than its subtitle implies. Towns and countryside are closely interwoven, and the English economy is very much a part of a European and, to some extent, an Asiatic economy.

———. *Medieval England—Towns, Commerce, and Crafts. 1086–1348.* London and New York: Longman, 1995. A companion volume to the previous work with a concentration on the towns and their inhabitants.

Pounds, N.J.G. *An Economic History of Medieval Europe.* 2nd ed. London and New York: Longman, 1994. A very good overall economic history.

Common Law

The Sources of the Law

Attenborough, F. L., ed. and trans. *The Laws of the Earliest English Kings.* New York: Russell and Russell, 1963. Covers the laws from Ethelbehrt (about 597) to those of Athelstan (925–939).

Bates, David. *Regesta regum Anglo-Normannorum: The Acts of William I, 1066–1087.* Oxford: Clarendon Press; New York: Oxford University Press, 1998. The Laws of William I.

Clanchy, M. T. *The Treatise on the Laws and Customs of the Realm of England Commonly Called Glanvill.* rev. ed. Oxford and New York: Oxford University Press, 1993.

Douglas, David C., and George W. Greenaway, eds. *English Historical Documents 1042–1189.* 2nd ed. London: Eyre Methuen; New York: Oxford University Press, 1981. Collected documents from this time period.

Downer, L. J., ed. and trans. *Leges Henrici Primi.* Oxford: Clarendon Press, 1972. The Laws of Henry I.

Drew, K. F. *The Lombard Laws.* Philadelphia: University of Pennsylvania Press, 1973.

Hall, G.D.G., ed. and trans. *The Treatise on the Laws and Customs of the Realm of England, Commonly Called Glanvill.* London: Nelson, 1965.

Robertson, A. J., ed. and trans. *The Laws of the Kings of England from Edmund to Henry I.* Cambridge: University of Cambridge Press, 1925. This volume not only contains the laws of the later Old English kings (including Cnut), but also the various regulations attributed to William I plus the "Coronation Charter of Henry I," Henry I's "Decree Concerning the Coinage," his "Decree Concerning the Hundred and County Courts," and his "London Charter."

Rothwell, Harry, ed. *English Historical Documents 1189–1327.* New York: Oxford University Press, 1975. Collected documents from this time period.

Stephenson, Carl, and Frederick George Marcham, eds. and trans. *Sources of English Constitutional History, A Selection of Documents from A.D. 600 to the Present.* New York and London: Harper, 1937. The Laws of William I.

Thorne, Samuel E., ed. and trans. *Henry de Bracton's De Legibus et Consuetudinibus Angliae: On the Laws and Customs of England.* 4 vols. Cambridge, UK: Published in Association with the Selden Society [by] the Belknap Press of Harvard University Press, 1968–1977.

On the Growth of the Common Law

Bartlett, Robert. *Trial by Fire and Water: The Medieval Judicial Ordeal.* Oxford: Clarendon Press; New York: Oxford University Press, 1986. This is a survey of the origins of the ordeal in Europe and the possible reasons for its prohibition to the clergy by the Fourth Lateran Council in 1215.

Brand, Paul. *The Making of the Common Law.* London and Rio Grande, OH: Hambledon Press, 1992. A collection of articles by Brand on a number of subjects related to the common law—courts, lawyers, legal treatises, specific causes—all in the thirteenth century.

———. *The Origins of the English Legal Profession.* Oxford and Cambridge, MA: Blackwell, 1992. A survey of law and court procedure in the eleventh and twelfth centuries, and the changes introduced in the thirteenth century that allowed (or necessitated) the growth of a legal profession not associated with the universities.

Davies, Wendy, and Paul Foreacre, eds. *The Settlement of Disputes in Early Medieval Europe.* Cambridge and New York: Cambridge University Press, 1986. This is a collection of articles by contemporary English medieval historians about dispute settlement in premodern France, Ireland, Spain,

Italy, and England. For the most part, these scholars are using records other than the laws: charters, records of dispute resolution, and chronicles. Their common theme is the importance of having the ability to record a decision in writing.

Grant, Raymond. *The Royal Forests of England.* Stroud, Gloucestershire, UK: Alan Sutton, 1991. A study of the forests in the thirteenth and fourteenth centuries primarily from the point of view of forest law and forest courts.

Hudson, John. *The Formation of the English Common Law: Law and Society in England from the Norman Conquest to Magna Carta.* London and New York: Longman, 1996. This work approaches the growth of the common law on the basis of court cases, not written laws.

————. *Land, Law, and Lordship in Anglo-Norman England.* Oxford and New York: Oxford University Press 1994. This is a study of the development of land law as it relates to feudal tenure in Anglo-Norman England.

Hyams, Paul R. *King, Lords, and Peasants in Medieval England: The Common Law of Villeinage in the Twelfth and Thirteenth Centuries.* Oxford and New York: Oxford University Press, 1980. This work is one of the very few attempts to generalize about the position of the peasant classes in medieval England. The result is somewhat confusing.

————. *Rancor and Reconciliation in Medieval England.* Ithaca, NY, and London, UK: Cornell University Press, 2003. Hyams argues that feud-like conditions similar to those on the Continent continued after the Norman Conquest through the thirteenth century, by which time the legal reforms of Henry II and his sons provided the "little" man with some protection against the "great."

Maitland, Frederic William, and Frederick Pollock. *The History of English Law before the Time of Edward I.* Cambridge: Cambridge University Press, 1895. This is the classic study of the medieval English law which, though modified in some respects, is still the place to begin the study of the English law.

Milsom, S.F.C. *Studies in the History of the Common Law.* London and Ronceverte, WV: Hambledon Press, 1985. An important work but extremely difficult to follow.

Palmer, Robert C. *The County Courts of Medieval England, 1150–1350.* Princeton, NJ: Princeton University Press, 1982. A workmanlike study of the role and procedure of the county courts during a period when the county courts were declining as the jurisdiction of the royal common law courts expanded.

Stenton, Doris Mary. *English Justice between the Norman Conquest and the Great Charter, 1066–1215*. Philadelphia: American Philosophical Society, 1964. A series of lectures based primarily on Lady Stenton's extensive knowledge of the judicial records.

Turner, Ralph V. *The English Judiciary in the Age of Glanvill and Bracton, c. 1176–1239*. Cambridge: Cambridge University Press, 1985. A careful study of the emergence of professional civil servants during the reigns of Henry II and his sons and grandson, with attention to the gradual shift of their duties from many types of administrative work to more professional jurists.

———. *Judges, Administrators and the Common Law in Angevin England*. London and Rio Grande, OH: Hambledon Press, 1994. A collection of Turner's papers on the subjects listed in the title.

Van Caenegem, R. C. *The Birth of the English Common Law*. Cambridge: Cambridge University Press, 1973. A very generalized study not worthy of this important author.

White, Stephen D. *Customs, Kinship, and Gifts to Saints: The Laudatio Parentum in Western France, 1050–1150*. Chapel Hill: University of North Carolina Press, 1988. This work does not deal with the development of the English common law, but it is set in part of the Angevin inheritance of Henry II. It is cited here for those students who may be interested in socio-legal theory as it relates to the emerging law of property descent.

Young, Charles R. *The Royal Forests of Medieval England*. Philadelphia: University of Pennsylvania Press, 1979. A general study of a topic largely neglected—the royal forests from the time of their establishment by William I until their decline in the later Middle Ages. Attention is given to their role in the baronial dispute with King John at the time of Magna Carta.

Biographies of Persons and Developments Related to Magna Carta

Strayer, Joseph R., ed. *Dictionary of the Middle Ages*, 13 vols. New York: Charles Scribner's Sons, 1982–1989. Gives brief biographies of the persons listed below as well as for other individuals and developments referred to in the text of this volume.

Alfred of Wessex

Abels, Richard P. *Alfred the Great: War, Kingship and Culture in Anglo-Saxon England*. London and New York: Longman, 1998. Abels is primarily a military historian, but in this volume he gives balanced weight to the importance of Alfred's predecessors and his own laws, administration, and cultural activities.

Keynes, Simon, and Michael Lapidge, trans. & introd. *Alfred the Great: Asser's Life of Alfred and Other Contemporary Sources*. Harmondsworth: Penguin Books, 1983. This is a translation of a contemporary biography of Alfred. Also included are a number of other contemporary sources, including extracts from Alfred's laws, his will, and selections from some of Alfred's translations.

Peddie, John. *Alfred the Warrior King*. Stroud, Gloucestershire, UK: Sutton Publishing, 1999. Primarily military history, lavishly illustrated with many sketches of military sites.

Thomas Becket (St. Thomas)

Barlow, Frank. *Thomas Becket*. Berkeley: University of California Press, 1986. A detailed study, generally unbiased.

Knowles, David. *Thomas Becket*. Stanford, CA: Stanford University Press, 1971. Knowles was a respected student of medieval church history, especially monastic history. But he could not write an unbiased history of Thomas Becket.

Urry, William. *Thomas Becket: His Last Days*. Stroud, Gloucestershire, UK: Sutton Publishing, 1999. Urry, as Keeper of the Manuscripts and Librarian of Canterbury Cathedral, had access to the papers of Becket as well as those of his opponents. He was not an admirer of Becket.

Winston, Richard. *Thomas Becket*. London: Constable, 1967. This is a popular biography of Becket and, as such, capitalizes on the color and passion of his career. Nonetheless, Winston has studied the sources, and his work can be useful.

Also see the items listed under Henry II.

Charlemagne and the Carolingian Empire

Collins, Roger. *Charlemagne*. Toronto: University of Toronto Press, 1998. Brief but competent.

Nelson, Janet L. *The Frankish World, 750–900*. London and Rio Grande, OH: Hambledon Press, 1996. A collection of papers by Janet Nelson on many aspects of the Carolingian world from the middle of the eighth century to the end of the ninth century.

Eleanor of Aquitaine

Kelly, Amy. *Eleanor of Aquitaine and the Four Kings*. Cambridge, MA: Harvard University Press, 1950. This is a fascinating biography, but bear in mind that it is based on the chroniclers, many of whom relied on the romances of the time.

Walker, Curtis Howe. *Eleanor of Aquitaine*. Durham: University of North Carolina Press, 1950. Another imaginative biography.

Wheeler, Bonnie, and John Carmi Parsons. *Eleanor of Aquitaine: Lord and Lady*. New York: Palgrave Macmillan, 2002. A collection of papers based on recent research.

Frederick II

Abulafia, David. *Frederick II: A Medieval Emperor*. London: Allen Lane The Penguin Press, 1998. An up-to-date study of Frederick's reign in Italy and Sicily: his achievements in Sicily, his frustration in Germany and northern Italy. There is a brief chapter on the culture of the court.

Van Cleve, Thomas Curtis. *The Emperor Frederick II of Hohenstaufen*. Oxford: Clarendon Press, 1972. A good scholarly study.

Henry II

Amt, Emilie. *The Accession of Henry II in England: Royal Government Restored, 1149–1159*. Woodbridge, Suffolk, UK, and Rochester, NY: Boydel Press, 1993. The subtitle of this work describes its content. Amt argues that by 1159, when Henry was foiled in his attempt to add Toulouse to his continental possessions, he had already created a kingdom that would support him financially and militarily in his endeavors.

Appleby, John T. *Henry II, the Vanquished King*. London: Bell, 1962. This is a popular biography but still useful. Appleby tends to overemphasize the tragedy of the revolt of Henry's sons.

Gillingham, John. *The Angevin Empire*. New York: Holmes & Meier, 1984. This is a very brief overview of the territories ruled by Henry II.

Warren, W. L. *Henry II*. Berkeley: University of California Press, 1973. This book is somewhat dated, but it is still the basic biography of Henry II.

White, Graeme J. *Restoration and Reform, 1153–1165: Recovery from Civil War in England*. Cambridge and New York: Cambridge University Press, 2000. A detailed study of the reign of Stephen and Henry II's first steps to restore the kingdom from the ravages of civil war.

Also see the volumes listed under Eleanor of Aquitaine, Richard I the Lionheart and John.

Sons of Henry II: Richard I the Lionheart and John

Brundage, James A. *Richard Lion Heart*. New York: Scribner, 1974. An unusual biography by a noted student of canon law.

Church, S. D. *The Household Knights of King John*. Cambridge and New York: Cambridge University Press, 1999. Heavily slanted toward military history but from a socioeconomic point of view.

————, ed. *King John: New Interpretations*. Woodbridge, Suffolk, and Rochester, NY: Boydell & Brewer, 1999. An interesting collection of essays on subjects relating to King John.

Gillingham, John. *The Life and Times of Richard I*. London: Weidenfeld and Nicolson, 1973. This is Gillingham's first biography of Richard I. It is a popular work, almost a coffee table version, but it also indicates Gillingham's interest in Richard as a legendary figure and a military hero.

————. *Richard Coeur de Lion: Kingship, Chivalry and War in the Twelfth Century*. London and Rio Grande, OH: Hambledon Press, 1994. This is a more serious study than the one listed above, but Gillingham's interests are still the same, with a little more attention given to Richard's actions as king.

————. *Richard I*. New Haven, CT: Yale University Press, 1999. This is Gillingham's third biography of Richard I and the most serious study. His themes remain the same but are studied in greater depth, with numerous quotations from contemporary authors.

Painter, Sidney. *The Reign of King John*. Baltimore, MD: Johns Hopkins University Press, 1949. An early attempt to free John from his "evil" image.

Turner, Ralph V. *King John*. London and New York: Longman, 1994. A balanced work relying heavily on John's interest in the administration of justice.

Turner, Ralph V., and Richard R. Heiser. *The Reign of Richard Lionheart*. Harlow, UK: Longman, 2000. Not as successful as Turner's *King John*.

Warren, W. L. *King John*. New York: W. W. Norton, 1961. Still very useful.

Innocent III

Cheney, C. F. *Pope Innocent III and England*. Stuttgart: Hiersemann, 1976. An exhaustive study published in a German series on popes and their papacies.

Moore, John C. *Pope Innocent III (1160/61–1216): To Root Up and to Plant.* Leiden and Boston: E. J. Brill, 2003. Relies heavily on translations of important writings of Innocent III.

Sayers, Jane. *Innocent III: Leader of Europe 1198–1216.* London and New York: Longman, 1994. A good introduction to the subject.

Stephen Langton

Powicke, F. M. *Stephen Langton.* New York: Barnes & Noble, 1965. This is a balanced work, the only biography in English.

Also see the volumes listed under John and Innocent III.

Louis IX (St. Louis)

Hallam, Elizabeth M. *Capetian France.* London and New York: Longman, 1980. A good text, excellent maps.

Hoyt, Robert S., and Stanley Chodorow. *Europe in the Middle Ages.* 3rd ed. New York: Harcourt Brace Jovanovich, 1976. A general text.

Jordan, William Chester. *Louis IX and the Challenge of the Crusade.* Princeton, NJ: Princeton University Press, 1979. A sound book but not easy to read.

Labarge, Margaret Wade. *Saint Louis: Louis IX, Most Christian King of France.* Boston: Little, Brown, 1968. Written in a popular style but reliable.

William Marshal

Crouch, David. *William Marshal: Court, Career and Chivalry in the Angevin Empire, 1147–1219.* London and New York: Longman, 1990. A reliable up-to-date book.

Painter, Sidney. *William Marshal Knight-errant, Baron, and Regent of England.* Toronto: Medieval Academy of America, 1982. A reprint of a well-known book published in 1933. Written before the *Histoire de Guillaume le Mareschal* had been subjected to a thorough criticism. William Marshal, like Eleanor of Aquitaine and Richard I the Lionheart, was a legendary as well as an historical figure. Throughout this work, he has been treated as an historical figure, although it is possible that a certain amount of legend has crept in through a biography written shortly after his death that was commissioned by his family and friends. This biography by a certain John is known as the *Histoire de Guillaume le Mareschal,* written in middle French.

Also see books listed under Eleanor of Aquitaine, Henry II, Richard I the Lionheart and John.

Simon de Montfort

Harding, Alan. *England in the Thirteenth Century.* Cambridge: Cambridge University Press, 1993. See general histories.

Lyon, Bryce. *Constitutional and Legal History of Medieval* England. 2nd ed. New York and London: Norton, 1980. See general histories.

Maddicott, J. R. *Simon de Montfort.* Cambridge: Cambridge University Press, 1994. A lengthy and meticulous work.

Philip II Augustus

Baldwin, John W. *The Government of Philip Augustus: Foundations of French Royal Power in the Middle Ages.* Berkeley: University of California Press, 1986. The standard work on this subject.

Bradbury, Jim. *Philip Augustus: King of France, 1180–1223.* London and New York: Longman, 1998. A serious study of the reigns of both Louis VII and Philip II as relating to the consolidation of royal power in France.

Hallam, Elizabeth M. *Capetian France.* London and New York: Longman, 1980.

See also works listed under Innocent III, John, and Stephen Langton.

Hubert Walter

Cheney, B. F. *Hubert Walter.* London: Nelson, 1967. A biography by a well-known church historian who is well informed on the relations between England and the church.

Young, Charles R. *Hubert Walter, Lord of Canterbury and Lord of England.* Durham, NC: Duke University Press, 1968. A careful study of Hubert Walter.

See also books referred to under Richard I the Lionheart and John.

William the Conqueror

Barlow, Frank. *William I and the Norman Conquest.* New York: Collier, 1965. Brief, readable, a good summary.

Bates, David. *William the Conqueror.* London: George Philip Ltd., 1989. A brief but up-to-date biography by an active Anglo-Norman scholar.

Douglas, David C. *William the Conqueror: The Norman Impact on England.* Berkeley: University of California Press, 1964. A solid biography covering both pre-conquest England and Normandy as known at the time of his victory.

Stenton, F. M. *William the Conqueror and the Rule of the Normans.* Rev. New York: Barnes & Noble, 1966. A long biography by the renowned Anglo-Saxon historian.

INDEX

Becket, Thomas, 6–8, 86–87, 101;
    biography, 63–67
Benevento, 78
Berengaria of Navarre, 76–77, 89
Bernard of Clairvaux, 72
Beverley, 17
Blanche of Castile, 77, 101–2, 106,
    117
Blois, 111
Blood feud, 161
Bohemund of Taranto, 156–57
Bologna, 37, 95
Boston, 17
Bouvines, 33, 94
Bracton, Henry de, 45
Bristol, 15
Britain, province, 13–14
Burgage tenure, 16, 46, 133, 144
Burgs, 15, 62
Burgundy, 22, 69
Byzantine Empire. *See* East Roman
    (Byzantine) Empire

Calixtus II, 12 n. 2
Canon law, 42, 48 n. 1, 64, 95
Canterbury, 15
Canterbury, archbishopric, 3–5,
    12 n. 5, 86; controversy over
    Stephen Langton, 98, 99–101;
    role in enforcing Confirmation
    of the Charters, 154
Capetians, 86, 112
Caroline script, 70
Carolingian Empire, 1, 21–22, 69–71
Carolingians, 52, 78, 111
Carucage, 9
Castle-guard, 133, 143
Cathars, 97, 108
Celestine III, 95
Chalus, 91, 106
Champagne, 83

Chancery, 23, 44, 119
Charlemagne, 1, 78, 111; biography,
    67–71
Charles of Anjou, Charles I of
    Sicily, 84, 102
Charles Martel, 69
Charter of the Forest, 47, 146–50
Chateau Gaillard, 114
Chester, 3, 62
Chiminage, 149
Chippenham, Peace of, 61
Christ Church, Canterbury, 32,
    35 n. 5
Church courts, 3, 48 n. 1
Church reform, 2–3, 155
Cinque Ports, 17, 142
Civil and canon law, 116, 120
Civil jurisdiction, 41
Civil law, 39, 42, 44, 120
Civitas, 13
Clerical taxation, 84
Clovis, 68
Cluny, 2, 79
Cnut, 3, 16, 24, 38
Coke, Edward, 58
Cold water ordeal, 164
Cologne, 83
Common counsel, 49–50, 131
Common pleas, 131, 142
Commons, The, 57
Community of the land, 152
Community of the realm, 152
Composition, 39
Compurgation, 39, 162
Concordat of Worms, 11 n. 2
Confirmation of the Charters, 56,
    150–52
Conrad III of German Roman Em-
    pire, 72, 158
Constance of Brittany, 93
Constance of Sicily, 80–81, 95–96

About the Author

KATHERINE FISCHER DREW is Lynette S. Autry Professor Emeritus of History, Rice University, Houston, TX. Professor Drew is past President of the Medieval Academy and is currently a Fellow. She is the editor of *The Lombard Laws*, among other works.